Ham Radio Bible
5 Books in 1

Comprehensive Guide for Mastery, Fun, and Preparedness in Every Situation
From Beginner to Advanced Techniques and Passing the Amateur Exam

American Radio Resilience Network (ARRN)

Copyright 2024. All Rights Reserved.

This document provides exact and reliable information regarding the topic and issues covered. The publication is sold with the idea that the publisher is not required to render accounting, officially permitted, or otherwise qualified services. If advice is necessary, legal or professional, a practiced individual in the profession should be ordered.

From a Declaration of Principles which was accepted and approved equally by a Committee of the American Bar Association and a Committee of Publishers and Associations.

In no way is it legal to reproduce, duplicate, or transmit any part of this document in either electronic means or printed format. Recording of this publication is strictly prohibited, and any storage of this document is not allowed unless with written permission from the publisher. All rights reserved.

The information provided herein is stated to be truthful and consistent. Any liability, in terms of inattention or otherwise, by any usage or abuse of any policies, processes, or Instructions contained within is the solitary and utter responsibility of the recipient reader.

Under no circumstances will any legal obligation or blame be held against the publisher for reparation, damages, or monetary loss due to the information herein, either directly or indirectly.

Respective authors own all copyrights not held by the publisher. The information herein is offered for informational purposes solely and is universal as such. The presentation of the data is without a contract or any guarantee assurance.

TABLE OF CONTENTS

BOOK 1 HAM Radio for Beginners: 7
- Introduction 8
- Chapter 1: Understanding HAM Radio Basics 9
- Chapter 2: The History and Evolution of HAM Radio 10
- Chapter 3: Getting Licensed: Your First Step into HAM Radio 12
- Chapter 4: Equipment Essentials for Beginners 13
- Chapter 5: Setting Up Your HAM Radio Station 14
- Chapter 6: The Language of HAM Radio: Q Codes and Terminology 16
- Chapter 7: Understanding Frequencies and Bands 17
- Chapter 8: Antennas for Beginners 18
- Chapter 9: Making Your First Contact 20
- Chapter 10: Joining the HAM Radio Community 21
- Chapter 11: Emergency Communication and Public Service 22
- Chapter 12: Digital Modes and New Technologies in HAM Radio 23
- Chapter 13: Operating Procedures and Best Practices 25
- Chapter 14: Troubleshooting Common Issues 26
- Chapter 15: Building and Customizing Equipment 27
- Chapter 16: Participating in Contests and Awards 29
- Chapter 17: Advanced Techniques for Experienced HAMs 30
- Chapter 18: Global Communication and Cultural Exchange 32
- Chapter 19: The Future of HAM Radio 33
- Chapter 20: Resources and Continuing Education 35
- Conclusion: 37

BOOK 2 The Ham Radio Advance Technik: 39
- Introduction 40
- Chapter 1: The Basics of Ham Radio 41
- Chapter 2: Setting Up Your First Station 43
- Chapter 3: Mastering Radio Frequencies 44
- Chapter 4: Antennas and Propagation 46
- Chapter 5: Transmitters and Receivers 47
- Chapter 6: Digital Modes of Communication 49
- Chapter 7: Morse Code in Modern Ham Radio 50
- Chapter 8: Emergency Communication Protocols 52

Chapter 9: Radio Wave Theory 53
Chapter 10: Operating Procedures and Etiquette 54
Chapter 11: Building a Ham Radio Community 56
Chapter 12: Advanced Tuning Techniques 57
Chapter 13: Exploring the World with DXing 58
Chapter 14: Contesting and Awards 59
Chapter 15: Satellite Communication with Ham Radio 61
Chapter 16: Software-Defined Radio (SDR) 62
Chapter 17: Advanced Electronics and Circuit Design 63
Chapter 17: Advanced Electronics and Circuit Design 65
Chapter 18: Signal Processing and Noise Reduction 66
Chapter 19: Legal Aspects and Regulations 67
Chapter 20: The Global Impact of Ham Radio 68
Conclusion: 70

BOOK 3 Exploring the World of Amateur Radio: 72
Introduction: 73
Chapter 1: "The History and Evolution of Amateur Radio" 75
Chapter 2: "Understanding Radio Waves and Frequencies" 76
Chapter 3: "Setting Up Your First Amateur Radio Station" 77
Chapter 4: "Radio Operating Procedures and Etiquette" 78
Chapter 5: "Antenna Basics and Design Principles" 80
Chapter 6: "Electronics and Components in Amateur Radio" 81
Chapter 7: "Digital Modes and Computer Integration in Amateur Radio" 82
Chapter 8: "Emergency Communication and Public Service" 83
Chapter 9: "Satellite Communication and Space Radio" 84
Chapter 10: "Radio Wave Propagation and Atmospheric Effects" 86
Chapter 11: "Advanced Antenna Systems and Design" 87
Chapter 12: "Building and Experimenting with Transceivers" 89
Chapter 13: "Regulations and Licensing in Amateur Radio" 91
Chapter 14: "Signal Processing and Noise Reduction Techniques" 92
Chapter 15: "Power Supplies and Safety Considerations" 93
Chapter 16: "DXing and Contesting in Amateur Radio" 95
Chapter 17: "Mobile and Portable Operations" 96
Chapter 18: "The Future of Amateur Radio" 97
Chapter 19: "Case Studies and Real-World Applications" 98

Chapter 20: "Building a Community: Clubs and Organizations" 99

Conclusion: 100

BOOK 4 Embracing the World of Ham Radio: 102

Introduction 103

Chapter 1: The Basics of Ham Radio – Understanding the Fundamentals 104

Chapter 2: Choosing Your Equipment – A Beginner's Guide 105

Chapter 3: Setting Up Your Ham Radio Station – Step-by-Step Instructions 107

Chapter 4: Understanding Radio Waves – The Science Behind the Signals 109

Chapter 5: Getting Licensed – Your Path to Becoming a Ham Radio Operator 110

Chapter 6: Operating Procedures – Best Practices and Etiquette 112

Chapter 7: Emergency Communication – Ham Radio in Crisis Situations 114

Chapter 8: Joining the Community – Clubs, Contests, and Events 115

Chapter 9: Digital Modes and Technologies – Modernizing Ham Radio 116

Chapter 10: Building and Modifying Equipment – A DIY Guide 118

Chapter 11: Antenna Design and Theory – Maximizing Your Signal 119

Chapter 12: Advanced Operating Techniques – Honing Your Skills 121

Chapter 13: Radio Wave Propagation – Understanding How Signals Travel 122

Chapter 14: Mobile and Portable Operations – Ham Radio on the Go 124

Chapter 15: Satellite Communication and Ham Radio – Reaching Beyond Earth 125

Chapter 16: Interference and Troubleshooting – Solving Common Problems 127

Chapter 17: The Future of Ham Radio – Trends and Emerging Technologies 128

Chapter 18: Global Communication and DXing – Connecting Worldwide 130

Chapter 19: Software-Defined Radio (SDR) – The New Frontier 131

Chapter 20: Legal Aspects and Regulations – Staying Compliant 132

Conclusion: 134

BOOK 5 The Radio Communication Handbook: 136

Introduction 137

Chapter 1: The Basics of Radio Waves 138

Chapter 2: Radio Hardware Components 140

Chapter 3: Setting Up Your Radio Station 142

Chapter 4: Antenna Design and Theory 144

Chapter 5: Transmission Lines and Feeders 145

Chapter 6: Modulation Techniques 147

Chapter 7: Radio Wave Propagation 148

Chapter 8: Building a Receiver 150

Chapter 9: Transmitter Design and Construction 151

Chapter 10: Power Supplies and Batteries 153

Chapter 11: Operating Procedures and Protocols 154

Chapter 12: Radio Spectrum and Frequency Allocation 156

Chapter 13: Digital Signal Processing in Radio 157

Chapter 14: Emergency and Mobile Radio Communications 158

Chapter 15: Radio Communication in Space 160

Chapter 16: Advanced Antenna Systems 161

Chapter 17: Software-Defined Radio (SDR) 162

Chapter 18: Radio Communication Security 164

Chapter 19: Troubleshooting and Maintenance 165

Chapter 20: The Future of Radio Communication 166

Conclusion: 167

BOOK 1
HAM Radio for Beginners:

QuickStart Guide for New HAMs

Exploring the World of HAM Radio:

A Gateway to Global Communication

Introduction

The realm of HAM radio, often regarded as a niche hobby, is in fact a rich and expansive world of communication that transcends geographical boundaries, cultures, and ages. This guide, "HAM Radio for Beginners: Quickstart Guide for New HAMs," is crafted to serve as a comprehensive introduction to the intriguing and multifaceted world of amateur radio. It is tailored to provide beginners with a solid foundation in HAM radio operations and practices, guiding them through the nuances of this technical yet immensely rewarding field.

Amateur radio, more popularly known as HAM radio, represents a unique blend of technology, communication, and community. It is an arena where individuals, irrespective of their background, come together to share knowledge, provide emergency communication, and explore the vast potential of radio frequencies. At its core, HAM radio is about harnessing the power of radio waves to connect with others, exchange ideas, and foster a global community of like-minded enthusiasts.

The allure of HAM radio is manifold. For some, it's the technical challenge and the thrill of building, experimenting with, and mastering radio equipment. For others, it's the excitement of making contact with people from different corners of the world, sometimes even astronauts aboard the International Space Station. Then there are those who see it as a vital public service, providing critical communication during emergencies when all other forms of connectivity fail. This multifaceted appeal makes HAM radio a continually evolving hobby, one that keeps pace with technological advancements while still retaining its classic charm.

The journey into the world of HAM radio begins with understanding its basics – the fundamental principles of radio communication. This knowledge is crucial as it lays the groundwork for all future learnings and operations in the field. The initial chapters of this guide are dedicated to unraveling these basics, ensuring a strong and clear foundation is set for the enthusiastic beginner.

Following the fundamentals, the guide delves into the historical context of HAM radio. Understanding its evolution is not just about tracing the technological advancements but also about appreciating the community's resilience and innovation. From the early days of radio to the modern era of digital communication, amateur radio has undergone significant transformations, each phase contributing to its rich heritage and shaping the community's ethos.

Another critical aspect covered in this guide is the process of obtaining a HAM radio license. Licensing is a mandatory step, ensuring that all operators have a basic level of proficiency and understanding of radio operations and regulations. This section provides detailed insights into preparing for the licensing exam, understanding the different types of licenses, and the responsibilities that come with being a licensed amateur radio operator.

Once the license is obtained, the next exciting phase is setting up the first HAM radio station. This guide provides practical advice on selecting equipment, understanding the nuances of different radio models, and tips for setting up an effective station within a budget. This section is particularly crucial as it translates theoretical knowledge into practical application, marking the true beginning of one's journey in HAM radio.

Beyond the equipment and setup, operating a HAM radio station requires familiarity with specific terminologies and codes, such as the Q codes, and an understanding of the operating procedures and etiquette. This guide aims to equip beginners with this essential knowledge, ensuring they can communicate effectively and respectfully with the global HAM radio community.

A significant portion of this guide is dedicated to the practical aspects of HAM radio operations. This includes making the first contact, which is a milestone for every amateur radio operator. There are chapters on how to join and engage with the HAM radio community, both locally and internationally, and the important role of HAM radio in emergency communication and public service. These sections highlight the practical applications of HAM radio, showcasing its relevance and importance in the modern world.

As the guide progresses, it introduces more advanced topics, such as digital modes of communication, DIY projects for customizing equipment, and participating in contests and awards. These chapters are designed to provide a path for growth and exploration within the hobby, encouraging beginners to expand their skills and engage more deeply with the community.

In conclusion, this guide is not just a technical manual; it is a gateway to a global community of communication enthusiasts. It offers a comprehensive overview of HAM radio for beginners, with a step-by-step approach that ensures a thorough understanding of the fundamentals, practical skills for setting up and operating a station, and a glimpse into the exciting possibilities that amateur radio offers. Whether one's interest in HAM radio is driven by a love for technology, a passion for communication, or a desire to serve the community, this guide is the perfect starting point on an endlessly fascinating journey.

Chapter 1: Understanding HAM Radio Basics

The journey into the fascinating world of HAM radio begins with understanding its core principles. This chapter provides a comprehensive introduction to the basics of HAM radio, including its fundamental concepts, equipment, and the science behind radio communication. This knowledge serves as the bedrock for all amateur radio enthusiasts, paving the way for effective and responsible radio operation.

HAM radio, at its essence, is about communicating over radio waves. Unlike standard AM/FM radio, HAM radio operators can both transmit and receive radio communications, which allows for two-way interaction. This capability forms the basis of the hobby, allowing for everything from casual conversation to emergency communication during disasters.

To start, it's important to grasp the basic science behind radio communication. Radio waves are a form of electromagnetic radiation with frequencies that fall within the electromagnetic spectrum. HAM radio operates on frequencies allocated specifically for amateur use, usually ranging from 1.8 MHz (160 meters) to 275 GHz (1 millimeter).

These frequencies are divided into different bands, each with its unique characteristics and uses. For example, lower frequency bands like 160 meters are great for long-distance communication at night, while higher frequency bands like 10 meters are better for daytime communication over shorter distances.

To illustrate this, consider a practical example: A HAM radio operator in New York wants to communicate with a friend in California using the 20-meter band during the daytime. The 20-meter band, operating around 14 MHz, is ideal for this long-distance communication during daylight hours due to its ability to bounce off the ionosphere and cover vast distances.

The next fundamental aspect is understanding the types of equipment used in HAM radio. A basic HAM radio setup includes a transceiver (a device that can both transmit and receive radio waves), an antenna, and a power source. The transceiver is the heart of the setup, allowing operators to tune into different frequencies and communicate with others.

Antennas play a crucial role in the effectiveness of radio communication. They come in various shapes and sizes, each designed for specific bands and purposes. For instance, a simple dipole antenna, which is relatively easy to build and install, can be an excellent starting point for beginners.

Power sources for HAM radios can vary, but most transceivers operate on 12 volts DC. This allows for flexibility in power options, ranging from portable battery packs to stationary power supplies.

An essential part of HAM radio basics is understanding the concept of modulation. Modulation is the process of varying a radio signal to convey information. The two primary types of modulation used in HAM radio are Amplitude Modulation (AM) and Frequency Modulation (FM). AM varies the signal's strength to convey information, while FM varies the frequency of the signal.

To give a practical example of modulation, imagine sending a voice signal over a radio wave. In AM, the voice causes variations in the signal's strength, while in FM, it causes changes in the signal's frequency. Each type of modulation has its advantages and is suited for different types of communication.

Another key component in HAM radio operation is the concept of repeaters. Repeaters are automated radio stations that receive a signal and retransmit it at a higher power, which allows for greater range and coverage. They are particularly useful in VHF and UHF bands, where radio waves typically travel in straight lines and can be limited by terrain.

For example, if a HAM operator wants to communicate from a valley, their direct signal might not reach far due to the surrounding hills. By using a repeater located on a high point, like a mountain or tall building, their message can be picked up and retransmitted over a much larger area, allowing for effective communication despite the challenging terrain.

Finally, this chapter touches on the ethical and legal aspects of HAM radio. All operators are expected to adhere to the regulations set by their country's communications authority, which in the United States is the Federal Communications Commission (FCC). These regulations include proper frequency usage, transmission power limits, and adherence to operational standards.

In conclusion, understanding the basics of HAM radio is crucial for anyone aspiring to be a part of the amateur radio community. This chapter has laid out the foundational knowledge required for effective communication, covering the science of radio waves, equipment essentials, modulation techniques, and the importance of repeaters, as well as legal and ethical considerations. With this groundwork, beginners are well-prepared to delve deeper into the world of HAM radio, exploring its myriad possibilities and embarking on a journey of lifelong learning and exploration.

Chapter 2: The History and Evolution of HAM Radio

The story of HAM radio is a tale of innovation, community, and the relentless pursuit of knowledge. This chapter takes you through the historical journey of amateur radio, from its earliest days to its current status as a global phenomenon. Understanding this history is not only about appreciating the technology but also recognizing the spirit of the HAM radio community that has thrived through various eras.

The origins of HAM radio can be traced back to the late 19th and early 20th centuries, a period marked by rapid advancements in radio technology. Pioneers like Guglielmo Marconi and Nikola Tesla were instrumental in demonstrating the practical applications of electromagnetic waves in communication. The early experiments in wireless telegraphy laid the groundwork for what would eventually become HAM radio.

One of the first notable milestones in amateur radio history was the establishment of the first amateur wireless clubs in the early 1900s. These clubs, formed by radio enthusiasts, were the precursors to modern HAM radio clubs. They provided a platform for exchanging ideas, conducting experiments, and advancing the technology of radio communication.

During World War I, the use of radio communication saw a significant uptick, and many amateur radio operators contributed to the war effort. However, the war also led to a temporary shutdown of amateur radio activities in many countries, including the United States. This was due to security concerns and the need to allocate radio frequencies for military use.

The 1920s and 1930s witnessed a resurgence of amateur radio. This era saw the refinement of technology and the establishment of regulations that would define amateur radio practices. One of the key developments was the allocation of specific frequency bands for amateur use, which provided a structured environment for HAM operations.

World War II again saw amateur radio operators contributing to the war effort, with many HAMs serving in communication roles. Post-war, the hobby saw a technological revolution, with advancements in equipment making radio more accessible to the average person. The introduction of transistors in the 1950s and 1960s further revolutionized HAM radio, allowing for more compact and efficient equipment.

To understand the evolution of HAM radio equipment, consider a practical example: In the early days, radio equipment was bulky and complicated, often requiring a significant amount of space and expertise to operate. A typical setup might include large vacuum tube transmitters and receivers, along with sizable antennas.

Fast forward to the present day, and HAM radio equipment is much more compact and user-friendly. Modern transceivers are small enough to fit in a backpack, yet powerful enough to communicate across continents. This evolution has made HAM radio more accessible to a broader range of people, contributing to the growth of the community.

The latter part of the 20th century and the early 21st century have seen HAM radio embracing digital technologies. Digital modes of communication, such as FT8 and PSK31, have become increasingly popular, allowing for efficient communication even under challenging conditions. The internet has also played a role in the evolution of HAM radio, with online resources and communities augmenting the traditional HAM experience.

One of the most exciting developments in recent years has been the involvement of HAM radio in space exploration. Amateur radio satellites (AMSAT) and the ability to communicate with astronauts aboard the International Space Station (ISS) have added a new dimension to the hobby. These advancements highlight the ongoing innovation and adaptability of the HAM radio community.

In conclusion, the history of HAM radio is a testament to human ingenuity and the desire to connect. From its humble beginnings in the early 20th century to its current status as a diverse and global community, HAM radio has continuously evolved, embracing new technologies while maintaining its core values of communication, education, and public service. This chapter not only chronicles the technological advancements in amateur radio but also celebrates the spirit of the HAM radio community, a spirit characterized by curiosity, collaboration, and a never-ending quest for knowledge.

Chapter 3: Getting Licensed: Your First Step into HAM Radio

Embarking on the journey of HAM radio begins with a crucial step - obtaining a license. This chapter demystifies the process of getting licensed, guiding you through the requirements, preparation, and examination. The importance of licensing in amateur radio cannot be overstated; it is not only a legal requirement but also a rite of passage that inducts you into the global community of amateur radio operators.

Licensing in HAM radio serves several purposes. It ensures that all operators have a basic understanding of radio theory, operating practices, and the legal and ethical responsibilities that come with the privilege of operating a radio station. It also helps in maintaining order on the airwaves by ensuring that operators adhere to allocated frequencies and power limits.

The first step in obtaining a license is understanding the different license classes. In the United States, the Federal Communications Commission (FCC) offers three classes of amateur radio licenses: Technician, General, and Amateur Extra. Each class grants different privileges in terms of frequency bands and modes of operation. The Technician class, being the entry-level license, provides access to all amateur radio frequencies above 30 MHz, ideal for local and regional communication. The General and Amateur Extra licenses offer progressively broader access to lower frequency bands, which allow for international communication.

The process of getting licensed involves passing an examination that tests your knowledge of radio theory, regulations, and operating practices. The Technician class exam, for example, typically covers basic principles of electricity and electronics, radio regulations, operating practices, and safety.

To illustrate the preparation process, let's consider a practical example: John, a budding amateur radio enthusiast, decides to get his Technician class license. He starts by gathering study materials, which include the FCC's Part 97 rules (the regulations governing amateur radio) and a study guide for the Technician class exam. John also joins a local amateur radio club where he attends classes and interacts with experienced HAM operators who offer him practical insights and advice.

As part of his preparation, John learns about basic concepts such as Ohm's Law, the different types of radio waves, and antenna theory. He also familiarizes himself with the FCC's rules on frequency allocation, station identification, and acceptable use of radio communication.

After several weeks of study and practice exams, John feels ready to take the test. The examination, which is administered by a team of volunteer examiners, consists of multiple-choice questions. John finds that the questions cover the topics he studied, including some practical scenarios that amateur radio operators might encounter.

Upon passing the exam, John submits his application to the FCC and soon receives his call sign, marking his official entry into the world of amateur radio. With his Technician class license, John can now operate on VHF and UHF frequencies, which are ideal for local communication via repeaters and even satellite communication.

This chapter also covers the importance of continuous learning in amateur radio. While obtaining a license is a significant milestone, the world of HAM radio is ever-evolving, with new technologies and modes of operation emerging regularly. Therefore, licensed operators are encouraged to keep abreast of these developments, perhaps even upgrading their license class to expand their operating privileges.

Additionally, this chapter touches on the ethical aspects of HAM radio. Licensed operators are expected to adhere to a code of conduct that promotes respect, courtesy, and cooperation on the airwaves. This includes proper use of language, adherence to frequency allocations, and consideration for other operators' rights to use the frequencies.

In conclusion, obtaining a HAM radio license is a journey that combines technical learning with an understanding of legal and ethical practices. This chapter provides a comprehensive guide to navigating this journey, offering practical advice, study strategies, and an overview of the examination process. Whether you aim to communicate locally or explore the far reaches of the radio spectrum, obtaining your license is the first step towards becoming a part of the global amateur radio community. With your license, a world of exploration, communication, and community service awaits.

Chapter 4: Equipment Essentials for Beginners

Venturing into the realm of HAM radio requires an understanding of the essential equipment that forms the foundation of this hobby. This chapter aims to guide beginners through the selection and understanding of basic HAM radio gear, ensuring they make informed decisions suited to their interests and objectives in amateur radio.

The cornerstone of any HAM radio setup is the transceiver. Transceivers are devices capable of both transmitting and receiving radio signals. For beginners, the choice of a transceiver is critical, as it dictates the range, modes of operation, and overall capabilities of their HAM radio experience. There are various types of transceivers, ranging from handheld models (often referred to as HTs, or "Handie-Talkies") to more sophisticated base station rigs.

For example, consider Sarah, a new HAM radio licensee. Her first purchase is a handheld VHF/UHF transceiver. This portable device is ideal for communicating via local repeaters and engaging in basic HAM radio activities. It's a cost-effective and user-friendly option for beginners.

Next in importance is the antenna. The antenna is a critical component of any HAM radio setup, as it significantly impacts the effectiveness of radio communication. There are several types of antennas, each suited for different bands and modes of operation. For VHF and UHF bands, which are commonly accessed by beginners, a simple vertical antenna or a Yagi antenna can be ideal choices.

Continuing with Sarah's example, she decides to complement her handheld transceiver with a simple vertical antenna mounted on her rooftop. This setup enhances her ability to communicate over longer distances than the transceiver's built-in antenna would allow.

For base station setups, especially for those interested in HF (High Frequency) communication, wire antennas such as dipoles or G5RV antennas are popular choices. These antennas are relatively easy to construct and can provide excellent performance for a wide range of frequencies.

Power supply is another crucial aspect. Most base station transceivers require a stable 12-volt power supply. Beginners can opt for a dedicated HAM radio power supply unit, which ensures the right voltage and current for their equipment. However, for a more budget-friendly option, a good quality 12-volt lead-acid battery can suffice.

Other essential pieces of equipment include coaxial cables to connect the antenna to the transceiver, a SWR (Standing Wave Ratio) meter to ensure the antenna is properly tuned, and various connectors and adapters. It's important for beginners to understand the role of each of these components and how they fit into their overall setup.

For a practical demonstration, let's consider the process of setting up a basic HAM radio station. After purchasing a transceiver, Sarah installs her vertical antenna. She connects the antenna to the transceiver using a length of coaxial cable. To ensure the antenna is properly tuned for the frequencies she intends to use, Sarah employs an SWR meter. This helps her avoid transmission issues and potential damage to her transceiver.

In addition to the primary equipment, there are several accessories that can enhance the HAM radio experience. These include headphones for clear audio reception in noisy environments, a microphone for better voice transmission, and even digital interfaces for those interested in exploring digital modes of HAM radio.

Understanding the function and selection of HAM radio equipment can seem daunting at first. However, this chapter aims to simplify these concepts, providing beginners with clear guidelines and practical examples. The goal is to empower new HAM radio enthusiasts to set up their first station effectively, paving the way for a fulfilling journey in amateur radio.

In summary, the right equipment is the key to a successful start in HAM radio. From choosing the appropriate transceiver to setting up an effective antenna system, each component plays a vital role in ensuring a rewarding experience. This chapter provides the foundational knowledge necessary for beginners to make informed decisions and start their adventures in HAM radio with confidence. With the basic setup in place, the world of amateur radio communication opens up, offering endless opportunities for learning, exploration, and connection.

Chapter 5: Setting Up Your HAM Radio Station

After acquiring the fundamental equipment, the next step for any aspiring HAM radio operator is to set up their station. This chapter walks you through the process of assembling a basic HAM radio station, offering practical advice and guidelines to ensure a smooth and efficient setup.

Setting up a HAM radio station involves more than just connecting equipment. It requires a thoughtful approach to location, equipment placement, and station ergonomics. The goal is to create a setup that is not only functional but also comfortable and safe for long-term use.

Firstly, choosing the right location for your station is crucial. Ideally, your station should be in a quiet area with minimal electronic interference. It should also be near a power source and have easy access to where your antenna will be placed. For most beginners, this might be a spare room, a corner of a living room, or even a garage space.

For instance, take the case of David, a new HAM enthusiast. David decides to set up his station in his home office, which offers a quiet environment and sufficient space for his equipment. He places his transceiver on a sturdy desk, ensuring it's at a comfortable height and position for operation.

The next step is installing the antenna. The choice of antenna and its placement significantly impacts the station's performance. For VHF and UHF operations, a simple vertical antenna or a Yagi antenna can be installed on the roof or balcony. For HF operations, wire antennas such as dipoles or end-fed wires might be more suitable.

David opts for a vertical antenna for VHF/UHF operations. He installs it on his rooftop, ensuring it's clear of obstructions for optimal signal transmission and reception. He then runs a coaxial cable from the antenna to his transceiver, carefully routing it to avoid potential tripping hazards and electromagnetic interference.

The electrical setup is another critical aspect. Ensuring a stable and safe power supply for your equipment is paramount. Most transceivers operate on 12 volts DC, and using a dedicated HAM radio power supply unit is advisable. It's also important to have proper grounding for your station to protect against electrical surges and improve overall performance.

David connects his transceiver to a 12-volt power supply, making sure to include a fuse for additional safety. He also grounds his equipment by connecting it to a grounding rod driven outside his home. This setup not only protects his equipment but also reduces unwanted electrical noise.

Configuring the transceiver is the next step. This involves setting the correct frequencies, modes, and other operational parameters. It's important to refer to the transceiver's manual and possibly seek advice from experienced HAM operators to optimize these settings.

For his first operation, David tunes his transceiver to a local repeater frequency. He sets the mode to FM (Frequency Modulation), as it's the most commonly used mode for VHF/UHF repeater communications. He also adjusts the squelch setting to eliminate background noise.

In addition to the hardware setup, a well-organized operating procedure is essential for efficient station operation. This includes logging contacts, adhering to proper frequency usage, and understanding the operational etiquette of HAM radio.

David prepares a logbook, both digital and paper, to record his contacts. He also familiarizes himself with the band plan, which outlines the frequency allocations for different modes and activities within the amateur radio bands.

Safety considerations are the final, but perhaps most important, aspect of setting up a HAM radio station. This includes electrical safety, ensuring proper ventilation for equipment to avoid overheating, and being mindful of RF exposure, especially when operating at higher power levels.

David ensures that all electrical connections are secure and that his equipment has enough space for proper heat dissipation. He also keeps a safe distance from his antenna while transmitting, particularly during high-power transmissions, to adhere to RF safety guidelines.

In summary, setting up a HAM radio station is a process that combines technical knowledge with practical considerations. This chapter provides a comprehensive guide to creating a functional, safe, and enjoyable operating environment. From choosing the right location to configuring your equipment and ensuring safety, each step is crucial in building a station that will serve as the launchpad for countless hours of radio exploration and communication. With a well-set-up station, beginners can confidently dive into the world of amateur radio, ready to connect with others and embark on a rewarding journey of discovery and learning.

Chapter 6: The Language of HAM Radio: Q Codes and Terminology

Effective communication in HAM radio involves more than just knowing how to operate the equipment; it also requires familiarity with the specific language and terminology used by amateur radio operators.

This chapter introduces you to the common phrases, abbreviations, and codes used in HAM radio, particularly the Q codes, which are essential for efficient and clear communication on the airwaves.

Q codes are a series of abbreviated codes used in radio communication to convey complex information quickly and efficiently. Originating from telegraphy, they have been adopted and adapted by the HAM radio community. These codes are universally recognized and can significantly streamline communication, especially in situations where brevity is vital, such as during contests or emergencies.

To illustrate the use of Q codes, consider the following example: Emily, an amateur radio operator, is in a conversation with another HAM. To inquire about the readability of her transmission, she asks, "How is my signal? Is it clear?" Instead of this long query, she could simply ask, "Q5?" This code is understood by the other operator to mean, "Is my signal perfectly readable?"

Q-CODE	MEANING	USAGE
QRM	Interference	There is QRM on your signal
QRN	Noise	There is QRN on this band
QRP	Low power	I am transmitting QRP now
QRT	Off and Clear	I am going QRT now
QRV	Ready to operate	I am QRV
QRX	Stand by or wait	Please QRX
QRZ	Who is calling	QRZ?
QSY	Change frequency	I will QSY to 20 Metres
QSB	Fading	There is QSB on your signal
QSL	All received	QSL on your last transmission
QSO	Contact	Thank you for the QSO
QTH	Location	My QTH is Melbourne

Apart from Q codes, there are other terminologies and phrases unique to HAM radio. For example, '73' is commonly used to mean 'best regards,' and '88' is used to convey 'love and kisses,' typically in conversations with family or close friends. These codes add a layer of personal touch and camaraderie to HAM radio communications.

Understanding band plans is another critical aspect of HAM radio communication. A band plan is a voluntary guideline for using different amateur radio bands. It helps in avoiding interference, as it designates specific sub-bands for various modes of operation, such as Morse code (CW), voice communication, and digital modes. For instance, the 20-meter band has specific portions allocated for CW and for single sideband (SSB) voice communication. Knowing these allocations helps operators choose the right frequency for their mode of operation.

Call signs are unique identifiers assigned to every licensed HAM radio operator. They consist of a prefix (one or two letters and a numeral indicating the region), and a suffix (one to three letters). For example, a call sign like 'N6XYZ' indicates an operator from the United States (N), in region 6, with the personal identifier 'XYZ'. Understanding and correctly using call signs is crucial for identifying oneself on the air and for logging contacts.

Proper radio etiquette is also a significant part of HAM radio communication. This includes identifying oneself by call sign at the beginning and end of a transmission and every ten minutes during communication. It also involves listening before transmitting to ensure the frequency is clear and being courteous and respectful to other operators.

Phonetics play a crucial role in ensuring clarity, especially when giving call signs or important information. The NATO phonetic alphabet is widely used in HAM radio for this purpose. For example, the call sign 'N6XYZ' would be phonetically communicated as "November Six X-ray Yankee Zulu."

Emily, in our earlier example, demonstrates proper radio etiquette and clear communication by identifying herself with her call sign, using phonetics, and employing Q codes and standard phrases. This not only makes her transmissions professional but also helps in building rapport and respect within the HAM radio community.

Understanding the language of HAM radio is not just about mastering a set of codes and phrases; it's about integrating into the global amateur radio community. It reflects a shared culture and set of practices that have evolved over decades. This chapter equips beginners with the essential terminology, codes, and practices needed for effective communication in HAM radio. With this knowledge, new operators can confidently navigate the airwaves, engage in meaningful conversations, and become active members of the HAM radio fraternity.

In conclusion, the language of HAM radio is a vital component of the hobby that enhances the experience of communication. It fosters a sense of belonging and mutual understanding among operators worldwide. By familiarizing themselves with this language, beginners can take a significant step forward in their journey into the fascinating world of amateur radio.

Chapter 7: Understanding Frequencies and Bands

The heart of HAM radio lies in its use of various frequencies and bands, each offering unique characteristics and opportunities for communication. This chapter aims to demystify the concept of radio frequencies and bands, helping beginners understand how to effectively navigate this crucial aspect of amateur radio.

Radio frequencies, measured in Hertz (Hz), refer to the number of cycles per second of a radio wave. In HAM radio, frequencies are divided into specific ranges, known as bands, each designated for different uses. These bands are identified by their wavelength, which is inversely proportional to the frequency.

To comprehend this concept, consider the relationship between frequency and wavelength. The frequency of a radio wave is determined by the number of times it oscillates per second. The higher the frequency, the

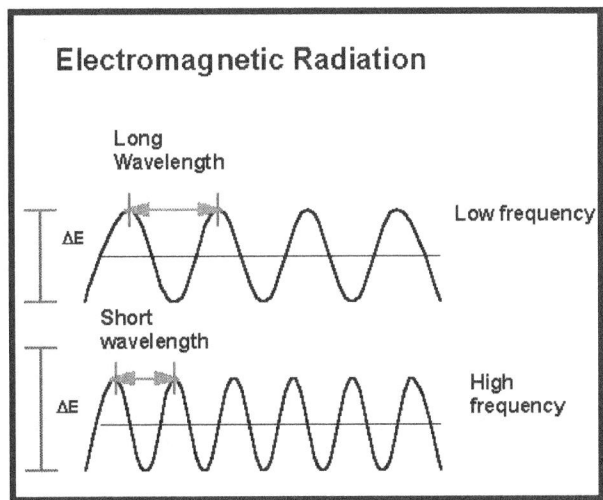

shorter the wavelength, and vice versa. For instance, a frequency of 14.250 MHz in the 20-meter band has a wavelength of about 20 meters.

The allocation of frequency bands for amateur radio use is regulated by international agreements and national regulations. Each band has its own characteristics, influenced by factors like time of day, solar activity, and atmospheric conditions. Understanding these characteristics is key to choosing the right band for your communication needs.

One fundamental concept in band selection is the difference between High Frequency (HF), Very High Frequency (VHF), and Ultra High Frequency (UHF) bands. HF bands (3 to 30 MHz) are known for their long-range communication capabilities, especially useful for international communication. VHF (30 to 300 MHz) and UHF (300 to 3000 MHz) bands, on the other hand, are typically used for local and regional communication.

For practical application, consider a HAM radio operator named Alex who wants to communicate locally. Alex would likely use a VHF band like 2 meters (144 to 148 MHz in the US) for clear line-of-sight communication within his region. However, if Alex wishes to reach an international audience, he would turn to an HF band, such as the popular 20-meter band (14 to 14.350 MHz), which allows for long-distance, global communication due to its ability to bounce off the ionosphere.

Each band also has its sub-bands and modes of operation, including Morse code (CW), voice (SSB, FM), and various digital modes. For instance, the 20-meter band has portions allocated specifically for CW and SSB voice communication. Adhering to these allocations is crucial to avoid interference with other operators and ensure efficient use of the spectrum.

Another critical aspect of frequency and band understanding is propagation. Propagation refers to how radio waves travel through the Earth's atmosphere. Different bands have different propagation characteristics, which can significantly affect communication. For instance, HF bands are greatly influenced by the ionosphere, allowing for skywave propagation, where radio waves bounce off the ionosphere and back to Earth, enabling long-distance communication.

To illustrate propagation, imagine Alex trying to make contact with another operator in a different continent. During the day, he might choose the 17-meter band (18.068 to 18.168 MHz), which offers good daytime long-distance propagation. At night, he might switch to the 40-meter band (7.000 to 7.300 MHz), which provides better night-time propagation.

Understanding the nuances of frequencies and bands is not just about technical knowledge; it's about making informed decisions to enhance your HAM radio experience. This chapter aims to provide beginners with the foundational understanding of these concepts, enabling them to choose the right frequencies and bands for their communication objectives.

In conclusion, mastering the frequencies and bands is a critical skill for any HAM radio operator. It allows for effective and responsible use of the radio spectrum, ensuring clear communication and minimizing interference with other users. With this knowledge, beginners can confidently explore the vast world of amateur radio, finding the bands and modes that best suit their interests and needs. Whether communicating locally or reaching out across the globe, understanding frequencies and bands is the key to unlocking the full potential of HAM radio.

Chapter 8: Antennas for Beginners

Antennas are a crucial component of any HAM radio setup, serving as the bridge between the airwaves and your radio equipment. This chapter aims to guide beginners through the basics of antennas, helping them understand the different types, their characteristics, and how to choose the right antenna for their specific needs.

An antenna is essentially a transducer that converts radio frequency (RF) fields into alternating current (AC) and vice versa. There are various types of antennas, each with its unique design and purpose. For beginners, understanding the basic types and their applications is essential to setting up an effective radio station.

One of the most common and simplest antenna types is the dipole antenna. A dipole consists of two metal wires or rods that emit and receive radio signals. It's typically half the wavelength of the frequency it's designed to operate on, making it a resonant antenna at that particular frequency.

For a practical example, consider a HAM operator named Lisa who wants to set up an antenna for the 20-meter band (around 14 MHz). To construct a dipole for this band, she would need a total length of approximately 10 meters (half the wavelength of 20 meters), divided into two 5-meter sections.

Another popular type of antenna, especially for VHF and UHF bands, is the Yagi antenna. A Yagi antenna consists of a driven element, reflectors, and directors, offering directionality and increased gain. This makes it ideal for communicating over long distances within specific directions.

For HAM operators interested in satellite communication or weak signal work on VHF/UHF bands, directional antennas like Yagis or parabolic dishes are often used. These antennas focus the radio energy in a particular direction, increasing the effective power and reception in that direction.

Antenna polarization is another critical concept. It refers to the orientation of the electric field of the radio wave concerning the Earth's surface. Vertical and horizontal polarizations are the most common, with vertical being more popular for VHF and UHF applications due to its omnidirectional pattern, ideal for local communications.

The importance of antenna height and placement cannot be understated. Generally, the higher the antenna, the better its performance, especially for VHF and UHF frequencies where the radio waves travel in a line-of-sight path. However, for HF bands, antenna height relative to the wavelength of the frequency in use is more critical.

Lisa, for instance, decides to install her dipole antenna for the 20-meter band at a height of 10 meters above the ground. This height ensures that her antenna performs efficiently, providing good coverage and allowing her to make contacts over various distances.

SWR (Standing Wave Ratio) is another term often associated with antennas. It's a measure of how effectively the radio's power is transmitted into the antenna. An SWR of 1:1 is ideal, meaning all the power is transmitted. However, anything below 2:1 is generally acceptable. High SWR readings indicate a problem with the antenna system, such as an impedance mismatch or a physical issue with the antenna itself.

To ensure her antenna system is functioning correctly, Lisa uses an SWR meter to measure the SWR of her dipole. By adjusting the length of the antenna elements and checking the connections, she aims to achieve the lowest SWR possible, ensuring maximum power is radiated from her antenna.

In conclusion, antennas are a vital part of any HAM radio setup, with their design and installation significantly impacting the overall performance of your station. This chapter provides beginners with a foundational understanding of the different types of antennas, their characteristics, and the factors to consider when choosing and installing an antenna. With this knowledge, beginners can confidently select and set up an antenna that best suits their operating goals, ensuring they can effectively communicate with the world through their HAM radio station. Whether it's local communication on VHF/UHF bands or global contacts on the HF bands, the right antenna is key to unlocking the full potential of your HAM radio adventures.

Chapter 9: Making Your First Contact

The moment you make your first contact (or "QSO" in HAM radio parlance) is a milestone in any amateur radio operator's journey. This chapter is dedicated to guiding beginners through the process of making their first contact, covering the preparation, the actual communication, and the post-contact procedures.

Before attempting your first contact, it's essential to ensure that your station is properly set up. This includes having your transceiver tuned to the right frequency, your antenna correctly installed and oriented, and all connections securely made. It's also vital to ensure that your station's output power is set appropriately for the band and mode you intend to use.

Let's consider a practical scenario with a new HAM operator named Tom. Tom has just set up his first HAM radio station, complete with a transceiver, a power supply, and a simple dipole antenna for the 20-meter band. He decides to attempt his first contact using single sideband (SSB) voice communication.

Before transmitting, Tom listens to the frequency to ensure it's not in use. This is a crucial step in HAM radio etiquette – always listen first to avoid interrupting ongoing conversations. Once he finds a clear frequency, he's ready to call CQ, which is an invitation for others to respond.

Tom speaks into his microphone, "CQ, CQ, CQ, this is [his call sign], [his call sign], [his call sign], calling CQ and standing by." He repeats this call a few times, then listens for a response.

After a few attempts, Tom hears a response. Another operator, using their call sign, acknowledges Tom's CQ call. Tom notes down the call sign and responds, confirming that he has heard the other operator. He speaks clearly, giving his location and a brief comment on his equipment or the weather, a common practice in initial contacts.

As the conversation progresses, Tom follows the rhythm of a standard QSO. This includes exchanging signal reports, which is a way of describing the quality of the reception. Signal reports are given using a readability, strength, and tone (RST) system. For instance, a report of "59" in voice communication means the signal is perfectly readable and very strong.

After a few minutes of conversation, Tom and the other operator sign off. The proper way to end a QSO is by thanking the other operator for the contact, giving your call sign, and using a standard sign-off phrase like "73," which means "best regards."

Tom's first QSO is a success. He records the details of the contact in his logbook, which is a critical practice in HAM radio. Logging each contact is not only a requirement in some cases but also a valuable record of your journey in amateur radio.

In conclusion, making your first contact is a thrilling experience and a significant achievement in the world of HAM radio. This chapter provides the necessary guidance to prepare for, execute, and complete a successful QSO. It covers the technical and operational aspects, including tuning your equipment, calling CQ, engaging in a conversation, and logging the contact.

For beginners like Tom, the first contact is just the start of an exciting journey of global communication. Each contact is an opportunity to learn, to share experiences, and to connect with fellow HAM radio enthusiasts around the world. With patience, practice, and adherence to radio etiquette, the world of amateur radio becomes an open book, full of fascinating stories and friendships waiting to be discovered.

Chapter 10: Joining the HAM Radio Community

Becoming a part of the HAM radio community extends beyond setting up a station and making contacts; it involves engaging with a global network of enthusiasts, joining clubs, participating in events, and contributing to the collective knowledge and culture of amateur radio. This chapter explores how new operators can immerse themselves in the HAM radio community, leveraging the camaraderie and resources it offers.

The HAM radio community is remarkably diverse, comprising individuals from various backgrounds and skill levels, all united by their passion for amateur radio. Engaging with this community can provide immense support, learning opportunities, and a sense of belonging.

One of the first steps to integrating into the HAM radio community is joining a local HAM radio club. These clubs are invaluable resources for beginners. They offer mentorship, access to equipment, and participation in group activities and events. Let's follow the journey of a new HAM operator, Emma, as she takes this step.

Emma, after making her first few contacts and gaining basic proficiency, seeks to join a local HAM radio club. She finds one in her area through an online search and decides to attend a meeting. At the meeting, Emma is welcomed by experienced operators who share her enthusiasm for radio communication. They offer advice, answer her questions, and invite her to participate in upcoming events.

Emma soon learns about the club's involvement in community services, such as providing communication support during local events and emergencies. This aspect of HAM radio appeals to her, and she decides to volunteer, gaining hands-on experience and contributing to her community.

Another significant aspect of the HAM radio community is participating in on-air activities and contests. These events are not only fun but also provide opportunities to hone operating skills and make numerous contacts worldwide. For example, Emma decides to participate in a Field Day event organized by her club. Field Day is an annual event where HAM operators set up temporary stations, often outdoors, and attempt to make as many contacts as possible over a 24-hour period.

Online forums and social media groups are also excellent platforms for engaging with the HAM radio community. These digital spaces offer a wealth of information, allow for the sharing of experiences, and provide a platform for asking questions and seeking advice. Emma joins a few online HAM radio forums and quickly becomes an active member, sharing her experiences and learning from others.

As Emma's journey in amateur radio progresses, she discovers the international scope of the HAM radio community. She makes contacts with operators from different parts of the world, learning about their cultures and experiences. This global connection is one of the most enriching aspects of HAM radio, fostering a unique sense of global camaraderie.

The chapter also highlights the importance of lifelong learning in amateur radio. The field of radio communication is constantly evolving, with new technologies and modes emerging. Continuous learning is key to staying current and fully enjoying the hobby. Emma, for instance, starts exploring digital modes of communication, adding a new dimension to her HAM radio experience.

In conclusion, joining and participating in the HAM radio community is a fulfilling and enriching experience. It provides support, learning opportunities, and a sense of belonging to a global network of enthusiasts. For beginners like Emma, it opens doors to new experiences, friendships, and a deeper understanding of the vast world of amateur radio. Whether through local clubs, on-air events, online forums, or global contacts, becoming an active member of the HAM radio community is an integral part of the amateur radio journey.

Chapter 11: Emergency Communication and Public Service

HAM radio is not just a hobby; it plays a crucial role in emergency communication and public service. This chapter explores how amateur radio operators provide vital communication support during emergencies, disasters, and community events, highlighting the importance of HAM radio as a reliable communication tool in times of need.

Amateur radio operators have historically been at the forefront of providing emergency communication services. When traditional communication networks fail or become overloaded during natural disasters, power outages, or other crises, HAM radio operators step in to fill the communication void, coordinating with emergency services and aiding in rescue and relief efforts.

Let's consider a practical example. Imagine a scenario where a severe storm hits a region, causing widespread power outages and disrupting cell phone and internet services. In this situation, local HAM radio operators, like John, a recently licensed amateur, spring into action.

John is a member of an Amateur Radio Emergency Service (ARES) group, a volunteer organization of amateur radio operators trained to assist in public service and emergency communications. Upon hearing of the storm, he promptly sets up his battery-powered HAM radio station, equipped with a multi-band antenna, and tunes into the local emergency communication net.

John's role involves relaying critical information between emergency responders and areas affected by the storm. He communicates reports of road closures, downed power lines, and rescue requests from people trapped in storm-affected areas. He also helps in passing welfare inquiries from family members outside the affected zone.

This chapter also covers the various ways HAM radio operators prepare for and participate in emergency communications. It includes training in emergency procedures, familiarization with various radio modes and frequencies used during emergencies, and participation in regular drills and simulations organized by groups like ARES and the Radio Amateur Civil Emergency Service (RACES).

In addition to emergency situations, amateur radio operators contribute to public service in other ways. Many participate in communication support for community events such as marathons, parades, and festivals. These events provide opportunities for operators to practice their communication skills in a less stressful environment while serving their communities.

For example, Emma, an enthusiastic amateur radio operator, volunteers to provide communication support for a local marathon. She sets up a station at one of the checkpoints, using her skills to coordinate the event's logistics, report runners' progress, and ensure the safety of participants.

The chapter emphasizes the importance of preparedness and training for effective emergency communication. This includes understanding the proper use of radio equipment, being familiar with emergency frequencies and protocols, and having a ready-to-go kit with essential radio gear and supplies.

Additionally, it discusses the ethical and legal aspects of operating in emergency situations. This includes understanding the limits of one's capabilities, respecting the chain of command in emergency response, and adhering to regulations regarding transmission during emergencies.

In conclusion, the role of amateur radio in emergency communication and public service is invaluable. It underscores the significance of HAM radio beyond being a hobby, highlighting its contribution to societal well-being and safety. For amateur radio operators like John and Emma, participating in emergency communication and public service is not only a duty but a fulfilling way to apply their skills and knowledge for the greater good. This chapter serves as a guide for beginners to understand the potential of HAM radio in emergencies and public service and encourages them to get involved, be prepared, and make a difference in their communities.

Chapter 12: Digital Modes and New Technologies in HAM Radio

As technology evolves, so does the world of amateur radio. Digital modes and new technologies have revolutionized HAM radio, offering operators innovative ways to communicate. This chapter delves into the various digital modes available to HAM operators, the technology behind them, and how these modes are shaping the future of amateur radio.

Digital modes in HAM radio refer to methods of communication that use digital data, rather than voice or Morse code, to convey messages. These modes have gained popularity due to their efficiency, especially in weak signal conditions, and their ability to connect operators across vast distances with minimal equipment.

One of the most popular digital modes is FT8, known for its ability to make contacts over long distances even with low power and modest antennas. FT8, part of the WSJT-X software suite developed by Nobel Prize laureate Joe Taylor, K1JT, uses a method of communication that is much more resistant to interference and noise than traditional modes.

Let's consider an example with an operator named Mike. Mike is interested in making international contacts but lives in an area with high noise levels and can only use a small antenna due to space constraints. By setting up a simple digital station using a computer, a sound interface, and his transceiver, Mike can use FT8 to make contacts worldwide, even with these limitations.

Another popular digital mode is PSK31, which allows for real-time, keyboard-to-keyboard communication, much like instant messaging. PSK31 is highly efficient in terms of bandwidth, making it ideal for crowded bands.

Digital Mobile Radio (DMR) is a rapidly growing digital mode, especially appealing to operators interested in VHF and UHF communications. DMR offers clear voice communication and the ability to connect to digital repeaters and networks, extending the range of communication significantly.

Emerging technologies in HAM radio also include software-defined radios (SDRs). SDRs differ from traditional radios in that they use software for processing radio signals, offering greater flexibility and the ability to implement different modes and functions via software updates.

For instance, Emma, an avid HAM operator, decides to explore SDRs. She purchases an entry-level SDR receiver and connects it to her computer. Using software, she can visually scan a wide range of frequencies, decode different digital modes, and even track satellites. SDRs open up a new realm of possibilities for experimenting and exploring the radio spectrum.

The chapter also covers the integration of HAM radio with the internet. Technologies like EchoLink and D-STAR allow operators to link their radio signals to the internet, enabling worldwide communication through repeaters connected to the internet. This technological integration extends the reach of amateur radio, breaking geographical barriers and bringing operators together from all corners of the globe.

In addition to exploring these modes and technologies, the chapter discusses the importance of keeping up with advancements and adapting to new technologies in the ever-evolving world of amateur radio. It encourages operators to experiment with different modes and technologies, find what interests them, and continue learning and growing within the hobby.

In conclusion, digital modes and new technologies have significantly expanded the capabilities and reach of amateur radio. They offer operators innovative ways to communicate, experiment, and explore the radio spectrum. From keyboard-to-keyboard digital conversations to worldwide contacts via internet-linked repeaters, these advancements have opened up new dimensions in amateur radio. For operators like Mike and Emma, these technologies not only enhance their experience but also connect them more closely to the global amateur radio community, heralding an exciting future for the hobby.

Chapter 13: Operating Procedures and Best Practices

Mastering the technical aspects of HAM radio is just one part of the equation; understanding and adhering to good operating procedures and best practices is equally important. This chapter provides a comprehensive guide to the etiquette, procedures, and best practices that every amateur radio operator should know to ensure effective, respectful, and safe communication on the airwaves.

Operating procedures in HAM radio encompass a wide range of practices, from how to initiate and end a communication to managing interference and observing frequency-specific protocols. These procedures are not only about following regulations but also about respecting other operators and maintaining the integrity of the amateur radio service.

Let's start with the basics of initiating a contact, often referred to as a QSO. The standard procedure involves listening to the chosen frequency to ensure it's not in use, followed by a call of "CQ" (a general call to any stations). For example, an operator named Robert, after tuning into an unoccupied frequency on the 20-meter band, calls, "CQ CQ CQ, this is [Robert's call sign], [Robert's call sign] calling CQ and standing by." He repeats this a few times and waits for a response.

Once a contact is established, maintaining proper communication etiquette is crucial. This includes clear and concise transmission, proper use of phonetics (especially when sharing call signs), and being patient and courteous throughout the conversation. For instance, during a QSO, Robert ensures he speaks clearly, uses standard phonetic alphabet to convey his call sign, and listens attentively to the other station, allowing for a smooth exchange.

Understanding and managing interference is another essential aspect of operating procedures. Interference, whether unintentional or intentional, can disrupt communication and cause frustration. Operators should strive to minimize their interference to others and handle any interference they encounter with patience and diplomacy.

For example, if Robert encounters interference during his communication, he first tries to adjust his frequency or antenna direction. If the interference persists, he politely contacts the interfering station (if possible) to resolve the issue.

Logging contacts is a best practice that serves multiple purposes. It keeps a record of communication, helps in managing awards and contests, and is a regulatory requirement in some cases. Operators should log the date, time, frequency, mode, and call sign of the other station at a minimum. Robert, for instance, maintains a digital logbook where he meticulously records all his QSOs.

Band plans are another critical aspect of operating best practices. These plans are voluntary guidelines that suggest how each portion of the amateur bands should be used. Respecting these plans helps in minimizing interference and ensures efficient use of the spectrum. Robert always refers to the latest band plan before operating, ensuring he's using the appropriate frequency and mode for his band of choice.

Safety in operating procedures cannot be overstressed. This includes not only electrical safety and proper grounding of equipment but also awareness of RF exposure limits. Operators should ensure that their station complies with national regulations regarding RF exposure, especially when operating with high power or in environments where others may be exposed to their signals.

Lastly, the chapter emphasizes the importance of continuous learning and adapting to changes. The world of amateur radio is dynamic, with technological advancements and regulatory changes occurring regularly. Staying informed and adaptable is key to being a responsible and effective HAM radio operator.

In conclusion, understanding and adhering to operating procedures and best practices is fundamental to the practice of amateur radio. It ensures efficient, respectful, and safe use of the radio spectrum, fosters a positive environment within the HAM radio community, and enhances the overall experience of the hobby. For operators like Robert, following these guidelines is not just about compliance; it's about contributing to the respected tradition of amateur radio and enjoying its benefits to the fullest.

Chapter 14: Troubleshooting Common Issues

In the world of amateur radio, encountering technical issues is a common experience. However, the ability to troubleshoot and resolve these issues is a vital skill for any HAM radio operator. This chapter focuses on identifying, diagnosing, and fixing common problems that operators may face with their equipment and setups.

Effective troubleshooting in HAM radio starts with a systematic approach – understanding the problem, breaking it down into potential causes, and methodically testing each possibility. The most common issues in HAM radio include problems with transmission and reception, antenna issues, interference, and equipment malfunctions.

Let's follow the experience of an operator named Alice as she troubleshoots a problem with her station. Alice notices that her transmissions are not being received by other stations, despite her equipment seeming to function correctly.

Step 1: Initial Assessment

Alice starts by verifying the basics: checking that her transceiver is powered on, the volume and squelch settings are correct, and the correct frequency and mode are selected. She also ensures her microphone is plugged in properly.

Step 2: Antenna and Cable Check

Suspecting an antenna issue, Alice visually inspects her antenna system. She looks for obvious signs of damage or wear, especially at connections and joins. She also inspects the coaxial cable running from her transceiver to the antenna, ensuring it's not frayed or kinked.

Step 3: SWR Measurement

Using an SWR meter, Alice checks the standing wave ratio (SWR) of her antenna. A high SWR reading would indicate a problem with the antenna or the feedline, such as a mismatch or damage.

Step 4: Power Output Check

Next, Alice checks the power output of her transceiver using a power meter. This helps her determine if the issue is with her transceiver's ability to transmit effectively.

Step 5: On-Air Testing

Having found no obvious issues with her equipment, Alice decides to conduct an on-air test.

She makes a transmission and asks for signal reports from any receiving stations. This helps her gauge if her signal is weak or distorted, indicating potential issues with her transmitter or antenna.

Step 6: Consulting Manuals and Online Resources

Still unable to resolve the issue, Alice consults her transceiver's manual for troubleshooting tips. She also searches online forums and HAM radio websites for advice from other operators who may have experienced similar issues.

Step 7: Seeking Assistance from Local HAM Community

As a final step, Alice reaches out to her local HAM radio club for assistance. Often, more experienced operators can provide valuable insights and hands-on help.

In Alice's case, a fellow club member identifies that the problem was due to a faulty connector on her antenna feedline, which was causing a significant loss of signal strength.

Other common issues that HAM operators may face include RF interference, both from within their own setup and from external sources. Interference issues can often be complex, requiring operators to methodically test for and eliminate potential sources of interference. This might involve using filters, adjusting antenna placement, or collaborating with neighbors and local authorities.

Maintaining a well-organized and documented station can also aid in troubleshooting. Keeping a record of equipment settings, changes, and past issues can provide valuable clues in diagnosing and resolving current problems.

In conclusion, troubleshooting is an essential skill in amateur radio, integral to maintaining an effective and efficient station. This chapter provides a framework for identifying and resolving common issues, empowering operators like Alice to tackle problems confidently and continue enjoying their hobby. The ability to troubleshoot not only enhances an operator's technical proficiency but also contributes to their overall growth and satisfaction in the world of HAM radio.

Chapter 15: Building and Customizing Equipment

One of the most rewarding aspects of HAM radio is the ability to build and customize your own equipment. This chapter dives into the world of DIY projects in amateur radio, offering guidance on how to get started, what projects to consider, and the skills you'll develop in the process.

Building your own HAM radio equipment not only enhances your understanding of how radio works but also allows you to tailor your setup to your specific needs. It can range from constructing simple antennas to designing complex transceivers.

Starting with Simple Projects

Beginners are advised to start with simpler projects and gradually move to more complex ones. A good starting point is building an antenna. Antennas are relatively easy to construct, require minimal components, and offer a great way to learn about radio wave propagation.

For instance, let's consider a project where a new HAM operator, Ben, decides to build a 2-meter band dipole antenna. The 2-meter band is a popular choice for VHF communication, and a dipole for this band can be made with basic materials like wire, coaxial cable, and some connectors.

Ben calculates the length of his dipole using the formula Length (in meters) =142.5 Frequency (in MHz) Length (in meters) = Frequency (in MHz)142.5. For a center frequency of 146 MHz, each leg of the dipole should be approximately 49 cm.

Intermediate Projects

As confidence and skills grow, operators can move on to more challenging projects. An intermediate project could involve building a simple receiver or a low-power (QRP) transceiver kit. These kits usually come with all the necessary components and detailed instructions, making them a great way to learn about the inner workings of radio equipment.

For example, Ben decides to take his hobby a step further by building a QRP transceiver kit for HF bands. He follows the instructions carefully, learning about components like resistors, capacitors, and transistors, and how they contribute to the functionality of the transceiver.

Advanced Projects

For the more experienced, designing and building a complex piece of equipment from scratch can be a highly rewarding challenge. This might include constructing a high-power amplifier or even designing a custom SDR (Software Defined Radio).

Learning and Applying Electronics Knowledge

Building and customizing equipment require a certain level of electronics knowledge. Operators often find themselves learning about electronic circuits, soldering, and RF design. There are plenty of resources available, from online tutorials to books and HAM radio club workshops, to help learn these skills.

The Satisfaction of DIY

The satisfaction of using equipment you've built yourself is immense. It adds a new dimension to the HAM radio experience, blending communication with experimentation and learning.

In Ben's case, the first contact he makes using his homemade dipole and QRP transceiver is a moment of great pride and achievement. He not only communicated over the airwaves but did so with equipment he built with his own hands.

Safety Considerations

It's crucial to emphasize safety when undertaking DIY projects. This includes understanding how to safely handle electronic components and tools, ensuring proper grounding and electrical safety, and being aware of RF exposure, especially when testing and using homemade transmitters.

Community and Sharing

Building equipment also opens up opportunities to engage with the wider HAM radio community. Many operators find joy in sharing their projects, seeking advice, and offering help to others. This exchange of knowledge and experience is a fundamental part of the amateur radio hobby.

In conclusion, building and customizing equipment is a deeply rewarding aspect of amateur radio that enhances both technical skills and on-air experience. Whether it's a simple antenna or a complex transceiver, DIY projects offer endless opportunities for learning, experimentation, and personal satisfaction. For operators like Ben, these projects are not just about the end product but about the journey of discovery and the joy of creating something that connects them to the world.

Chapter 16: Participating in Contests and Awards

Participation in contests and pursuit of awards are activities that many HAM radio operators find immensely rewarding. These activities not only add an element of excitement to the hobby but also improve operational skills and knowledge. This chapter introduces the concept of HAM radio contests and awards, offering insights into how to get involved, prepare for, and enjoy these aspects of amateur radio.

Understanding HAM Radio Contests

HAM radio contests are competitive events where operators attempt to make as many contacts as possible within a set period. Contests vary in their rules and objectives. Some focus on contacting as many stations as possible, while others might be about contacting stations in as many different countries or regions as possible.

For a beginner like Clara, participating in a contest is an excellent way to improve her operating skills. She decides to enter a simple domestic contest designed for new operators. The contest requires participants to make as many contacts as possible within a 24-hour period, using only a specific band.

Preparation for Contests

Preparation is key to successful contest participation. This includes ensuring that all equipment is functioning correctly, understanding the contest rules, and planning operating strategies, such as the best times to operate and which frequencies to use.

Clara spends time studying the band plan and contest rules. She also ensures her transceiver is properly set up and that her antenna is tuned to the contest band.

Participating in the Contest

During the contest, Clara experiences the thrill of rapid-fire contacts. She quickly learns the importance of efficient communication and accurate logging of each contact. As the contest progresses, Clara finds her confidence and proficiency growing.

Post-Contest Activities

After the contest ends, participants typically submit their logs to the contest organizers for verification. Clara carefully reviews her log, ensuring all information is accurate before submission. She then waits eagerly for the contest results, excited to see how she fared against other operators.

Pursuing Awards

Apart from contests, pursuing various awards offered in the HAM radio community is another engaging activity. These awards are typically based on achieving certain milestones, such as contacting a set number of countries or regions.

For instance, Clara sets her sights on an award for making contact with operators in 100 different countries. She diligently tracks her contacts, using various modes and bands to reach her goal. Each new country contacted brings a sense of achievement and brings her closer to earning the award.

Awards for Special Achievements

There are also awards for special achievements, like contacting remote islands, participating in emergency communication, or making contacts via satellite. These awards encourage operators to explore different aspects of amateur radio.

Learning and Growth

Through contests and awards, operators like Clara not only enhance their operating skills but also deepen their understanding of radio propagation, antenna theory, and global geography. These activities also offer a fun and engaging way to interact with the global HAM radio community.

In Conclusion

Participating in contests and pursuing awards can be one of the most thrilling and rewarding aspects of amateur radio. They provide goals to strive for, skills to hone, and a global playground to explore. Whether a newcomer or a seasoned operator, contests and awards offer endless opportunities for enjoyment, learning, and personal achievement in the world of HAM radio.

Chapter 17: Advanced Techniques for Experienced HAMs

For the seasoned amateur radio operator, delving into advanced techniques offers a path to enhanced communication capabilities and a deeper understanding of radio science. This chapter explores various advanced aspects of HAM radio, including sophisticated operating methods, complex equipment, and cutting-edge technologies, tailored for experienced operators looking to expand their horizons.

Exploring Advanced Modes and Techniques

Advanced HAM radio operators often experiment with various modes and techniques that require more knowledge and skill. These include weak signal communication modes like Moonbounce (EME - Earth-Moon-Earth) and meteor scatter communication, which involve bouncing signals off the moon or ionized trails of meteors, respectively.

Consider an operator named Daniel, an experienced HAM enthusiast who decides to explore EME communication. This mode requires a highly directional antenna system, low-noise amplifiers, and a robust transceiver capable of handling weak signals. Daniel sets up a large Yagi antenna array and connects it to a preamplifier and a high-power transceiver in his shack.

Digital Signal Processing (DSP) and Software-Defined Radio (SDR)

Digital Signal Processing (DSP) in HAM radio is a technique that uses digital technology to filter and process radio signals, enhancing signal clarity and reducing noise and interference. Experienced operators like Daniel often integrate DSP into their stations for improved performance.

Software-Defined Radio (SDR) takes this a step further. SDRs use software for processing radio signals, offering unparalleled flexibility and control over how signals are transmitted and received. With an SDR, operators can easily switch between different modes, bands, and signal processing techniques using just their computer and software.

Satellite and Space Communication

Satellite communication is another area where experienced operators can expand their skills. This involves communicating through amateur radio satellites (AMSATs) orbiting the Earth, some of which even offer transponder capabilities for relaying signals.

Daniel decides to add satellite communication to his repertoire. He sets up a station with a rotatable antenna system capable of tracking satellites as they move across the sky, a computer-controlled transceiver for adjusting frequencies in real-time, and software for tracking satellite orbits.

Advanced Antenna Systems

For the advanced operator, antenna systems become more sophisticated. This includes phased arrays, steerable beams, and antennas optimized for specific modes like EME or satellite communication. Understanding and constructing such antennas require a deep knowledge of antenna theory and radio wave propagation.

Daniel, in his pursuit of EME communication, constructs a phased array of Yagi antennas, carefully designed to focus radio energy towards the moon, maximizing his chance of successful moonbounce communications.

Remote Station Operation

Remote station operation is an advanced aspect of HAM radio where operators control their stations from a different location, often via the internet. This is particularly useful for operators who live in areas with poor propagation conditions or restrictive antenna installations.

Daniel sets up a remote operation system, allowing him to control his station from his city apartment, where installing a large antenna system is not feasible.

Engaging in Technical Research and Development

Experienced HAM operators often engage in technical research and development, experimenting with new equipment designs, propagation studies, and digital communication techniques. They contribute to the amateur radio community by sharing their findings and innovations.

Daniel, with his interest in EME, conducts experiments on signal propagation and shares his findings with the community through articles, presentations, and online forums.

Mentoring and Education

Finally, experienced operators like Daniel often take on mentoring roles, sharing their knowledge and expertise with newcomers to the hobby. They may conduct workshops, write articles, or offer one-on-one guidance, helping to foster the next generation of HAM radio enthusiasts.

In conclusion, advanced techniques in HAM radio offer experienced operators like Daniel a wide array of fascinating areas to explore. From moonbounce and satellite communication to advanced antenna systems and digital technologies, these techniques not only enhance personal communication capabilities but also contribute to the broader amateur radio community. Engaging in these advanced aspects of HAM radio is a journey of continuous learning and discovery, pushing the boundaries of what is possible in amateur radio communication.

Chapter 18: Global Communication and Cultural Exchange

HAM radio transcends the boundaries of conventional communication, offering a unique platform for global interaction and cultural exchange. This chapter delves into the aspects of HAM radio that enable operators to connect with people from diverse cultures and regions, exploring the ways in which amateur radio fosters international understanding and friendship.

Bridging Distances with HF Communication

High Frequency (HF) bands are the gateway to long-distance, international communication in HAM radio. These bands allow operators to reach across continents, making contacts thousands of miles away. This is where much of the cultural exchange in HAM radio takes place.

Consider an operator named Elena, who regularly uses the 20-meter band to communicate globally. She sets up a schedule to talk with a fellow operator in Japan, a country she's always been fascinated with. Through these conversations, Elena not only practices her radio skills but also learns about Japanese culture, language, and traditions.

Special Event Stations and DX-peditions

Special event stations and DX-peditions (expeditions to rare or remote locations) are significant aspects of global communication in HAM radio. These events often celebrate cultural or historical milestones and attract attention from operators worldwide.

Elena participates in a special event station commemorating a significant cultural festival. She contacts operators from different parts of the world who are also participating, exchanging greetings and learning about each other's cultures.

Language and Communication

While English is commonly used in HAM radio, operators often encounter and learn phrases in other languages. This adds an enriching dimension to the hobby, as language is a key component of cultural exchange.

Elena, for example, learns basic greetings in several languages. She uses these to start her contacts, showing respect and appreciation for other cultures, which is always warmly received.

International Contests and Awards

International contests and award programs in HAM radio encourage operators to make contacts with as many countries as possible. These activities not only provide a competitive aspect to the hobby but also encourage cultural exchange.

Elena participates in an international contest, aiming to contact as many countries as she can over a weekend. Each contact brings a new opportunity to interact with operators from different cultural backgrounds.

QSL Cards and Cultural Exchange

QSL cards, sent to confirm radio contacts, often feature images and information about the operator's locale and culture. These cards are treasured by HAM operators as tokens of their global connections.

Elena has a collection of QSL cards from around the world, each card offering a glimpse into the life and culture of the operator who sent it. She also designs her own QSL cards, showcasing aspects of her local culture and scenery.

Educational and Cultural Programs

Many HAM radio operators participate in educational and cultural exchange programs, connecting schools and communities across different countries. This often involves scheduled contacts where topics of cultural and educational significance are discussed.

For instance, Elena sets up a contact between a local school and a school in Brazil. Students exchange questions and information about their daily lives, educational systems, and cultural practices.

HAM Radio and Diplomacy

HAM radio also plays a role in international diplomacy and understanding. By fostering direct, person-to-person communication across borders, amateur radio helps break down barriers and misconceptions, promoting peace and friendship.

Elena reflects on her contacts and realizes how her perceptions have broadened. Through her HAM radio interactions, she's gained a deeper appreciation of the diversity and richness of different cultures.

In conclusion, global communication and cultural exchange are fundamental aspects of HAM radio, offering unique opportunities for operators to connect with people from various backgrounds. For operators like Elena, amateur radio becomes a bridge to the world, not just in a technical sense, but in a cultural and educational sense as well. It's a hobby that not only spans frequencies but also narrows the gaps between different cultures, fostering a sense of global community and understanding.

Chapter 19: The Future of HAM Radio

The world of amateur radio is constantly evolving, shaped by technological advancements, regulatory changes, and the shifting interests of its community. This chapter explores the potential future directions of HAM radio, examining emerging trends, technologies, and the changing landscape of communication.

Embracing Digital Technologies

Digital modes and internet-linked communications are becoming increasingly prevalent in amateur radio. These technologies offer new ways to communicate, bringing efficiency and global connectivity to the forefront.

Consider a young operator named Lucas, who represents the new generation of HAM enthusiasts. Lucas is particularly interested in digital modes like FT8 for weak signal communication and uses internet-linked systems such as D-STAR and EchoLink to connect with repeaters and operators around the world.

Integration of Software-Defined Radio (SDR)

Software-Defined Radio (SDR) is set to play a significant role in the future of amateur radio. Its flexibility and adaptability make it a powerful tool for experimentation and development.

Lucas sets up an SDR station, which allows him to explore a wide range of frequencies and modes with a simple click. The visual interface of SDR software also helps him better understand signal propagation and band conditions.

Advancements in Satellite and Space Communication

The involvement of amateur radio in space exploration, including communication with satellites and the International Space Station (ISS), is likely to grow. These aspects of the hobby capture the imagination and offer a glimpse into the future of communication.

Lucas participates in a scheduled contact with an astronaut aboard the ISS, using a satellite ground station setup. This experience not only excites him but also inspires him to learn more about space communication.

The Role of HAM Radio in Emergency Communication

The importance of amateur radio in emergency and disaster communication remains paramount. With climate change and natural disasters, the role of amateur radio as a reliable backup communication system is likely to become more critical.

Lucas volunteers with a local Amateur Radio Emergency Service (ARES) group. He participates in training and drills, preparing to provide essential communication in times of crisis.

Youth Involvement and Education

The future of HAM radio depends significantly on attracting younger generations. Educational initiatives, STEM (Science, Technology, Engineering, and Mathematics) programs, and youth-oriented activities are crucial for bringing new blood into the hobby.

Lucas, aware of this need, starts a club at his school to introduce other students to amateur radio. He organizes demonstrations and workshops, sparking interest among his peers.

Regulatory Challenges and Opportunities

The amateur radio community faces ongoing regulatory challenges, including spectrum allocation and licensing procedures. Balancing the needs of a growing and technologically advancing hobby with the regulatory frameworks is crucial for the future of amateur radio.

Lucas stays informed about regulatory issues and participates in discussions and advocacy efforts to protect and expand amateur radio's access to the radio spectrum.

The Continuing Importance of Clubs and Organizations

HAM radio clubs and organizations will continue to play a vital role in the hobby's future. They provide support, advocacy, education, and a sense of community for operators of all ages and experience levels.

Lucas's involvement in his local club and national organizations like the ARRL (American Radio Relay League) connects him with a wider community of amateur radio enthusiasts, offering support and opportunities for growth.

Globalization and Cultural Exchange

As the world becomes more interconnected, the role of amateur radio in promoting international friendship and understanding becomes even more important. HAM radio offers a unique platform for cross-cultural communication and global connectivity.

Lucas regularly participates in international events and contests, making contacts worldwide and learning about different cultures through amateur radio.

In conclusion, the future of HAM radio looks vibrant and diverse, driven by technological innovation, community involvement, and global connectivity. For operators like Lucas, the hobby offers endless possibilities for exploration, learning, and contribution. The evolution of amateur radio reflects the changing world, adapting to new technologies and challenges while maintaining its core values of communication, education, and community service.

Chapter 20: Resources and Continuing Education

In the dynamic world of amateur radio, continuous learning and access to quality resources are key to staying informed and proficient. This chapter highlights the various resources and educational opportunities available to HAM radio operators, emphasizing the importance of ongoing education and skill development in the hobby.

Books and Publications

There is a wealth of written material available for amateur radio enthusiasts. Books and publications covering a wide range of topics, from beginner guides to advanced technical manuals, are invaluable resources.

Consider Sarah, an intermediate-level HAM operator who is keen to expand her knowledge. She turns to classic texts like the "ARRL Handbook for Radio Communications" and "The ARRL Antenna Book," which provide in-depth information on almost every aspect of amateur radio.

Online Resources and Websites

The internet has become a treasure trove of information for HAM radio operators. Websites, forums, and online communities offer up-to-date information, tutorials, and platforms for discussion and advice.

Sarah frequently visits websites like QRZ.com for call sign lookups and eHam.net for equipment reviews and forums. She also subscribes to YouTube channels that specialize in amateur radio topics, offering visual guides and demonstrations.

HAM Radio Blogs and Podcasts

Blogs and podcasts run by experienced HAM radio operators are excellent sources of information, news, and insights into the hobby. They provide a more personal touch and often cover the latest trends and discussions in the amateur radio community.

Sarah follows a few well-known amateur radio blogs and regularly listens to podcasts like "HAM Nation" and "The ARRL Audio News," which keep her informed about the latest developments in the hobby.

Workshops and Webinars

Many HAM radio clubs and organizations host workshops and webinars on various aspects of amateur radio. These events are great for learning new skills, understanding emerging technologies, and meeting other HAM operators.

Sarah attends workshops hosted by her local HAM radio club and signs up for webinars offered by national and international amateur radio organizations. These events not only enhance her knowledge but also provide networking opportunities.

HAM Radio Clubs and Organizations

Joining a HAM radio club or organization is perhaps one of the most valuable steps an operator can take. Clubs provide mentorship, resources, and opportunities to practice and learn in a supportive environment.

Sarah is an active member of her local HAM radio club and also a member of the ARRL (American Radio Relay League). These affiliations provide her with access to resources, help in setting up her station, and guidance on improving her operating skills.

Licensing and Upgrade Classes

For those looking to obtain or upgrade their amateur radio license, there are numerous classes available. These classes not only prepare operators for licensing exams but also provide a deeper understanding of radio theory and operation.

Sarah, aiming to upgrade her license, enrolls in an online class that prepares her for the General class license exam. The class covers technical topics, regulations, and operating practices.

Conventions and HAMfests

HAM radio conventions and HAMfests are gatherings where operators can attend lectures, meet vendors, and see the latest equipment and technologies. These events are excellent for learning and experiencing the broader HAM radio culture.

Sarah plans to visit the annual Dayton Hamvention, one of the largest amateur radio gatherings in the world. She looks forward to attending seminars, viewing new products, and interacting with fellow HAM enthusiasts from around the globe.

Self-Experimentation and Projects

Finally, one of the best ways to learn in amateur radio is through self-experimentation and DIY projects. Building antennas, setting up stations, and experimenting with different modes and setups provide practical, hands-on learning experiences.

Sarah spends her weekends working on various radio projects, such as building a new antenna and setting up a digital mode station. These projects not only enhance her technical skills but also provide a sense of accomplishment.

In conclusion, the resources and opportunities for continuing education in amateur radio are abundant and varied. For operators like Sarah, these resources are invaluable for enhancing knowledge, skills, and enjoyment of the hobby. Whether through reading, online learning, community involvement, or hands-on experimentation, continuous learning is a cornerstone of the amateur radio experience, keeping operators engaged, informed, and connected to the ever-evolving world of HAM radio.

Conclusion:

The Endless Journey in HAM Radio

The journey of a HAM radio operator is one of continuous exploration, learning, and community engagement. This book, "HAM Radio for Beginners: QuickStart Guide for New HAMs," has endeavored to provide a comprehensive foundation for anyone embarking on this fascinating adventure. In concluding, we reflect on the essence of amateur radio, its impact on individuals and communities, and the ongoing journey that lies ahead for every operator.

The Lifelong Learning Experience

HAM radio is a hobby where learning never stops. From the first steps of understanding basic concepts to exploring advanced technologies and modes, the hobby offers endless opportunities for growth and development. Every new frequency tuned, every antenna built, and every contact made is a step forward in this enriching journey.

Take the example of an operator named Alex. Alex started his HAM radio journey as a teenager, building simple antennas and making local contacts. Over the years, he expanded his skills, exploring digital modes, participating in contests, and eventually engaging in satellite communication. His journey in amateur radio has been a constant source of learning and personal fulfillment.

Community and Friendship

One of the most rewarding aspects of HAM radio is the sense of community it fosters. HAM operators worldwide share a common passion that transcends geographical, cultural, and political boundaries, creating a global network of friends and mentors. This community aspect is not just about making contacts but about sharing experiences, offering help, and working together.

Alex recalls the friendships he has formed over the airwaves, some of which have lasted decades. He also cherishes the support he received from other operators when setting up his station or when he volunteered for emergency communication during a natural disaster.

Contributing to Society

Amateur radio also plays a significant role in public service and emergency communication. Operators like Alex often volunteer their skills and equipment during emergencies, providing critical communication links when other systems fail. This aspect of the hobby underscores its relevance and importance in the modern world.

Embracing Change and Innovation

The world of amateur radio is constantly evolving with technological advancements. Operators are continually adapting to new technologies, whether it's the latest digital mode, software-defined radio, or satellite communication. This adaptability and willingness to embrace change are what keep the hobby vibrant and relevant.

Alex, for instance, has witnessed the transition from analog to digital modes and has embraced SDR technology. He enjoys experimenting with new software and equipment, constantly adding to his knowledge and capabilities.

The Personal Journey

Every HAM operator's journey is unique, shaped by their interests, experiences, and the paths they choose to explore. For some, the hobby is about technical experimentation and innovation; for others, it's about communication and community service. But for all, it's a journey of discovery and enjoyment.

Alex's journey in amateur radio has been multifaceted. He has delved into technical projects, participated in community service, and enjoyed the simple pleasure of casual conversations with operators from around the world.

In Conclusion

As we conclude this book, it's clear that the journey in HAM radio is as diverse and expansive as the hobby itself. It's a journey that offers not just a pastime, but a lifetime of learning, exploration, and connection. Whether you are a beginner like Sarah, an intermediate enthusiast like Elena, or an experienced operator like Alex, amateur radio has something to offer everyone.

The world of HAM radio awaits, ready to be explored and experienced. As you continue on your journey, remember that each step you take enriches not just your own experience, but also the broader amateur radio community. May your journey be filled with clear signals, interesting contacts, and endless learning.

BOOK 2
The Ham Radio Advance Technik:

An Overview of Ham Radio's Rich History and Evolution

Introduction

In the ever-evolving world of communication technology, amateur radio, commonly known as ham radio, stands out as a fascinating and enduring cornerstone. This book, "The Ham Radio Advance Technik", delves into the intricate and captivating world of ham radio, offering a comprehensive guide that caters to both novices and seasoned enthusiasts. The purpose of this book is not only to educate but also to inspire a deeper appreciation and understanding of ham radio's unique place in both historical and modern communication landscapes.

Ham radio's inception dates back to the late 19th century, emerging almost concurrently with the birth of radio technology itself. Initially, radio waves were a newfound phenomenon, a mysterious form of communication that could traverse long distances without the need for physical connections. The early experimenters and pioneers of this technology were primarily amateurs, driven by curiosity and a passion for innovation. These individuals laid the groundwork for what would become a global hobby, a tool for emergency communication, and a means of connecting people across continents and cultures.

The essence of ham radio is communication over radio waves using various types of equipment and frequencies. Unlike commercial radio, television, or professional broadcasting, ham radio is characterized by its two-way communication nature. Operators, known as hams, engage in conversations, exchange messages, and share knowledge with fellow enthusiasts worldwide. This unique aspect of interaction and learning is what continually draws people to this hobby.

A critical aspect of ham radio is the requirement of licensing. Unlike other forms of wireless communication, operating a ham radio station requires an operator to pass examinations and obtain a license from their national regulatory authority. This process ensures that all operators have a basic understanding of radio theory, operating principles, and legal regulations. Licensing also serves as a rite of passage, inducting new members into a global community that values responsibility, technical proficiency, and mutual respect.

This book is structured to provide a comprehensive journey through the world of ham radio. It begins by laying the foundational knowledge required for anyone interested in taking up this hobby. This includes understanding the basic concepts of radio frequencies, equipment, and the licensing process. Following chapters build upon this foundation, exploring more advanced topics such as antenna design, propagation, digital communication modes, and satellite communication. Each chapter is designed to progressively deepen the reader's understanding and skills in various aspects of ham radio.

The technological aspect of ham radio cannot be understated. This book delves into the intricacies of transmitters, receivers, antennas, and other equipment that form the backbone of a ham radio setup. Readers will learn how to select the right equipment for their needs, understand the principles behind their operation, and even delve into building and modifying their own gear. This hands-on approach is a significant part of the hobby's appeal, as it allows enthusiasts to tailor their experience and engage with the technology at a fundamental level.

Another fascinating aspect of ham radio explored in this book is the use of Morse code. Despite being one of the oldest forms of electronic communication, Morse code remains relevant in the ham radio community. It exemplifies the blend of historical tradition and modern technology that is characteristic of ham radio. Learning and using Morse code connects today's hams with the pioneers of radio communication, providing a sense of continuity and tradition.

Emergency communication is another critical area where ham radio plays a vital role, which is extensively covered in this book. In times of natural disasters or other emergencies, when conventional communication infrastructures are compromised, ham radio operators often step in to provide vital communication links. This role underscores the importance of ham radio not just as a hobby but as a public service.

The scientific principles underlying ham radio are explained in detail, including radio wave theory, signal propagation, and the impact of various atmospheric conditions on radio communication. This technical knowledge is essential for any ham radio operator, as it allows them to optimize their equipment and understand the nuances of radio wave behavior.

Furthermore, this book addresses the social and cultural impact of ham radio. It is a hobby that transcends borders, languages, and cultures, connecting people from all walks of life. Ham radio fosters a sense of global community and friendship, bound together by a shared passion for communication and technology.

Advanced topics such as contesting, awards, and satellite communication are also covered. These aspects add competitive and exploratory dimensions to the hobby, challenging operators to hone their skills and expand their horizons.

In conclusion, "The Ham Radio Advance Technik" is not just a technical guide; it is a testament to the enduring fascination and relevance of ham radio. As technology continues to advance, ham radio adapts and evolves, integrating new technologies while preserving its core principles of communication, experimentation, and community. This book aims to equip readers with the knowledge and inspiration to join this ever-evolving journey, embracing the future of ham radio while honoring its rich past.

Chapter 1: The Basics of Ham Radio

Understanding the Fundamentals: Frequencies, Equipment, and Licensing

The journey into the world of amateur radio begins with mastering its fundamentals – frequencies, equipment, and licensing. This chapter aims to provide a comprehensive introduction to these basic elements, along with a practical example to illustrate their application in the real world.

Frequencies and Bands

The radio frequency spectrum is vast, with amateur radio operators having access to specific bands allocated by regulatory bodies like the Federal Communications Commission (FCC) in the United States. These bands are segments of the radio frequency spectrum designated for amateur radio use, each having its unique characteristics and uses.

For example, the 2-meter band (144-148 MHz) is one of the most popular VHF bands among amateur radio enthusiasts. It's ideal for local communications over a range of up to 100 miles, depending on the terrain and equipment. This band is commonly used for both base station and handheld transceivers, making it a versatile choice for various communication needs.

Equipment Basics

The basic equipment required for a ham radio setup includes a transceiver (a combined receiver and transmitter), an antenna, and a power source. The choice of equipment depends on various factors, including the operator's budget, the intended use, and the bands they plan to operate on.

For our practical example, let's consider setting up a station for the 2-meter band. A typical setup would include:

1. **Transceiver**: A VHF transceiver capable of operating in the 144-148 MHz range. This could be a mobile unit installed at a home station or a handheld device for portable use.

2. **Antenna**: A simple 1/4 wavelength vertical antenna would suffice for local communications. Antennas can be homemade or commercially purchased. The antenna's height and placement significantly impact its performance.
3. **Power Source**: For a base station, this could be a 12-volt power supply. Handheld transceivers usually come with their rechargeable batteries.

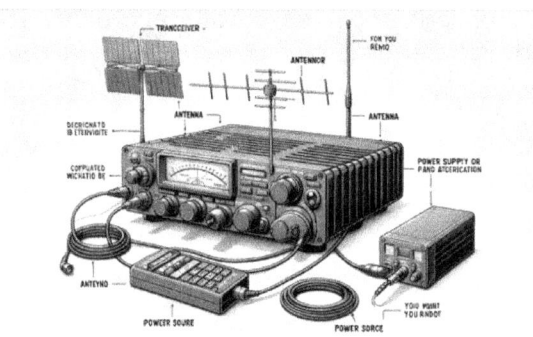

Licensing

Obtaining a ham radio license is a critical step. In the United States, the FCC offers three levels of licenses – Technician, General, and Extra. Each level grants increasing access to different bands and modes of operation. The Technician license, being the entry-level license, is a great starting point for beginners.

The licensing process involves passing an examination that tests knowledge of basic regulations, operating practices, and electronics theory. Preparation for this exam can be done through self-study, online courses, or local ham radio clubs.

Practical Example: Setting Up a Station for the 2-Meter Band

Let's walk through a practical example of setting up a basic ham radio station for the 2-meter band. This setup is ideal for someone who has just acquired their technician license.

1. **Choosing a Transceiver**: For our example, we select a dual-band mobile transceiver that covers both the 2-meter and 70-centimeter bands. This transceiver can be installed at a home station or used in a vehicle.
2. **Antenna Selection and Installation**: We opt for a 1/4 wavelength ground-plane antenna for the 2-meter band. This antenna is mounted on the roof of the home, ensuring it's above any obstructions for optimal signal transmission and reception. The antenna is connected to the transceiver using coaxial cable.
3. **Powering the Station**: A 12-volt power supply is connected to the transceiver, providing a stable power source. For handheld use, the transceiver's battery is kept charged.
4. **Initial Setup and Testing**: After installing the equipment, the next step is to test the setup. We tune the transceiver to a local repeater frequency and perform a radio check. Adjustments to the antenna position might be necessary to achieve the best performance.
5. **Making the First Contact**: Using the local repeater, we make our first contact. This involves listening to the frequency to ensure it's clear, keying the microphone, and following proper operating procedure to call another station.
6. **Logging and Learning**: Every contact made is logged, including the date, time, frequency, and call sign of the stations contacted. This log serves as a record and a tool for learning and improving operating skills.

Through this practical example, a new ham radio operator can experience the thrill of setting up their first station and making initial contacts. This process not only provides a solid foundation in operating a ham radio station but also sparks the curiosity and enthusiasm that drive the amateur radio hobby.

As we progress through this book, more advanced topics and techniques will be explored. However, the basics outlined in this chapter form the cornerstone upon which all further ham radio knowledge and skills are built.

Chapter 2: Setting Up Your First Station

A Step-by-Step Guide: Equipment Selection, Location, and Installation

After understanding the fundamentals of ham radio, the next crucial step is setting up your first station. This chapter provides a detailed guide on selecting the right equipment, finding the perfect location, and installing your station, complemented by a practical example to illustrate these concepts.

Equipment Selection

The heart of any ham radio station is its equipment, which primarily includes a transceiver, an antenna, and a power source. The selection of this equipment is critical and depends on several factors such as the operator's budget, the type of communications they wish to engage in, and the space available for the setup.

1. **Transceiver**: Choose a transceiver based on the bands you plan to operate on. For beginners, a dual-band VHF/UHF transceiver is often recommended as it allows access to two of the most popular amateur radio bands.
2. **Antenna**: The antenna is perhaps the most crucial component of your setup. The choice of antenna depends on the space available and the bands you wish to operate on. For most beginners, a simple dipole or a vertical antenna for the VHF/UHF bands is a good start.
3. **Power Supply**: A stable and reliable power supply is essential. Most base station transceivers require a 12-volt power supply. Ensure that the power supply can handle the maximum power output of the transceiver.

Location Selection

The location of your station plays a significant role in its performance. When choosing a location, consider factors like:

1. **Space**: Ensure there is enough room for your equipment and any future expansions.
2. **Interference**: Avoid locations with high levels of electrical noise, such as near large electronic appliances or power lines.
3. **Antenna Placement**: The location should allow for optimal antenna placement, ideally in a high and clear area.

Installation

Setting up your station involves connecting all the components and ensuring they function correctly together. Follow these steps:

1. **Assembling the Transceiver**: Place the transceiver in a well-ventilated area to prevent overheating. Connect it to the power supply, ensuring all connections are secure.
2. **Antenna Setup**: Install the antenna as high as possible, away from obstructions. Ensure it is properly grounded for safety and performance.
3. **Connecting the Antenna to the Transceiver**: Use quality coaxial cable to connect the antenna to the transceiver. The length and quality of the cable can significantly affect the station's performance.
4. **Testing the Setup**: Once everything is connected, power up the transceiver and check for proper operation. Test the SWR (Standing Wave Ratio) to ensure the antenna is tuned correctly.

Practical Example: Setting Up a VHF/UHF Station

Let's walk through a practical example of setting up a basic VHF/UHF station, ideal for local and regional communication.

1. **Choosing Equipment**: For our example, we select a dual-band VHF/UHF transceiver, a simple vertical antenna for VHF/UHF, and a 12-volt power supply.
2. **Finding the Location**: We choose a spare room in a house with a window facing a clear, open area for the antenna.
3. **Installing the Antenna**: The vertical antenna is installed on a mast on the roof of the house. It's positioned to have a clear view of the sky, away from large obstructions. The antenna is properly grounded.
4. **Setting Up the Transceiver**: The transceiver is placed on a desk, with ample space around it for ventilation. It is connected to the power supply and the coaxial cable from the antenna.
5. **Connecting and Testing**: After ensuring all connections are secure, we turn on the transceiver and perform a radio check. We tune to a local repeater and listen for activity, ensuring the system is receiving well.
6. **Making Adjustments**: The SWR meter is used to check the antenna's tuning. Minor adjustments are made to the antenna length for optimal tuning.
7. **First Contact**: We make our first contact using the local repeater, introducing ourselves and engaging in a brief conversation with another local ham operator.

Through this practical example, the new ham radio operator gains hands-on experience in setting up a basic yet functional amateur radio station. This process not only equips them with the necessary skills but also instills confidence in their ability to communicate effectively using ham radio.

The setup described here represents the foundation upon which many ham radio enthusiasts build their lifelong hobby. As skills and interests develop, operators often expand their stations with more advanced equipment and antennas, exploring wider aspects of amateur radio communication. However, the principles and steps outlined in this chapter provide a solid starting point for anyone embarking on their ham radio journey.

Chapter 3: Mastering Radio Frequencies

Navigating the Spectrum: Frequency Bands and Their Uses in Ham Radio

In this chapter, we delve into the world of radio frequencies, a crucial aspect of ham radio. Understanding the frequency bands and their specific characteristics is key to becoming an effective operator. This chapter will guide you through the different frequency bands, their properties, and practical applications, culminating in a hands-on example.

Understanding Frequency Bands

The radio frequency spectrum is divided into different bands, each with unique properties and uses. These bands range from Very Low Frequency (VLF) to Extremely High Frequency (EHF). For ham radio operators, the most commonly used bands are High Frequency (HF), Very High Frequency (VHF), and Ultra High Frequency (UHF).

1. **High Frequency (HF)**: Ranging from 3 to 30 MHz, HF bands are known for their long-distance communication capabilities, facilitated by their ability to reflect off the ionosphere.
2. **Very High Frequency (VHF)**: Spanning 30 to 300 MHz, VHF bands are primarily used for local and regional communications, offering clearer audio quality but shorter range compared to HF.

3. **Ultra High Frequency (UHF)**: Covering 300 MHz to 3 GHz, UHF bands are used for very local communications and can penetrate urban landscapes but have a limited range.

Each of these bands has its specific advantages and limitations, influenced by factors like time of day, solar activity, and atmospheric conditions.

Propagation and Its Effects

Understanding radio wave propagation is crucial for effective communication. Propagation refers to how radio waves travel through the atmosphere. Factors affecting propagation include:

1. **The Ionosphere**: Plays a significant role in HF band propagation, reflecting radio waves back to Earth, enabling long-distance communication.
2. **Line of Sight**: Essential for VHF and UHF communications, as these frequencies generally travel in straight lines and are obstructed by physical barriers.
3. **Weather Conditions**: Can impact signal strength and quality, particularly for VHF and UHF frequencies.

Equipment for Different Bands

The choice of equipment varies depending on the band of operation. For HF bands, operators often use large antennas like dipoles or verticals, and transceivers capable of handling the specific frequency range. For VHF and UHF, smaller antennas and handheld or mobile transceivers are common.

Practical Example: Tuning into Different Bands

Let's explore a practical scenario where an operator tunes into different bands and experiences their unique characteristics.

1. **HF Exploration**: The operator sets up a dipole antenna and tunes the transceiver to the 20-meter band (14 MHz). They find that during the day, the band is active with international communications, thanks to ionospheric propagation.
2. **VHF Communication**: Using a 2-meter band handheld transceiver with a small vertical antenna, the operator communicates with local ham radio enthusiasts. The communication is clear and limited to a shorter range, typical of VHF.
3. **UHF Experimentation**: On the 70-centimeter band, the operator uses a mobile transceiver with a UHF antenna. They notice that the communication range is further limited, but the signal penetrates urban areas effectively.
4. **Logging and Observing**: The operator logs all contacts and notes the differences in signal clarity, range, and propagation effects across the bands.
5. **Antenna Adjustments**: To optimize HF reception, the operator experiments with antenna height and orientation, noticing significant changes in signal reception.
6. **Participating in a Net**: Joining a local VHF net, the operator experiences organized communication, gaining insight into the operational nuances of different bands.

Through this example, the operator gains a hands-on understanding of how different frequency bands function, the importance of propagation, and the practical aspects of operating on each band. This knowledge is indispensable for any ham radio enthusiast and forms the basis for more advanced explorations into the world of amateur radio.

Mastering the nuances of radio frequencies and their respective bands is a journey that every ham radio operator undertakes. This chapter serves as a stepping stone into that journey, providing the foundational knowledge and practical insights needed to navigate the vast and fascinating spectrum of ham radio frequencies.

Chapter 4: Antennas and Propagation

Design and Theory: Building and Optimizing Antennas for Maximum Range

Antennas are a critical component in ham radio, serving as the interface between the radio waves traveling through the air and the electronic equipment used by ham radio operators. This chapter delves into the theory, design, and practical aspects of antennas, as well as the principles of radio wave propagation that affect their performance.

Understanding Antennas

An antenna is a transducer that converts radio frequency (RF) electrical signals into electromagnetic waves and vice versa. The efficiency, design, and placement of an antenna can significantly affect communication range and clarity.

Types of Antennas

There are various types of antennas, each with its characteristics and specific uses:

1. **Dipole Antennas**: Simple, effective, and commonly used for HF bands. They consist of two metal wires or rods with a feedline in the center.
2. **Yagi-Uda Antennas**: Directional antennas that provide increased gain, ideal for VHF/UHF bands.
3. **Vertical Antennas**: Common for mobile and maritime use, offering an omnidirectional pattern suitable for VHF and UHF.
4. **Loop Antennas**: Known for their small size and efficiency, particularly in confined spaces.
5. **Wire Antennas**: Versatile and easy to construct, suitable for various bands.

Antenna Theory

The performance of an antenna is influenced by several factors:

1. **Resonance**: The frequency at which an antenna naturally resonates, resulting in the most efficient transmission and reception.
2. **Impedance Matching**: Ensuring the antenna and the transmitter have the same impedance for efficient power transfer.
3. **Polarization**: The orientation of the electromagnetic field produced by the antenna, which can be horizontal, vertical, or circular.
4. **Gain**: A measure of how much power is transmitted in a particular direction.
5. **Bandwidth**: The range of frequencies over which the antenna can operate effectively.

Propagation Principles

Understanding how radio waves propagate is crucial in optimizing antenna performance. Factors affecting propagation include:

1. **Ground Reflection**: The interaction of radio waves with the earth's surface, affecting signal strength and reach.
2. **Atmospheric Absorption**: The loss of signal strength due to atmospheric conditions.
3. **Ionospheric Reflection**: Particularly relevant for HF bands, where radio waves can be reflected back to Earth.
4. **Line of Sight**: Essential for VHF and UHF frequencies, as these waves travel in straight lines.

Practical Example: Building and Testing a Dipole Antenna

Let's go through a practical example of constructing and testing a dipole antenna for the 20-meter band (14 MHz).

1. **Calculating Antenna Length**: For a half-wave dipole, the formula is Length (in meters)=300frequency (in MHz)×0.5Length (in meters)=frequency (in MHz)300×0.5. For a 14 MHz dipole, this would be approximately 10.7 meters in total length, with each leg being about 5.35 meters.
2. **Construction**: Using two pieces of wire, each 5.35 meters long, and an insulator at the center where the feedline will connect. The antenna is assembled and hung horizontally at a height, ideally more than half a wavelength above the ground.
3. **Feedline Connection**: A coaxial cable is attached to the center insulator, ensuring proper impedance matching.
4. **Testing Resonance**: Using an antenna analyzer or an SWR meter to test the resonance of the antenna. Adjustments are made to the length of the wires until the lowest SWR is achieved at the desired frequency.
5. **On-Air Testing**: The antenna is connected to a transceiver, and a test transmission is made. Signal reports from other stations can provide feedback on the antenna's performance.
6. **Logging and Analysis**: All contacts and signal reports are logged, and any patterns or issues noted are used to further refine the antenna setup.

Through this example, the operator gains practical experience in antenna theory, design, and testing. The knowledge and skills acquired are not only gratifying but also empower the operator to experiment with other types of antennas, enhancing their understanding and capabilities in ham radio.

Antenna design and optimization are an art and a science that lie at the heart of effective ham radio communication. The concepts and practices outlined in this chapter provide a foundation for amateurs to build upon, encouraging experimentation and learning in the pursuit of the perfect antenna setup.

Chapter 5: Transmitters and Receivers

Core Components Explained: How They Work and How to Choose Them

Transmitters and receivers are the fundamental components of any ham radio setup, enabling communication over vast distances. This chapter will delve into their workings, how to choose the right ones for your needs, and a practical example to illustrate these concepts.

Understanding Transmitters

A transmitter converts electrical signals into radio waves, which are then transmitted through the antenna. The key aspects of a transmitter include:

1. **Frequency Generation**: The transmitter generates the carrier frequency on which the signal is transmitted.
2. **Modulation**: This process varies the carrier wave to encode the information. Common modes include Amplitude Modulation (AM), Frequency Modulation (FM), and Single Sideband (SSB).
3. **Power Amplification**: Increases the strength of the signal to be sent over long distances.
4. **Filtering**: Ensures the transmission stays within the designated frequency band and reduces interference.

Understanding Receivers

A receiver captures radio waves from the air and converts them back into electrical signals. Its main components are:

1. **Antenna**: Captures the incoming radio waves.
2. **Tuner**: Selects the desired frequency and rejects others.
3. **Demodulation**: Extracts the audio or data signal from the modulated carrier wave.
4. **Amplification**: Boosts the extracted signal to a level suitable for output devices like speakers or headphones.

Choosing Transmitters and Receivers

When selecting a transmitter and receiver, consider:

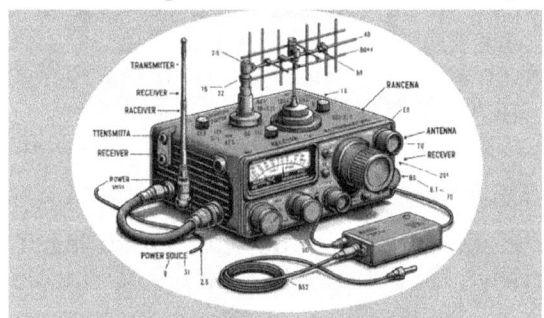

1. **Frequency Range**: Ensure they cover the bands you intend to operate in.
2. **Power Output**: Higher power transmitters can transmit over greater distances but may require additional licensing.
3. **Sensitivity and Selectivity**: For receivers, sensitivity refers to the ability to detect weak signals, while selectivity is the ability to distinguish between closely spaced signals.
4. **Features and Functionality**: Look for features like digital signal processing, filters, and built-in tuners, depending on your needs.

Practical Example: Setting Up and Testing a Transceiver

Let's consider a practical scenario of setting up a transceiver (a combined transmitter and receiver) for amateur radio use.

1. **Selection**: Choose a transceiver suitable for HF band operation, with a power output of 100 watts, SSB capability, and a built-in antenna tuner.
2. **Antenna Connection**: Connect a multi-band dipole antenna to the transceiver. Ensure the antenna covers the HF bands you plan to operate on.
3. **Power Source**: Connect the transceiver to a 12-volt power supply, ensuring it provides enough current for the transceiver's maximum power output.
4. **Initial Configuration**: Set up the transceiver's basic settings, such as frequency, mode (SSB, AM, FM), and filters according to the operation's requirements.

5. **Testing Transmission**: Tune the transceiver to a clear frequency in the 20-meter band. Adjust the antenna tuner for the lowest SWR. Transmit a test signal and request a signal report from any responding station.
6. **Receiving Signals**: Adjust the receiver's settings, such as the RF gain and filters, to optimize the reception of signals. Scan through the band and listen to different stations, noting the clarity and strength of received signals.
7. **Logging Contacts**: Log each contact made, noting the frequency, mode, and signal reports. This data will help in assessing the performance of your setup.

Through this example, the operator gets practical experience in setting up and operating a transceiver, understanding the intricacies of both transmission and reception. This foundational knowledge is crucial for effective communication and further exploration in the world of amateur radio.

The mastery of transmitters and receivers is a vital skill for any ham radio enthusiast. It involves not only technical understanding but also a practical hands-on approach to ensure effective communication. The concepts and practices outlined in this chapter provide a robust framework for amateurs to understand and optimize their radio setups, paving the way for a rewarding experience in the ham radio community.

Chapter 6: Digital Modes of Communication

Embracing Modernity: Understanding Digital Transmission in Ham Radio

The advent of digital technology has revolutionized the world of ham radio, introducing various digital modes of communication that offer enhanced efficiency, reliability, and new functionalities. This chapter explores the digital landscape in amateur radio, covering the basics of digital modes, how they work, and a practical example of setting up and using a digital mode.

Understanding Digital Modes

Digital modes involve the transmission of data over radio waves using digital signals rather than traditional analog methods. These modes can offer clearer communications with less power and are often more resistant to noise and interference.

Popular Digital Modes

1. **RTTY (Radio Teletype)**: One of the oldest digital modes, it transmits data by varying the frequency of the carrier wave.
2. **PSK31 (Phase Shift Keying, 31 Baud)**: A highly efficient mode allowing real-time, low-power communications, ideal for keyboard-to-keyboard chatting.
3. **FT8**: A newer, fast mode designed for weak-signal conditions, perfect for making contacts over long distances even with modest equipment.
4. **D-STAR (Digital Smart Technologies for Amateur Radio)**: Developed for voice and data transmission, it allows for global communication through interconnected repeaters and the internet.
5. **WSJT-X Modes (including JT65, JT9)**: Designed for weak signal communication, these modes are excellent for DXing (long-distance communication).

The Basics of Digital Communication

In digital modes, voice or data is first converted into digital form. This digital data is then used to modulate a carrier wave, typically through methods like Frequency Shift Keying (FSK), Phase Shift Keying (PSK), or Quadrature Amplitude Modulation (QAM).

Equipment for Digital Modes

1. **Transceiver**: Most modern transceivers support digital modes either directly or through an interface.
2. **Computer**: A PC is typically used to run digital mode software and process the digital signals.
3. **Interface**: Connects the transceiver to the computer, handling the conversion between audio and digital signals.
4. **Software**: Programs like WSJT-X, FLdigi, or DigiPan are used to operate in various digital modes.

Practical Example: Making Contacts using FT8

For our practical example, we will set up a station to operate in the FT8 digital mode.

1. **Software Installation**: Install the WSJT-X software on a computer. This software supports FT8 and other digital modes.
2. **Connecting the Transceiver**: Connect the transceiver to the computer using a signal interface. This interface will handle the conversion of digital signals between the transceiver and the computer.
3. **Software Configuration**: Configure the WSJT-X software with the correct settings for your transceiver, including COM port, audio input/output, and transmission settings.
4. **Time Synchronization**: Ensure the computer's clock is accurately synchronized to UTC, as precise timing is critical for FT8.
5. **Tuning the Transceiver**: Select an appropriate frequency for FT8 within the ham bands (e.g., 14.074 MHz for the 20-meter band).
6. **Making Contacts**: Open WSJT-X and start monitoring for incoming FT8 CQ calls. When you spot a CQ, click on it to reply and initiate a QSO (contact).
7. **Logging Contacts**: Each completed QSO should be logged, noting the call sign, signal report, time, and frequency.

Through this example, the operator experiences the unique aspects of digital mode communication, including the setup and actual operation. The use of software and digital processing opens up new avenues for communication that are less affected by noise and signal strength, enabling contacts that might be challenging or impossible with traditional analog methods.

Digital modes have significantly expanded the scope and capabilities of amateur radio, allowing operators to continue their pursuit of communication and experimentation in this digital age. Understanding and utilizing these modes not only enhances the ham radio experience but also keeps the hobby in line with modern technological advancements. The practical knowledge and skills gained from operating digital modes are invaluable assets in the toolbox of any contemporary ham radio enthusiast.

Chapter 7: Morse Code in Modern Ham Radio

The Timeless Language: Learning and Utilizing Morse Code

Morse Code, a method of transmitting textual information as a series of on-off tones, lights, or clicks, has been a fundamental aspect of radio communication since its earliest days. Despite the advent of more advanced technologies, Morse Code remains a valuable skill for amateur radio operators. This chapter explores the relevance of Morse Code in modern ham radio, how to learn it, and its practical application.

The Relevance of Morse Code Today

While it might seem antiquated, Morse Code is highly efficient in weak signal conditions and is a mode that requires minimal bandwidth. It's particularly effective during emergencies or in situations where sophisticated equipment is not available.

Learning Morse Code

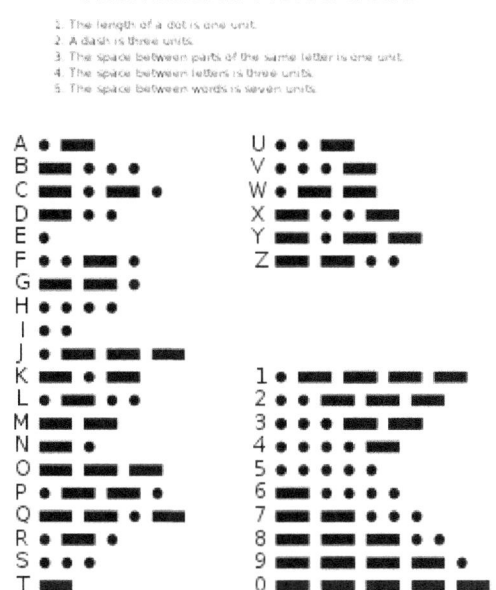

1. **Understanding the Basics**: Morse Code represents each letter of the alphabet and each numeral by a unique sequence of dots (short signals) and dashes (long signals).
2. **Practice**: Regular practice is essential. Start with learning a few letters and numbers each day, gradually increasing speed and complexity.
3. **Listening**: Listening to Morse Code transmissions can significantly improve proficiency. There are many online resources and practice tools available.
4. **Joining a Community**: Engaging with a community of Morse Code enthusiasts can provide support and motivation.

Equipment for Morse Code Transmission

1. **Key or Paddle**: Used to manually send Morse Code. A straight key is the traditional option, while paddles are used for faster, electronic keying.
2. **Transceiver**: Most modern transceivers have a Morse Code mode (CW – Continuous Wave).
3. **Decoding Software**: There are software options available that can decode Morse Code transmissions, useful for beginners.

Practical Example: Communicating with Morse Code

Let's set up a scenario where an amateur radio operator uses Morse Code for communication.

1. **Equipment Setup**: Connect a straight key to a transceiver set to the CW mode. For this example, use the 20-meter band (around 14.060 MHz, a common Morse Code frequency).
2. **Sending a CQ Call**: Start by sending a CQ call in Morse Code. For instance, "CQ CQ CQ DE [Your Call Sign] K" where "DE" means "from" and "K" is an invitation for any station to respond.
3. **Receiving Responses**: Listen for responses from other stations. It may take time to distinguish the Morse Code tones.
4. **Making a QSO (Contact)**: When a station responds, proceed with the QSO. Exchange information like signal report, location, and operator's name.
5. **Logging the Contact**: Log the details of the contact, including the call sign of the other station, time, band, and any other relevant details.
6. **Practice and Improvement**: Regular practice in sending and receiving Morse Code will improve speed and accuracy. Participate in Morse Code nets or contests to enhance skills.

Through this practical exercise, the operator gains experience in Morse Code communication, appreciating its simplicity and efficiency. Morse Code offers a unique and satisfying way to communicate, connecting today's operators with the roots of wireless communication.

Despite being one of the oldest forms of electronic communication, Morse Code continues to hold a special place in the world of amateur radio. Its resilience over time is a testament to its effectiveness and the fondness with which it is regarded in the ham radio community. Learning and using Morse Code not only enriches the amateur radio experience but also ensures that this timeless skill is preserved for future generations of radio enthusiasts.

Chapter 8: Emergency Communication Protocols

Preparedness and Response: Ham Radio's Role in Emergencies

In times of crisis, when conventional communication systems often fail or become overloaded, amateur radio has repeatedly proven to be a reliable means of emergency communication. This chapter covers the critical role of ham radio in emergencies, the protocols involved, and a practical example of setting up an emergency communication (EmComm) station.

Understanding Ham Radio's Role in Emergencies

Amateur radio operators are uniquely positioned to provide essential communication services during emergencies. They can establish networks rapidly over wide areas, making ham radio a critical component of disaster response.

Key Aspects of Emergency Communication

1. **Reliability**: Ham radio does not rely on the internet or cellular networks, making it operational even when other systems fail.
2. **Flexibility**: Operators can quickly adapt to changing situations and frequency conditions.
3. **Coverage**: With the right equipment, ham radio can cover local, national, and international areas.
4. **Interoperability**: Ham radio can interface with other communication systems, providing a bridge between different agencies and groups.

Protocols and Best Practices

1. **Training and Certification**: Operators involved in emergency communication should undergo specific training, such as the Amateur Radio Emergency Service (ARES) training in the USA.
2. **Standard Operating Procedures (SOPs)**: Having clear SOPs ensures efficient and coordinated communication during emergencies.
3. **Net Operations**: Understanding how to participate in a directed net, where a net control station manages communications, is crucial.
4. **Message Handling**: Operators should be proficient in accurately passing written messages, often using standard forms like the Radiogram or ICS forms.

Equipment for Emergency Communication

1. **Transceiver**: A reliable, multi-band transceiver with battery backup is essential.
2. **Antennas**: Portable and easily deployable antennas are preferred.
3. **Power Source**: Having multiple power options, like batteries, solar panels, or generators, is crucial.
4. **Additional Gear**: Accessories such as headsets, spare cables, and portable digital devices for decoding and sending digital messages.

Practical Example: Setting Up an Emergency Ham Radio Station

Let's walk through the setup of an emergency communication station:

1. **Transceiver Setup**: Choose a transceiver that can operate on HF and VHF/UHF bands. Connect it to a power source like a rechargeable battery pack.
2. **Antenna Assembly**: Set up a portable antenna, such as a wire dipole or a collapsible vertical antenna. Ensure it's properly erected for optimal reception and transmission.

3. **Power Management**: Connect the transceiver to the battery pack. Have solar chargers or a generator as backup power sources.
4. **Testing the Equipment**: Perform a test transmission on various bands to check the equipment's functionality and the clarity of the signal.
5. **Joining Emergency Nets**: Tune into known emergency nets or frequencies, such as local ARES frequencies or HF hurricane watch nets, to practice net operations and message handling.
6. **Mock Emergency Drill**: Participate in a simulated emergency drill. Practice sending and receiving messages, including using digital modes and handling formal message traffic.
7. **Logging and Debriefing**: Log all communications and review the operation's effectiveness. Note any areas for improvement or equipment adjustments needed.

Through this practical scenario, the operator gains hands-on experience in setting up and operating an emergency communication station. Such exercises are crucial in preparing amateur radio operators to respond effectively in real-world emergencies.

Emergency communication is a significant aspect of the amateur radio service, demonstrating its value beyond hobbyist activities. Operators skilled in emergency communication protocols can make a substantial difference in disaster response efforts, showcasing the enduring relevance and importance of amateur radio in modern society.

Chapter 9: Radio Wave Theory

Understanding the Science: How Radio Waves Travel and Interact

Radio wave propagation, the process by which radio waves travel from a transmitter to a receiver, is a fundamental aspect of ham radio. This chapter delves into the science behind radio wave propagation, including how various atmospheric conditions and geographical factors affect these waves. Understanding these principles is crucial for effective communication in amateur radio.

Fundamentals of Radio Wave Propagation

Radio waves are a form of electromagnetic radiation with a frequency lower than that of visible light. The behavior of these waves, including their travel path and how they interact with the environment, is influenced by several factors:

1. **Frequency**: Different frequencies have distinct propagation characteristics. Lower frequencies (HF) can travel longer distances by reflecting off the ionosphere, while higher frequencies (VHF/UHF) typically have line-of-sight propagation.
2. **Ionosphere Layers**: The ionosphere, an upper layer of the atmosphere ionized by solar radiation, plays a critical role in long-distance HF communication by reflecting radio waves back to Earth.
3. **Ground Wave Propagation**: Low-frequency waves can travel along the Earth's surface, making them effective for local communications.
4. **Tropospheric Propagation**: For VHF and UHF, the troposphere can occasionally allow for longer-than-normal range communication.
5. **Solar Activity**: Solar flares and sunspots can significantly affect ionospheric propagation, either enhancing or degrading long-distance communication.

Antenna and Wave Interaction

The design and placement of antennas are also integral to the propagation of radio waves:

1. **Antenna Height**: The higher an antenna, the better it can transmit and receive signals, especially for VHF/UHF frequencies.

2. **Directionality**: Some antennas are designed to focus energy in specific directions, enhancing communication in those areas.
3. **Polarization**: The orientation of the radio wave, vertical or horizontal, should match between transmitting and receiving antennas for optimal signal strength.

Practical Example: Experimenting with HF and VHF Propagation

Let's illustrate these concepts through a practical example:

1. **HF Communication at Night**: Set up a transceiver with a dipole antenna for the 40-meter band. As evening approaches, start making contacts. Observe how the range of communication increases after sunset due to improved ionospheric propagation conditions.
2. **VHF Line-of-Sight Experiment**: Using a 2-meter band handheld transceiver with a vertical antenna, attempt to establish contacts at various distances. Note the direct relationship between line-of-sight, antenna height, and communication range.
3. **Ground Wave Testing on Low Frequencies**: On a lower frequency band like 80 meters, conduct tests to see how far ground wave propagation allows for communication. This can be done during the day when ionospheric propagation is less effective for these frequencies.
4. **Solar Activity Monitoring**: Regularly check solar activity reports and sunspot numbers. Correlate these with your HF communication experiences, noting any patterns in signal clarity or range.
5. **Logging Observations**: Keep a detailed log of all experiments, including time, frequency, antenna type, and environmental conditions. Over time, this log will serve as a valuable reference to understand how different factors affect radio wave propagation.

Through this hands-on approach, the amateur radio operator gains a deeper understanding of the principles of radio wave theory and their practical application in real-world scenarios. These experiments are not only educational but also immensely satisfying, offering a glimpse into the invisible yet fascinating world of radio wave propagation.

Radio wave theory is not just an academic topic; it is a practical science that directly impacts every aspect of amateur radio operation. By understanding the nuances of how radio waves travel and interact with their environment, ham radio enthusiasts can optimize their setups for maximum effectiveness, no matter the operating conditions. This knowledge is not only essential for achieving successful communication but also for fostering a deeper appreciation of the natural phenomena that make amateur radio possible.

Chapter 10: Operating Procedures and Etiquette

The Art of Communication: Best Practices for Effective and Courteous Operation

Effective communication in amateur radio involves more than just understanding the technical aspects of radio operation. It also encompasses a set of operating procedures and etiquette that ensure smooth, respectful, and efficient use of the radio spectrum. This chapter outlines these practices and provides a practical example to demonstrate their application in real-world scenarios.

Basics of Operating Procedures

1. **Frequency Usage**: Always check if a frequency is in use before transmitting. This can be done by listening for any ongoing communication and asking if the frequency is clear.
2. **Calling CQ**: When initiating a call, use the standard format: "CQ CQ CQ, this is [Your Call Sign], [Your Call Sign] calling CQ and standing by."
3. **Responding to Calls**: When responding to a CQ call, reply with the station's call sign followed by your own. Ensure clarity and brevity in communication.

4. **Signal Reports**: Use the RST (Readability, Signal Strength, Tone) system for reporting the quality of received signals.
5. **Handling Interference**: If your communication is interfering with others, be prepared to adjust your frequency or power level.

Etiquette in Ham Radio

1. **Respect and Courtesy**: Treat other operators with respect, regardless of their experience level or the quality of their equipment.
2. **Emergency Traffic**: Always yield to emergency traffic. If you hear a station declaring an emergency, clear the frequency immediately.
3. **Use of Language**: Maintain professionalism in language and avoid controversial topics.
4. **Acknowledging Mistakes**: If you make an error, acknowledge it, apologize if necessary, and learn from the experience.

Special Operating Events

Participating in special events like contests or field days requires additional considerations:

1. **Understanding the Rules**: Be familiar with the rules and objectives of the event.
2. **Efficient Operating**: In fast-paced environments like contests, keep communications brief and to the point.
3. **Logging Contacts**: Accurate and timely logging is crucial during these events.

Practical Example: Operating in a Contest

Let's apply these principles in a practical scenario – participating in a ham radio contest.

1. **Preparation**: Research the contest rules and objectives. Set up your station, ensuring it is functioning optimally for the bands in use.
2. **Frequency Management**: Start by finding a clear frequency. Listen first, then ask if the frequency is in use.
3. **Making Contacts**: Once you establish a clear frequency, begin calling CQ following the contest format. When stations respond, exchange the required information as per the contest rules – typically a signal report and a serial number.
4. **Handling Pile-ups**: If many stations respond simultaneously, manage the pile-up efficiently by selecting one call sign at a time.
5. **Logging**: Log each contact accurately, including call signs, exchanged information, and time of contact.
6. **Respecting Rules and Operators**: Throughout the contest, maintain courteous communication, adhere to the rules, and respect the operating procedures of other participants.
7. **Post-Contest**: Review your log for accuracy and submit it to the contest organizers within the specified timeframe.

Participating in this contest scenario reinforces the importance of proper operating procedures and etiquette. It provides practical experience in managing a station under various conditions, handling communications efficiently, and respecting the rules and other operators.

Operating procedures and etiquette form the backbone of effective and harmonious communication in the amateur radio community. They ensure that all operators, regardless of experience level, can participate in a respectful and orderly manner. By adhering to these standards, amateur radio operators not only contribute to the smooth functioning of the radio spectrum but also uphold the tradition of camaraderie and mutual respect that is a hallmark of the ham radio community.

Chapter 11: Building a Ham Radio Community

Networking and Clubs: Fostering Connections Among Enthusiasts

The ham radio community is a global network of individuals united by a shared passion for amateur radio. This chapter explores how to engage with and contribute to this vibrant community, the benefits of joining ham radio clubs, and how to leverage these networks for learning and sharing knowledge.

The Importance of Community in Ham Radio

Amateur radio is not just about the radios and the technology; it's about the people who use them. Being part of a community offers numerous benefits:

1. **Knowledge Sharing**: Experienced operators share their knowledge with newcomers, fostering a culture of learning and mentorship.
2. **Support and Assistance**: Community members can offer technical support, advice on equipment purchases, and assistance in setting up stations.
3. **Friendship and Camaraderie**: Ham radio brings together people from diverse backgrounds, creating lifelong friendships and a sense of belonging.
4. **Organized Activities**: Clubs often organize activities like field days, contests, and educational sessions that enhance the amateur radio experience.

Joining Ham Radio Clubs

Joining a local or online ham radio club is one of the best ways to connect with the community:

1. **Finding a Club**: Look for local clubs through national amateur radio organizations or online directories.
2. **Participation**: Attend meetings, join club nets, and participate in club events.
3. **Volunteering**: Offer your skills and time for club activities and initiatives.

Building Networks

Building a personal network within the ham radio community can lead to various opportunities:

1. **Mentorship**: Seek out mentors who can guide you through the learning process.
2. **Collaborative Projects**: Collaborate with other hams on projects like antenna building, station setup, or experimenting with new modes.
3. **Public Service**: Engage in public service activities like emergency communications, providing a valuable service to the community.

Practical Example: Organizing a Field Day

Let's put these concepts into practice by organizing a field day, a popular ham radio activity:

1. **Planning the Event**: Form a committee within your local club to plan the field day. Decide on the date, location, and equipment needed.
2. **Publicizing**: Promote the event within the club and to the local community. Use social media, club newsletters, and local media to spread the word.
3. **Setting Up**: On the day of the event, set up stations, antennas, and operating areas. Ensure safety and accessibility for all participants.

4. **Operating**: Encourage all attendees, regardless of skill level, to operate the stations. Offer guidance and support, especially to newer operators.
5. **Educational Activities**: Include workshops or demonstrations on various aspects of amateur radio, such as antenna building, digital modes, or emergency communication.
6. **Socializing**: Foster camaraderie by including social activities like a barbecue or picnic.
7. **Debriefing**: After the event, gather feedback to learn what worked well and what could be improved.

Organizing and participating in a field day is an excellent way to experience the ham radio community's spirit. It provides an opportunity for hands-on learning, networking, and fun.

The ham radio community is a rich and diverse network of individuals, each contributing their unique skills and perspectives. By actively engaging in this community, amateur radio operators not only enrich their own experiences but also contribute to the growth and vitality of this fascinating hobby. Networking, club participation, and community activities are not just ways to enjoy amateur radio; they are also means to preserve and pass on this valuable legacy to future generations.

Chapter 12: Advanced Tuning Techniques

Fine-Tuning Your Skills: Advanced Methods for Signal Optimization

In amateur radio, the ability to fine-tune your equipment and techniques is crucial for enhancing communication quality and range. This chapter delves into advanced tuning methods, focusing on optimizing transceiver settings, antenna adjustments, and utilizing advanced digital tools for signal enhancement.

Understanding the Nuances of Tuning

Advanced tuning goes beyond the basic setup of a radio station. It involves a deep understanding of how different components interact and how minor adjustments can lead to significant improvements in performance.

1. **Transceiver Settings**: Advanced tuning involves optimizing various transceiver settings such as IF (Intermediate Frequency) bandwidth, RF (Radio Frequency) gain, and squelch settings for different operating conditions.
2. **Antenna Tuning**: Precisely tuning an antenna to resonate at the desired frequency is crucial. This involves understanding SWR (Standing Wave Ratio) and using tools like antenna analyzers for fine adjustments.
3. **Interference Reduction**: Implementing filters and noise reduction techniques to minimize interference and enhance signal clarity.
4. **Digital Signal Processing (DSP)**: Modern transceivers equipped with DSP can significantly improve reception by filtering out unwanted noise and enhancing desired signals.

Advanced Tuning Equipment

1. **Antenna Analyzers**: Used to measure SWR and impedance, helping to fine-tune antennas for optimal performance.
2. **Signal Generators**: Can be used for testing and calibrating equipment.
3. **Software-Defined Radio (SDR)**: Offers a visual approach to tuning and can be used for precise control over signal processing.

Practical Example: Optimizing an HF Station

Let's apply these advanced tuning techniques in a practical scenario of optimizing an HF station:

1. **Initial Setup**: Start with a basic HF station setup including a transceiver connected to a dipole antenna.
2. **Using an Antenna Analyzer**: Connect the analyzer to the antenna and measure the SWR across the desired band. Adjust the antenna length for the lowest SWR at the operating frequency.
3. **Transceiver Adjustments**: On the transceiver, fine-tune the IF bandwidth to suit the mode of operation. For SSB, a narrower bandwidth might improve voice clarity, while for CW, an even narrower setting is preferable.
4. **Implementing DSP**: If the transceiver has DSP capabilities, experiment with different DSP settings to reduce noise and improve signal quality.
5. **Testing and Logging**: Make several contacts across the band, noting the settings that yield the best results. Log these settings along with the signal reports received from other stations.
6. **Iterative Adjustments**: Based on the initial tests, make further small adjustments to the antenna, transceiver settings, and DSP. Each adjustment should be followed by practical tests to gauge its impact.
7. **Long-Term Observation**: Over several days or weeks, continue to observe the station's performance under different conditions, making notes of any required adjustments.

Through this process, the operator gains a deep understanding of how each component and setting affects the overall performance of their station. This knowledge is invaluable for maximizing the capabilities of their setup and can be applied to various operating conditions and scenarios.

Advanced tuning is both an art and a science, requiring patience, precision, and a willingness to experiment. By mastering these techniques, amateur radio operators can significantly enhance their communication experience, making it more efficient and enjoyable. This chapter not only provides the technical know-how but also encourages a mindset of continuous learning and improvement, essential in the world of amateur radio.

Chapter 13: Exploring the World with DXing

Long-Distance Communication: Strategies and Excitement of Making Distant Contacts

DXing, a term derived from "distance" and "x" (meaning unknown), refers to the activity of making long-distance contacts in amateur radio. This chapter explores the exhilarating world of DXing, offering strategies for successful long-distance communication and a hands-on example of making a DX contact.

Understanding DXing

DXing is one of the most thrilling aspects of ham radio, involving communication with distant stations, often in other countries or continents. Success in DXing requires not only technical skill but also knowledge of propagation, geography, and sometimes, just a bit of luck.

Key Aspects of Successful DXing

1. **Propagation Knowledge**: Understanding how radio waves travel and are affected by atmospheric conditions is crucial for successful DXing.
2. **Equipment Optimization**: Using a well-tuned antenna system and a powerful enough transmitter to reach distant stations.
3. **Operating Skills**: Proficiency in operating practices, such as recognizing and using the best times for DX contacts on different bands.
4. **Patience and Persistence**: DXing can be challenging, requiring patience to wait for the right conditions and persistence to make the contact.

Strategies for Effective DXing

1. **Band Selection**: Choose bands known for long-distance communication, such as the 20-meter or 40-meter HF bands.
2. **Time of Day**: Consider the best times for DXing, which vary depending on the band and target region. For example, nighttime is often better for HF bands.
3. **Listening Skills**: Develop the ability to pick out weak signals and identify DX stations amidst noise and interference.
4. **QSL Cards**: Sending and receiving QSL cards (confirmation of contact) is a popular aspect of DXing, serving as a tangible record of the achievement.

Practical Example: Making a DX Contact

Let's go through a step-by-step process of making a DX contact:

1. **Preparing the Station**: Ensure that your antenna is properly tuned for the target band. If you have a directional antenna, like a Yagi, aim it towards the region you're targeting.
2. **Choosing the Right Time**: Based on propagation predictions, choose the best time to attempt a DX contact. For instance, early morning or late evening might be optimal for certain regions.
3. **Tuning the Band**: Slowly scan through the band, listening for distant stations. Pay attention to faint signals.
4. **Calling DX Stations**: Once you identify a DX station, wait for a gap in the conversation and then call using standard DX protocol – your call sign followed by "DX".
5. **Managing a Pile-up**: If you're on a sought-after frequency, you might experience a pile-up with several stations calling you simultaneously. Handle this by calmly selecting one call sign at a time.
6. **Logging the Contact**: After a successful contact, log the details, including the time, frequency, and call sign of the DX station. This information is crucial for sending QSL cards later.
7. **Reflecting and Learning**: Review each DX attempt to understand what worked and what didn't. This reflection is key to improving your DXing skills.

Making a DX contact can be one of the most rewarding experiences in amateur radio, offering a sense of accomplishment and connection to the global ham radio community.

DXing brings a unique excitement to amateur radio, combining technical challenges with the thrill of making connections across the globe. It exemplifies the spirit of adventure and exploration inherent in the hobby, pushing operators to expand their skills and understanding of the world. Through DXing, amateur radio operators not only communicate across vast distances but also bridge cultural and geographical divides, fostering a sense of global community and mutual understanding.

Chapter 14: Contesting and Awards

Competitive Spirit: Participating in Ham Radio Contests and Earning Awards

Ham radio contests, a staple of the hobby, offer operators a chance to test their skills, improve their stations, and enjoy the thrill of competition. This chapter delves into the world of amateur radio contests, outlining various types of contests, strategies for success, and the process of earning awards.

Understanding Ham Radio Contests

Contests in amateur radio are organized events where operators attempt to make as many contacts as possible within a set period. They vary in format, rules, and objectives, but all share the goal of promoting skill and participation in the hobby.

Types of Contests

1. **DX Contests**: Focus on making long-distance contacts, often with specific regions or countries.
2. **VHF/UHF Contests**: Involve making contacts on the VHF and UHF bands, emphasizing line-of-sight communication.
3. **QRP Contests**: For operators using low-power transmitters, testing skill in making contacts with limited power.
4. **Field Day**: A popular event combining a contest with emergency preparedness, where operators set up portable stations in the field.

Contest Strategies

1. **Preparation**: Ensure your equipment is in top condition and understand the contest rules and objectives.
2. **Operating Efficiently**: Develop a rhythm for making contacts quickly and accurately. Efficiency is key in contests.
3. **Band and Mode Strategy**: Choose bands and modes that maximize your chances of making contacts based on conditions and your station's capabilities.
4. **Logging Accurately**: Use contest logging software for real-time logging and to avoid duplicate contacts.

Earning Awards

Many organizations offer awards for contesting achievements, such as making a certain number of contacts or contacting a set number of countries.

Practical Example: Participating in a Worldwide DX Contest

Let's walk through an example of participating in a worldwide DX contest:

1. **Pre-Contest Setup**: Check all equipment, ensuring the transceiver and antenna are functioning optimally. Install and set up contest logging software.
2. **Understanding the Rules**: Review the contest rules, including allowed bands, modes, and the point system.
3. **Contest Start**: Begin operating at the start of the contest, searching for and contacting as many stations as possible. Rotate between bands based on propagation conditions.
4. **Efficient Operation**: Use a consistent and clear exchange format. For DX contests, this usually includes signal report and location or a serial number.
5. **Handling Pile-ups**: Manage any pile-ups efficiently, selecting call signs and responding quickly.

6. **Logging Contacts**: Log each contact immediately and accurately. The logging software will help manage duplicates and tally scores.
7. **End of Contest**: At the end of the contest period, double-check the log for accuracy, then submit it to the contest organizers by the deadline.
8. **Review and Reflection**: After the contest, review your performance. Note what strategies worked well and areas for improvement.

Participating in a contest, especially a competitive DX contest, can be an exhilarating experience. It tests an operator's skills in station setup, operating efficiency, and strategic thinking.

Contesting in amateur radio is more than just a competition; it's a celebration of the skills, technology, and community that make up this fascinating hobby. Whether competing for personal achievement, awards, or simply for the joy of participation, contests offer a dynamic and engaging way to experience the diverse aspects of amateur radio. Through these events, operators not only improve their skills but also contribute to the vibrancy and growth of the amateur radio community worldwide.

Chapter 15: Satellite Communication with Ham Radio

Reaching for the Stars: Using Satellites for Advanced Ham Radio Communication

Satellite communication represents a sophisticated and exhilarating aspect of amateur radio, allowing operators to communicate over incredibly long distances by bouncing signals off satellites orbiting the Earth. This chapter introduces the basics of amateur radio satellite communication, the equipment needed, and a practical guide to making your first satellite contact.

Introduction to Amateur Radio Satellites

Amateur radio satellites, often built and operated by amateur radio organizations, orbit the Earth and act as repeaters in space. They receive signals from the ground and retransmit them back, covering vast areas far beyond the reach of traditional ground-based communication.

Types of Amateur Radio Satellites

1. **Low Earth Orbit (LEO) Satellites**: Orbit close to the Earth and are easier to access but have shorter pass times.
2. **Geostationary Satellites**: Remain in a fixed position relative to the Earth, offering continuous coverage over a specific area but require more sophisticated equipment.

Equipment for Satellite Communication

1. **Dual-Band Transceiver**: Capable of transmitting and receiving on VHF and UHF bands.
2. **Antennas**: Directional antennas like Yagis are preferred for tracking satellites.
3. **Rotator System**: For automatic tracking of satellites as they move across the sky.
4. **Software**: Tracking software to predict satellite passes and aid in aligning antennas.

Practical Example: Making Contact Through a LEO Satellite

Here's a step-by-step guide to making your first contact using a LEO amateur radio satellite:

1. **Research and Planning**: Begin by researching which amateur radio satellites are accessible from your location. Websites like AMSAT provide schedules and orbital information.
2. **Setting Up the Station**: Set up your dual-band transceiver and connect it to the computer running satellite tracking software. Assemble your directional antenna and connect it to the rotator system.
3. **Tracking the Satellite**: Use the software to predict when the satellite will be passing over your location. Align your antenna with the satellite's predicted path.
4. **Tuning the Transceiver**: Tune your transceiver to the satellite's uplink frequency (for transmitting) and downlink frequency (for receiving). Adjust for Doppler shift as the satellite approaches.
5. **Making Contact**: As the satellite comes into range, transmit your call sign and listen for replies. Due to the high speed of the satellite, contacts will be brief.
6. **Logging Contacts**: Log any successful contacts, including the satellite's name, pass time, and the call signs of stations contacted.
7. **Evaluating and Adjusting**: After the pass, evaluate your performance. Adjust your tracking and antenna aiming techniques for future passes.

Making contact through an amateur radio satellite is a remarkable achievement that combines technical skills, planning, and precise execution. It opens up a new dimension of amateur radio, connecting operators across continents and cultures.

Satellite communication in amateur radio showcases the innovative spirit of the hobby, merging radio communication with space technology. It offers a unique and advanced aspect of amateur radio that challenges operators to expand their skills and understanding of radio wave propagation. By successfully making satellite contacts, amateur radio enthusiasts not only enjoy a highly rewarding experience but also contribute to the pioneering spirit of space exploration and communication.

Chapter 16: Software-Defined Radio (SDR)

The Future of Ham Radio: Exploring the Capabilities of Software-Defined Radio

Software-Defined Radio (SDR) represents a significant leap in the evolution of radio technology, offering unparalleled flexibility and new capabilities to amateur radio enthusiasts. This chapter delves into SDR, explaining how it differs from traditional radio, its advantages, and a step-by-step guide to setting up and using an SDR system.

Understanding Software-Defined Radio

Unlike traditional radios where hardware (like mixers, filters, amplifiers, modulators/demodulators, etc.) is used for processing radio signals, SDR relies on software to perform these functions. This software can be updated to implement new features or adapt to different communication standards, making SDRs extremely versatile.

Advantages of SDR in Ham Radio

1. **Wide Frequency Range**: SDRs typically have a broad frequency range, enabling access to a wide spectrum of bands.
2. **Signal Processing**: Advanced signal processing capabilities offer better reception, filtering, and noise reduction.

3. **Modulation Flexibility**: SDRs can easily switch between different modulation types and support new modes as they develop.
4. **Spectrum Visualization**: Most SDRs provide a visual display of the radio spectrum, allowing for more effective signal searching and monitoring.

SDR Equipment and Software

1. **SDR Hardware**: Ranges from inexpensive dongles for entry-level use to more advanced, dedicated SDR transceivers.
2. **Computer**: A PC or laptop capable of running the SDR software and processing the radio signals.
3. **Software**: Programs like SDRSharp, HDSDR, or GNU Radio, which provide the interface and tools for operating the SDR.

Practical Example: Setting Up and Using an SDR for Reception

Let's explore a practical example of setting up an SDR for receiving a wide range of signals:

1. **SDR Hardware Setup**: Connect an SDR dongle to your computer. Attach an appropriate antenna to the dongle – a simple discone antenna is a good all-around choice for a wide range of frequencies.
2. **Software Installation**: Install SDR software on your computer. Software like SDRSharp or HDSDR is user-friendly and suitable for beginners.
3. **Initial Configuration**: Open the SDR software and configure it to recognize the SDR dongle. Set up the basic settings such as frequency range and audio options.
4. **Tuning and Exploring**: Start tuning to different frequencies. Explore various bands and notice the different types of signals, such as commercial FM radio, amateur radio bands, aircraft communications, and more.
5. **Using Software Features**: Experiment with the software's features like filtering, noise reduction, and spectrum analysis. Observe how these tools affect the reception and clarity of the signals.
6. **Logging and Researching**: Log interesting signals and research them to understand more about what you are receiving. This could include amateur radio frequencies, international broadcasts, or even signals from satellites.
7. **Exploring Digital Modes**: If your SDR software supports digital decoding, try decoding digital modes like RTTY, PSK31, or FT8. You may need additional software plugins or applications for this.

Through this example, the operator becomes familiar with the operation of an SDR, exploring the vast array of signals accessible with this technology. SDR opens up new possibilities for experimentation and learning in amateur radio, making it an invaluable tool for modern radio enthusiasts.

SDR technology represents a paradigm shift in amateur radio, offering a blend of traditional radio concepts with the power of modern computing. It not only simplifies the process of exploring a wide range of frequencies but also provides a platform for continuous learning and experimentation. As the technology evolves, SDR is poised to become an integral part of the amateur radio experience, pushing the boundaries of what can be achieved with radio communication.

Chapter 17: Advanced Electronics and Circuit Design

DIY Approach: Building and Modifying Your Own Ham Radio Equipment

For many amateur radio enthusiasts, the ability to build and modify their own equipment is a highly rewarding aspect of the hobby. This chapter explores the advanced world of electronics and circuit design in amateur radio, providing insights into the skills required and a practical example of a DIY radio project.

Understanding Electronics in Ham Radio

Ham radio electronics range from simple circuits like antenna tuners to more complex designs like transceivers. A strong foundation in electronic principles is essential for anyone looking to venture into building or modifying radio equipment.

Skills and Knowledge Base

1. **Basic Electronic Components**: Understanding resistors, capacitors, transistors, inductors, and integrated circuits and their roles in different circuits.
2. **Circuit Design and Analysis**: Ability to read and understand schematics, and the skills to design simple circuits.
3. **Soldering and Assembly**: Proficiency in soldering and assembling electronic components is crucial for building equipment.
4. **Testing and Troubleshooting**: Skills in using test equipment like multimeters, oscilloscopes, and signal generators to test and troubleshoot circuits.
5. **Safety**: Knowledge of safe working practices to prevent accidents, especially when working with high voltages.

Tools and Equipment

A well-equipped workspace is key, with tools like soldering irons, wire strippers, pliers, and a variety of electronic components.

Practical Example: Building a QRP (Low-Power) Transceiver

As a practical project, let's build a simple QRP transceiver suitable for CW (Morse code) communication on the 40-meter band.

1. **Design and Planning**: Start with a proven QRP transceiver design. Source the schematic from reliable amateur radio publications or online resources.
2. **Gathering Components**: Collect all necessary components such as resistors, capacitors, transistors, a crystal for the desired frequency, and a PCB (Printed Circuit Board) if using one.
3. **Assembly**: Carefully solder each component onto the PCB, following the schematic. Pay attention to the orientation of polarized components like electrolytic capacitors and transistors.
4. **Initial Testing**: Once assembled, perform initial checks for short circuits or incorrect connections using a multimeter.
5. **Powering Up**: Connect a power source, initially keeping the power low to check for any issues.
6. **Alignment and Adjustment**: Follow the alignment procedure in the design, which typically involves adjusting inductors or variable capacitors for optimal performance.
7. **Connecting Antenna and Key**: Attach a suitable antenna and a Morse code key to the transceiver.
8. **On-Air Testing**: Test the transceiver by attempting to make contacts. Adjust the antenna and transceiver settings for best performance.
9. **Documentation**: Keep a detailed record of the build process, adjustments, and on-air experiences. This documentation can be invaluable for future projects or troubleshooting.

Building your own QRP transceiver is a fantastic way to deeply understand the inner workings of radio equipment. It also provides a platform for experimentation and further modifications.

The process of designing, building, and operating your own equipment is at the heart of amateur radio DIY culture. It not only reinforces the technical knowledge of electronics and radio theory but also instills a sense of accomplishment and independence. For many, this aspect of the hobby is as rewarding as making contacts on the air, embodying the spirit of innovation and self-reliance that has long defined amateur radio.

Chapter 17: Advanced Electronics and Circuit Design

DIY Approach: Building and Modifying Your Own Ham Radio Equipment

For many amateur radio enthusiasts, the ability to build and modify their own equipment is a highly rewarding aspect of the hobby. This chapter explores the advanced world of electronics and circuit design in amateur radio, providing insights into the skills required and a practical example of a DIY radio project.

Understanding Electronics in Ham Radio

Ham radio electronics range from simple circuits like antenna tuners to more complex designs like transceivers. A strong foundation in electronic principles is essential for anyone looking to venture into building or modifying radio equipment.

Skills and Knowledge Base

1. **Basic Electronic Components**: Understanding resistors, capacitors, transistors, inductors, and integrated circuits and their roles in different circuits.
2. **Circuit Design and Analysis**: Ability to read and understand schematics, and the skills to design simple circuits.
3. **Soldering and Assembly**: Proficiency in soldering and assembling electronic components is crucial for building equipment.
4. **Testing and Troubleshooting**: Skills in using test equipment like multimeters, oscilloscopes, and signal generators to test and troubleshoot circuits.
5. **Safety**: Knowledge of safe working practices to prevent accidents, especially when working with high voltages.

Tools and Equipment

A well-equipped workspace is key, with tools like soldering irons, wire strippers, pliers, and a variety of electronic components.

Practical Example: Building a QRP (Low-Power) Transceiver

As a practical project, let's build a simple QRP transceiver suitable for CW (Morse code) communication on the 40-meter band.

1. **Design and Planning**: Start with a proven QRP transceiver design. Source the schematic from reliable amateur radio publications or online resources.
2. **Gathering Components**: Collect all necessary components such as resistors, capacitors, transistors, a crystal for the desired frequency, and a PCB (Printed Circuit Board) if using one.
3. **Assembly**: Carefully solder each component onto the PCB, following the schematic. Pay attention to the orientation of polarized components like electrolytic capacitors and transistors.
4. **Initial Testing**: Once assembled, perform initial checks for short circuits or incorrect connections using a multimeter.
5. **Powering Up**: Connect a power source, initially keeping the power low to check for any issues.

6. **Alignment and Adjustment**: Follow the alignment procedure in the design, which typically involves adjusting inductors or variable capacitors for optimal performance.
7. **Connecting Antenna and Key**: Attach a suitable antenna and a Morse code key to the transceiver.
8. **On-Air Testing**: Test the transceiver by attempting to make contacts. Adjust the antenna and transceiver settings for best performance.
9. **Documentation**: Keep a detailed record of the build process, adjustments, and on-air experiences. This documentation can be invaluable for future projects or troubleshooting.

Building your own QRP transceiver is a fantastic way to deeply understand the inner workings of radio equipment. It also provides a platform for experimentation and further modifications.

The process of designing, building, and operating your own equipment is at the heart of amateur radio DIY culture. It not only reinforces the technical knowledge of electronics and radio theory but also instills a sense of accomplishment and independence. For many, this aspect of the hobby is as rewarding as making contacts on the air, embodying the spirit of innovation and self-reliance that has long defined

Chapter 18: Signal Processing and Noise Reduction

Enhancing Clarity: Techniques for Clearer Transmission and Reception

Effective communication in amateur radio is not just about transmitting signals; it's equally about ensuring those signals are clear and understandable. This chapter focuses on advanced signal processing and noise reduction techniques, essential for enhancing the clarity of both transmission and reception in ham radio.

Understanding Signal Processing

Signal processing in amateur radio involves manipulating the signal to improve its clarity, strength, and readability. This can be achieved through various methods, both in hardware and software.

Noise Reduction Techniques

1. **Bandpass Filtering**: This technique allows only a specific range of frequencies to pass through, reducing interference from signals outside the desired bandwidth.
2. **Digital Signal Processing (DSP)**: Modern transceivers often include DSP chips that can reduce noise, improve signal clarity, and even decode digital signals.
3. **IF (Intermediate Frequency) Shift and Notch Filtering**: These are used to eliminate or reduce interference from nearby strong signals.
4. **Automatic Gain Control (AGC)**: Adjusts the receiver's gain to maintain a steady output volume despite varying signal strengths.

Advanced Hardware for Signal Enhancement

1. **External DSP Units**: For radios without built-in DSP, external units can provide similar benefits.
2. **Preselectors and Preamps**: Used at the receiver's front end to improve sensitivity and selectivity, especially for weak signals.
3. **Noise-Canceling Headphones**: Useful for operators to manually distinguish between signal and noise.

Practical Example: Reducing Noise in an HF Station

Let's walk through an example of implementing noise reduction techniques in a typical HF station:

1. **Assessing the Noise Level**: Start by assessing the ambient noise level on your primary operating bands. Use the transceiver's S-meter as a rough guide.
2. **Adding Bandpass Filters**: Install bandpass filters for the bands you frequently operate on. This will help in attenuating out-of-band noise.
3. **Setting Up DSP**: If your transceiver has built-in DSP, explore different settings like noise reduction, notch filtering, and IF shift to find the optimal configuration for different types of noise.
4. **External DSP Unit**: For radios without built-in DSP, connect an external DSP unit. Adjust its settings to achieve the best noise reduction.
5. **On-Air Testing**: After setting up, go on-air and test the effectiveness of the adjustments. Engage in regular communication and ask for signal reports from other operators.
6. **Fine-Tuning**: Based on feedback and your own observations, fine-tune the DSP settings, filter choices, and antenna orientation for optimal performance.
7. **Logging and Analysis**: Keep a log of the noise levels, settings used, and the quality of reception. Over time, this data will help in further refining your noise reduction approach.

Implementing advanced signal processing and noise reduction techniques significantly enhances the quality of both received and transmitted signals, leading to more enjoyable and effective communication experiences.

Signal processing and noise reduction are critical in the crowded and often noisy RF spectrum that ham radio operators navigate. By effectively implementing these techniques, operators can overcome challenging conditions, making their station more effective and their time on the air more productive and satisfying. As technology advances, the tools and methods for signal processing continue to evolve, offering ever-greater opportunities for clarity and precision in amateur radio communications.

Chapter 19: Legal Aspects and Regulations

Staying Compliant: Understanding the Legal Framework Surrounding Ham Radio

Navigating the legal aspects of amateur radio is crucial for every operator. This chapter provides an in-depth look into the regulations governing ham radio, including licensing requirements, frequency allocations, and operational rules, along with a practical example demonstrating compliance with these regulations.

Understanding Amateur Radio Regulations

The regulations for amateur radio are designed to ensure responsible use of the radio spectrum, a public resource. They vary by country but generally cover areas like:

1. **Licensing**: Requirements and procedures for obtaining an amateur radio license, which may include passing an examination.
2. **Frequency Allocations**: Specific frequency bands allocated for amateur radio use.
3. **Power Limits**: Maximum allowed power output levels for different license classes.
4. **Operational Rules**: Guidelines on how to operate legally and ethically, including identification requirements and prohibited transmissions.
5. **Interference Management**: Rules regarding the avoidance and resolution of interference with other services.

International Regulations

1. **ITU Regulations**: The International Telecommunication Union (ITU) sets global guidelines, which are then adapted into national laws.
2. **Reciprocal Licensing**: Agreements between countries that allow hams to operate internationally under certain conditions.

Legal and Ethical Operating Practices

1. **Station Identification**: Regularly identifying your station with your call sign as per legal requirements.
2. **Avoiding Prohibited Communications**: Staying clear of commercial, encrypted, or offensive transmissions.
3. **Interference Resolution**: Addressing any interference issues with other services promptly and courteously.

Practical Example: Setting Up a Legal Ham Radio Station

Let's go through the steps of setting up and operating a ham radio station while adhering to legal and regulatory requirements:

1. **Obtaining a License**: If you're new to amateur radio, start by studying for and passing the licensing exam. Once passed, you'll receive a call sign which is your legal identifier on the air.
2. **Understanding Frequency Allocations**: Familiarize yourself with the frequency bands allocated for your license class. This information can be found in national regulatory authority publications or online resources.
3. **Setting Up the Station**: When setting up your station, ensure your equipment complies with the power limits and technical standards specified for your license class.
4. **Station Identification**: Make it a habit to identify your station by transmitting your call sign at the beginning and end of a communication, and periodically during longer transmissions, as required by regulations.
5. **Logging and Monitoring**: Keep a log of your transmissions, including frequency, time, mode, and power level. Regularly monitor your transmissions for unintended interference and be prepared to adjust your setup if necessary.
6. **Engaging in International Communication**: If you plan to communicate with stations in other countries, make sure to be aware of international regulations and reciprocal agreements.
7. **Participating in On-Air Activities**: Whether engaging in casual QSOs, contests, or emergency communication, always operate within the bounds of your licensing conditions and operational rules.

By following these steps, you not only ensure legal compliance but also contribute to the orderly and responsible use of the radio spectrum.

The legal framework surrounding amateur radio is essential for maintaining order and fairness in the use of a shared global resource. By understanding and adhering to these regulations, amateur radio operators demonstrate their commitment to the hobby and their respect for the wider community. This chapter not only serves as a guide to legal compliance but also as a reminder of the responsibility each operator has in preserving the integrity and future of amateur radio.

Chapter 20: The Global Impact of Ham Radio

Bridging Cultures: How Ham Radio Connects People Across the World

Amateur radio transcends geographical boundaries and cultural differences, making it a unique global phenomenon. This chapter explores the wide-reaching impact of ham radio on international understanding and cooperation, highlighting its role in emergency communication, cultural exchange, and technological innovation.

The Universal Language of Ham Radio

Ham radio operators, often referred to as hams, come from diverse backgrounds, yet share a common language in their passion for radio communication. This shared interest fosters a sense of global community and mutual respect.

Cultural Exchange and Understanding

1. **International QSOs**: Regular communication with operators from around the world naturally leads to cultural exchanges, building understanding and friendships across nations.
2. **Special Event Stations**: Commemorating global events or historical milestones, these stations promote international awareness and camaraderie.
3. **DXpeditions**: Expeditions to rare or remote locations not only challenge operators' skills but also bring attention to those areas, sometimes highlighting their culture and challenges.

Ham Radio in Global Emergencies

Amateur radio plays a vital role in emergency communication, particularly in disaster-stricken areas where traditional communication infrastructure has failed.

Technological Innovation and Collaboration

The global ham community has been at the forefront of many technological advancements in radio communication, often collaborating across borders on projects and experiments.

Ham Radio and Education

Many educational institutions around the world incorporate amateur radio into their curriculum, using it as a practical tool to teach science, technology, engineering, and mathematics (STEM) subjects.

Practical Example: Organizing an International Ham Radio Event

To illustrate the global impact of ham radio, let's organize an international ham radio event focused on cultural exchange:

1. **Event Planning**: Collaborate with ham radio clubs worldwide to organize a special event station or a series of stations. Decide on a theme that promotes cultural exchange, like 'World Heritage Sites on the Air'.
2. **Publicizing the Event**: Use various channels such as social media, amateur radio forums, and newsletters to promote the event globally.
3. **On-Air Activities**: During the event, encourage participants to share information about their local culture and heritage. This could include local music, stories, or historical facts.
4. **QSL Cards as Cultural Tokens**: Design special QSL cards for the event that reflect aspects of each participating country's culture.
5. **Real-time Interaction**: Utilize digital modes and live streaming to enable real-time interaction, allowing participants to visually share their cultural elements.
6. **Post-Event Compilation**: Compile the experiences, stories, and images shared during the event into a digital booklet or a web page, creating a lasting record of this cultural exchange.
7. **Feedback and Reflection**: After the event, gather feedback from participants and reflect on the learnings and insights gained about different cultures and communities.

By organizing such an event, amateur radio operators can actively participate in and contribute to cross-cultural understanding and global cooperation.

Amateur radio's ability to connect people across continents and cultures is one of its most remarkable aspects. It not only facilitates communication but also serves as a conduit for cultural exchange, international friendship, and mutual understanding. The global impact of ham radio extends beyond individual hobbyists to encompass educational, technological, and humanitarian spheres, making it a powerful tool for global connectivity and cooperation.

Conclusion:

The Ongoing Journey of Ham Radio

Embracing the Future while Honoring the Past

The journey through the world of amateur radio, as explored in this book, reveals a hobby that is as dynamic as it is enduring. From its early beginnings to its current standing in the digital age, ham radio has continually evolved, integrating new technologies while preserving its core values of communication, experimentation, and community. In this conclusion, we reflect on the multifaceted nature of ham radio, its impact on individuals and societies, and its prospective future.

The Ever-Evolving Nature of Ham Radio

Ham radio has consistently adapted to technological changes. It has embraced digital modes, software-defined radio, and satellite communication, all while maintaining traditional practices like Morse code and voice communication. This adaptability ensures the hobby remains relevant and engaging, offering something for every kind of enthusiast, from the builder and tinkerer to the global communicator and emergency responder.

Ham Radio's Impact on Individuals

For many, ham radio is more than a hobby; it's a lifelong passion that fosters continuous learning and personal growth. It cultivates a unique set of skills—from technical know-how to global awareness—making its practitioners well-rounded individuals.

Community and Camaraderie

Perhaps the most enduring aspect of ham radio is the sense of community it fosters. This community transcends geographical, political, and cultural boundaries, creating a global network of friends and collaborators. Events like field days, contests, and DXpeditions are not just about the radio but about the people behind the radio.

Educational Value

In the realm of education, ham radio is an invaluable tool. It provides a practical application for STEM subjects, sparking interest in science and technology among young minds. By participating in school clubs and amateur radio events, students gain hands-on experience that can inspire future careers.

Emergency Communication

Ham radio's role in emergency communication cannot be overstated. In disaster situations where traditional communication infrastructure fails, amateur radio operators have repeatedly proved to be lifesavers, relaying critical information and aiding rescue operations.

The Future of Ham Radio

Looking ahead, the future of ham radio appears vibrant. Emerging technologies like AI and continued advancements in digital communication are poised to open new avenues for experimentation. The integration of ham radio with other hobbies like drone flying and space exploration hints at exciting possibilities.

Practical Example: A Ham Radio Operator's Journey

To encapsulate the essence of this conclusion, consider the journey of Alex, a ham radio enthusiast:

1. **Initial Interest**: Alex starts as a teenager, intrigued by the magic of radio waves. He studies and obtains his amateur radio license.
2. **Building a Station**: Over the years, Alex builds his station, starting with a simple setup and gradually adding more sophisticated equipment like a software-defined radio and a satellite tracking system.
3. **Engaging with the Community**: Alex becomes a regular participant in local ham radio clubs, contests, and field days, building friendships and exchanging knowledge with fellow enthusiasts.
4. **Emergency Services**: Alex volunteers for emergency communication services, providing crucial assistance during natural disasters.
5. **Mentorship**: As an experienced ham, Alex mentors new entrants to the hobby, passing on his knowledge and passion.
6. **Exploring New Technologies**: Keen on innovation, Alex experiments with new technologies in ham radio, constantly learning and adapting.

Alex's journey mirrors the evolving landscape of amateur radio—a blend of tradition and innovation, personal fulfillment, and community service.

Final Reflections

Amateur radio is not just about the radios; it's about the people, the learning, and the endless possibilities that the airwaves offer. It is a hobby that continues to inspire, connect, and serve, adapting to the times while retaining its core essence. The ongoing journey of ham radio is a testament to its enduring relevance and its capacity to continually offer new horizons to explore.

BOOK 3
Exploring the World of Amateur Radio:

Foundations and Innovations

Introduction:

"Exploring the World of Amateur Radio: Foundations and Innovations"

Amateur radio, often referred to as ham radio, represents a unique blend of technology, community, and communication. It's a hobby that transcends geographic, political, and cultural barriers, uniting enthusiasts across the globe through the airwaves. This book, "Exploring the World of Amateur Radio: Foundations and Innovations," is designed to be a comprehensive guide, providing insight into the various facets of amateur radio, from its history and technological foundations to its current applications and future potential.

The appeal of amateur radio lies in its versatility and the myriad of opportunities it presents for experimentation, learning, and communication. From casual conversations with individuals in distant lands to providing critical communication during emergencies, ham radio encompasses a wide range of activities. This book aims to cater to both the novice eager to set up their first station and the seasoned operator seeking to delve deeper into advanced aspects of the hobby.

The history of amateur radio is a testament to human ingenuity and the relentless pursuit of knowledge and communication. The early days of radio saw pioneers experimenting with wireless technology, leading to the development of the first amateur radio stations. These enthusiasts were not only instrumental in advancing radio technology but also laid the groundwork for a global community of amateur radio operators. The book's first chapter delves into this rich history, tracing the evolution of amateur radio from its rudimentary beginnings to the sophisticated practice it is today.

Understanding the science behind radio technology is crucial for any amateur radio enthusiast. The book dedicates significant coverage to the fundamentals of radio waves, frequencies, and how they are utilized in amateur radio. This includes a detailed examination of different frequency bands, their characteristics, and their specific uses in ham radio. This technical foundation is essential for anyone looking to deeply engage with the hobby and become proficient in various aspects of radio communication.

Setting up an amateur radio station is a journey of its own. The book provides comprehensive guidance on selecting the right equipment, including transceivers, antennas, and other accessories. It also offers practical advice on setting up antennas, dealing with interference, and optimizing the station for different modes of communication. This is complemented by a chapter on operating procedures and etiquette, ensuring that readers are well-equipped not just technically, but also in understanding the norms and practices that govern communication on the airwaves.

Antennas play a critical role in any radio setup, and the book dedicates considerable attention to this topic. Starting with antenna basics and design principles, it gradually moves towards more advanced concepts and designs. This progression allows readers to build their understanding and experiment with different antenna types and configurations.

The integration of digital modes and computer technology has revolutionized amateur radio, opening up new avenues for communication and experimentation. The book explores these digital modes, covering how they work, their applications, and how they integrate with traditional radio setups. This includes a look at software-defined radio (SDR), a technology that has brought about significant changes in the amateur radio landscape.

Amateur radio plays a vital role in emergency communication and public service. The book examines how amateur radio operators provide critical communication services during natural disasters and other emergencies when traditional communication networks are unavailable. This chapter not only highlights the practical aspects of emergency communication but also underscores the social responsibility aspect of amateur radio.

With the advancement of technology, amateur radio has extended its reach beyond Earth. The book delves into the fascinating world of satellite communication and space radio, providing insights into how amateurs can communicate via satellites and even engage with the International Space Station (ISS). This chapter not only serves as a guide to satellite communication but also illustrates the forward-looking nature of the hobby.

Radio wave propagation is another critical area covered in the book. Understanding how radio waves travel and are affected by various atmospheric conditions is essential for effective communication. The book explains the principles of wave propagation, including how different environmental factors influence signal strength and quality. This knowledge is crucial for operators looking to optimize their communication strategies.

As the book progresses, it delves into more specialized topics such as advanced antenna systems, building and experimenting with transceivers, and the regulatory aspects of amateur radio. These chapters are designed to provide in-depth knowledge and practical skills for those looking to enhance their capabilities and fully engage with all aspects of the hobby.

Signal processing and noise reduction are key areas of focus for any radio operator. The book provides comprehensive coverage of various techniques and strategies to improve signal clarity and reduce interference. This is particularly important in today's environment, where the airwaves are increasingly crowded, and maintaining clear communication is more challenging.

Power supplies and safety considerations are often overlooked aspects of amateur radio. The book addresses these critical topics, offering guidance on choosing the right power supply and implementing safety practices to prevent accidents and equipment damage. This information is vital for ensuring a safe and enjoyable amateur radio experience.

DXing and contesting represent the competitive side of amateur radio. The book explores the exciting world of long-distance communication (DXing) and amateur radio contests, providing tips and strategies for those interested in these aspects of the hobby. This includes advice on equipment, operating techniques, and how to successfully participate in and enjoy these activities.

Mobile and portable operations have become increasingly popular in the amateur radio community. The book offers practical advice for setting up and operating mobile and portable stations, including tips for effective communication while on the move. This chapter is particularly relevant for those who enjoy combining amateur radio with travel and outdoor activities.

Looking towards the future, the book speculates on the potential developments and technological advancements in amateur radio. This includes emerging technologies, potential changes in regulations, and the evolving nature of the hobby. The chapter encourages readers to stay curious and open-minded, embracing the continuous evolution of amateur radio.

The book concludes with a focus on the social aspects of amateur radio, emphasizing the importance of clubs, organizations, and communities. These entities play a crucial role in supporting and nurturing the amateur radio community, providing opportunities for learning, collaboration, and fellowship. This chapter highlights how amateur radio is more than just a technical hobby; it's a community and a shared passion that connects people around the world.

In summary, "Exploring the World of Amateur Radio: Foundations and Innovations" is a comprehensive guide that covers the breadth and depth of amateur radio. From its historical roots to its modern-day applications and future potential, the book provides readers with the knowledge and skills needed to fully engage with this fascinating hobby. Whether you're a beginner looking to set up your first station or an experienced operator seeking to expand your knowledge, this book is an invaluable resource for anyone interested in the world of amateur radio.

Chapter 1: "The History and Evolution of Amateur Radio"

The history of amateur radio is a captivating journey that mirrors the evolution of modern communication technology. From the early experiments with wireless telegraphy to the sophisticated digital communications of today, amateur radio has been a constant bedrock of innovation, community, and technical advancement.

In the late 19th century, the foundation of what would become amateur radio was laid by pioneers like Guglielmo Marconi and Nikola Tesla. They experimented with wireless telegraphy, demonstrating that it was possible to transmit signals over long distances without wires. Marconi's successful transmission across the Atlantic in 1901 marked a significant milestone in wireless communication, paving the way for the development of radio technology.

The early 20th century saw rapid advancements in radio technology, and with it, the rise of amateur radio operators. These early enthusiasts were often self-taught, experimenting with homemade equipment to communicate over increasing distances. The appeal of amateur radio lay in its ability to connect people across vast distances, a novelty in an era when long-distance communication was limited and expensive.

During World War I, the importance of radio technology became evident, leading to significant advancements but also temporary restrictions on amateur radio activities. Many amateur radio operators put their skills to use for military communication. After the war, the restrictions were lifted, and the hobby saw a resurgence. The 1920s were a golden era for amateur radio, with operators pushing the boundaries of what was possible with their modest equipment.

One practical example of the innovation during this era was the creation of the 'superheterodyne' receiver by Edwin Armstrong in 1918. This receiver significantly improved the ability to select desired signals and reject unwanted ones, revolutionizing radio reception. To illustrate, let's consider a practical scenario where an amateur radio operator in the 1920s, let's call him John, is building his own superheterodyne receiver.

John gathers the necessary components: vacuum tubes, a tuner, capacitors, and a set of headphones. He carefully assembles these components based on the designs published in a radio enthusiast magazine. The process requires precise tuning and calibration. John connects an antenna to his receiver and begins to adjust the dials. After several adjustments, he hears a clear voice through the headphones — he has successfully received a transmission from another amateur radio operator several hundred miles away. This moment signifies not just a personal achievement for John but also a testament to the spirit of innovation and community that amateur radio fosters.

The 1930s and 1940s witnessed further technological advancements, with the introduction of frequency modulation (FM) and single-sideband (SSB) modulation. These developments allowed for more efficient use of the radio spectrum and better quality of transmissions, respectively. The amateur radio community was quick to adopt and experiment with these new technologies, further enhancing their capabilities.

World War II again saw amateur radio operators contributing to the war effort, with many serving as wireless operators and communication experts. Post-war, the hobby saw another resurgence, with technological advancements from the war years filtering down to civilian use. The 1950s and 1960s were marked by further experimentation and the expansion of amateur radio bands, allowing operators to explore new frequencies and modes of communication.

The late 20th century introduced computer technology to amateur radio, leading to digital modes of communication such as packet radio and later, internet-linked communication like EchoLink and D-STAR. These digital modes allowed for new forms of communication, including data transmission, further expanding the capabilities of amateur radio.

As the 21st century dawned, amateur radio continued to evolve with advancements in digital technology. Software-defined radios (SDRs) emerged, offering unprecedented flexibility and control over radio communications. The hobby also began to intersect with other technological hobbies, such as DIY electronics and maker culture, leading to a new wave of innovation and interest.

Throughout its history, amateur radio has consistently demonstrated its resilience and adaptability. It has embraced new technologies while retaining its core ethos of experimentation, community, and communication. The hobby has not only been a catalyst for technological innovation but also a means of bridging cultural and geographical divides.

Amateur radio's history is also a story of regulation and organization. Early on, the need for a regulatory framework became evident to prevent interference and allocate frequencies fairly. This led to the establishment of national and international bodies to regulate amateur radio activities. The American Radio Relay League (ARRL), founded in 1914, played a pivotal role in advocating for amateur radio operators' interests and establishing operational standards.

Looking at the modern amateur radio landscape, it is evident that the hobby has come a long way from its humble beginnings. Today, amateur radio operators have at their disposal an array of technologies and modes of communication, from traditional Morse code to digital voice and data modes. The community continues to thrive, with clubs and organizations around the world fostering the spirit of amateur radio.

As we delve deeper into the subsequent chapters, we will explore the technical aspects of amateur radio in detail. From setting up a station to understanding radio wave propagation and engaging in digital modes, this book aims to provide a comprehensive guide for anyone interested in this enduring and ever-evolving hobby.

Chapter 2: "Understanding Radio Waves and Frequencies"

Radio waves, the carriers of wireless communication, are a fascinating aspect of physics and a fundamental element in amateur radio. To appreciate and excel in the hobby of amateur radio, an understanding of how radio waves work and how different frequencies are applied is essential. This chapter delves into the scientific principles of radio waves and explores the practical use of various frequency bands in amateur radio.

Radio waves are a type of electromagnetic radiation, similar to light waves, but with much longer wavelengths. They travel at the speed of light and can be reflected, refracted, and absorbed by various materials. Radio waves are characterized by their frequency, measured in hertz (Hz), and their wavelength, inversely proportional to the frequency. The radio spectrum is divided into several bands, each with unique properties and uses in amateur radio.

To comprehend how radio waves are generated and used for communication, let's consider a practical example involving a simple amateur radio setup. Imagine an amateur radio operator, Sarah, setting up a basic transmitter and receiver. Her transmitter includes an oscillator that generates an alternating current at a specific frequency, which in turn produces radio waves. Sarah connects an antenna to the transmitter, which radiates these waves into the air.

The antenna's design is crucial as it must resonate at the frequency of the radio waves to be efficient. Sarah uses a half-wave dipole antenna, which is simple yet effective for her frequency of operation. She adjusts the length of the antenna to match the wavelength of her chosen frequency, ensuring optimal transmission.

Once Sarah's radio waves are airborne, they travel outward until they reach another antenna connected to a receiver, like the one at her friend's amateur radio station. This receiver is tuned to the same frequency as Sarah's transmitter, allowing it to pick up her signal from among the myriad of other signals on the airwaves.

The receiver converts the radio waves back into electrical signals, which are then processed to retrieve the original information, be it voice, Morse code, or digital data.

The choice of frequency is critical in amateur radio as different bands have different properties. Lower frequency bands, like the 160-meter band (1.8 to 2.0 MHz), have longer wavelengths and are capable of long-distance communication, especially at night. These bands are ideal for Sarah if she wants to reach distant stations. On the other hand, higher frequency bands, like the 2-meter band (144 to 148 MHz), have shorter wavelengths and are generally used for local communication.

Each band has its own challenges and advantages. For instance, the very high frequency (VHF) and ultra-high frequency (UHF) bands offer clearer quality and support a wider range of modes, but they have a shorter range and are more line-of-sight. This makes them suitable for local communication and activities like contesting and emergency communication.

In addition to frequency, modulation is a key concept in radio communication. Modulation is the process of varying a radio wave to carry information. The two primary types of modulation are amplitude modulation (AM), where the amplitude of the wave is varied, and frequency modulation (FM), where the frequency of the wave is varied. Each type has its specific applications and characteristics. For example, FM is less susceptible to noise and is widely used in VHF and UHF communication.

As Sarah experiments with different frequencies and modes, she learns about the effects of atmospheric conditions on radio waves. Lower frequencies can bounce off the ionosphere, a layer of the Earth's atmosphere, allowing them to travel over the horizon and cover greater distances. This phenomenon, known as skywave propagation, is most effective at night when the ionosphere is more stable. Higher frequencies, on the other hand, tend to travel in straight lines and are more affected by obstacles like buildings and terrain.

Understanding the radio spectrum and its allocation is also crucial for amateur radio operators. The spectrum is a limited resource, managed and allocated by national and international bodies to prevent interference between different users. Amateur radio operators must adhere to these allocations and operate within designated frequency bands.

Safety is another important aspect when working with radio waves. High power levels and certain frequencies can pose health risks, so amateur radio operators must be aware of and adhere to safety guidelines to protect themselves and others.

In conclusion, the world of radio waves and frequencies is both complex and fascinating. It requires a blend of scientific understanding and practical experimentation. For amateur radio enthusiasts like Sarah, mastering these concepts opens up endless possibilities for communication and exploration.

Chapter 3: "Setting Up Your First Amateur Radio Station"

Setting up an amateur radio station is an exciting venture, combining elements of technology, craftsmanship, and experimentation. This chapter aims to guide beginners through the process of establishing their first amateur radio station, addressing key components such as equipment selection, station layout, and antenna construction.

When embarking on setting up an amateur radio station, the first step is understanding the types of equipment needed. The essential components include a transceiver (a combined transmitter and receiver), a power supply, an antenna, and various connecting cables and accessories. Each piece plays a crucial role in the station's operation, and selecting the right equipment is crucial for a successful setup.

Let's consider a practical example: Michael, a new amateur radio enthusiast, is setting up his first station. Michael begins by selecting a transceiver. He chooses a basic, entry-level model that covers the HF bands (high frequency) and includes modes like SSB (single sideband) and CW (continuous wave, used for Morse code). This choice suits his interest in long-distance (DX) communication and provides room for growth as he gains experience.

Next, Michael focuses on the power supply. His transceiver requires a 13.8V DC power supply. He opts for a regulated power supply with enough amperage to handle his transceiver's maximum power output plus a margin for additional accessories.

The antenna is perhaps the most critical component of the station. Michael decides to start with a simple half-wave dipole antenna for the 20-meter band. This choice is influenced by his interest in DX communication and the physical space he has available for the antenna. The half-wave dipole is a good starter antenna as it's relatively easy to construct and effective for its size.

Michael measures and cuts two pieces of wire, each a quarter wavelength of the 20-meter band, and attaches them to a central insulator. He then attaches a coaxial cable to the insulator and ensures the other end is connected to his transceiver. He mounts the antenna as high as possible in his backyard, ensuring it's clear of obstructions and safely away from power lines.

With the transceiver, power supply, and antenna in place, Michael turns his attention to the station layout. He arranges his equipment on a sturdy desk in a quiet room of his house, with the transceiver in a central, easily accessible spot. He also invests in a comfortable chair, as he plans to spend significant time operating the station.

Michael's station also includes a few additional accessories: a SWR (standing wave ratio) meter to ensure his antenna is properly tuned, a set of headphones for clear audio reception, and a microphone for voice communication. He also adds a key for Morse code operation, as he's interested in learning and using this traditional mode.

Once everything is set up, Michael powers on his station and tunes to a frequency within the 20-meter band. He carefully adjusts the controls on his transceiver, listening for signals. After a few minutes, he hears a station calling CQ (a general call to any station). Excitedly, he responds, making his first contact. This moment marks the beginning of his journey into the world of amateur radio.

Safety is a critical aspect of setting up and operating an amateur radio station. Michael ensures that all electrical connections are secure and that his equipment is grounded to protect against electrical surges. He also familiarizes himself with the recommended power levels and exposure limits to radio frequency energy, ensuring a safe operating environment.

In summary, setting up an amateur radio station involves careful planning and thoughtful selection of equipment. It's a process that combines technical knowledge with hands-on skills. For beginners like Michael, starting with basic equipment and a simple antenna is a practical approach, allowing for learning and experimentation. As they gain experience, amateur radio operators can expand and upgrade their stations, exploring new bands, modes, and technologies.

Chapter 4: "Radio Operating Procedures and Etiquette"

In amateur radio, effective communication is not just about the technical setup but also about understanding and adhering to established operating procedures and etiquette. These protocols ensure orderly and respectful use of the radio spectrum, facilitating smooth and enjoyable interactions between operators. This chapter aims to provide a comprehensive guide to the standard operating procedures and the unspoken rules of etiquette in the amateur radio community.

Amateur radio is a hobby that is as much about community and respect as it is about technology. There are established norms and protocols that have been developed over many years, which help maintain a friendly and cooperative atmosphere on the airwaves. Understanding and following these protocols is essential for every amateur radio operator.

Let's consider a practical example to illustrate the importance of operating procedures and etiquette. Emily, a newly licensed amateur radio operator, is keen to make her first contact. She has her station set up and is ready to go, but first, she needs to understand the basics of making a call.

Before transmitting, Emily listens to the frequency to ensure it's not in use. This is a fundamental rule in amateur radio: always listen before transmitting. After a few minutes of listening and hearing no activity, Emily decides it's safe to make a call.

She presses the transmit button on her microphone and clearly states her call sign, followed by "CQ" three times. "CQ" is a general call to any station, and it stands for "seek you." Her call sounds like this: "This is [call sign], CQ CQ CQ." She then releases the transmit button and waits for a response, making sure to leave a gap for others to join in.

Soon, another operator responds with his call sign. Emily acknowledges the response by repeating the other operator's call sign, followed by her own. This exchange of call signs is crucial as it establishes a clear connection between the two stations.

As the conversation proceeds, Emily adheres to the principles of good amateur radio communication. She speaks clearly and at a moderate pace, allowing time for the other operator to understand her words. She avoids using jargon or slang that may not be familiar to all operators, sticking to plain language. When passing the conversation back to the other operator, she uses the term "over" to indicate that she has finished speaking and is waiting for a response.

Throughout the conversation, Emily remains courteous and patient. She avoids interrupting the other operator and listens attentively to what is being said. This respect for the other operator is a key aspect of amateur radio etiquette.

After a pleasant exchange, Emily ends the conversation by thanking the other operator for the contact and wishes them well. She concludes with her call sign, a standard practice to formally end a transmission. The conversation might end with, "Thank you for the QSO (conversation), 73 (best regards), [call sign]."

In addition to one-on-one conversations, Emily also learns about other aspects of amateur radio communication. She familiarizes herself with the concept of a "net," which is a scheduled gathering of amateur radio operators on a specific frequency at a predetermined time. Participating in a net requires understanding and following specific procedures, such as checking in when the net controller calls for participants.

Another key aspect of operating procedures and etiquette is understanding and adhering to the band plan. The band plan is a voluntary guideline outlining the suggested use of different frequencies within amateur bands. For example, certain frequencies might be designated for Morse code (CW), while others are reserved for digital modes. Respecting these guidelines helps reduce interference and ensures that all operators can enjoy their preferred modes of communication.

Moreover, Emily learns about the importance of signal reports. A signal report is a standard format to describe the quality of a received signal, typically using the RST (Readability, Signal Strength, Tone) system. Giving accurate and helpful signal reports is a courtesy that helps fellow operators adjust their equipment for optimal performance.

In summary, the chapter emphasizes the importance of understanding and adhering to amateur radio operating procedures and etiquette. These norms and protocols are not just about maintaining order on the airwaves but also about fostering a sense of community and mutual respect among operators. For new operators like Emily, learning these guidelines is an essential step towards becoming an integral part of the amateur radio community.

Chapter 5: "Antenna Basics and Design Principles"

The antenna is a critical component in any amateur radio setup, serving as the bridge between the airwaves and the radio equipment. A well-designed antenna can significantly enhance the performance of a radio station, making effective communication possible even under challenging conditions. This chapter is dedicated to understanding the basics of antennas and their design principles, providing guidance for amateur radio enthusiasts looking to build or choose the right antenna for their station.

At its core, an antenna is a device that converts electrical signals into radio waves and vice versa. The efficiency of this conversion process is dependent on various factors, including the antenna's design, construction, and placement. Understanding these factors is crucial for any amateur radio operator.

Let's consider a practical example to illustrate the principles of antenna design and operation. Tom, an amateur radio enthusiast, decides to build a simple yet effective antenna for his HF (High Frequency) radio station. He opts to construct a quarter-wave vertical antenna for the 40-meter band.

Tom starts by calculating the length of the antenna. The formula for a quarter-wave vertical antenna is Length (in meters) = 71.5 / frequency (in MHz). For the 40-meter band (around 7 MHz), this calculation gives a length of approximately 10.2 meters. Tom cuts a piece of wire to this length and attaches it to a non-conductive support, ensuring it stands vertically.

Next, Tom addresses the issue of grounding. A quarter-wave vertical antenna requires a good ground plane to function effectively. Tom installs a series of radials, which are wires extending outward from the base of the antenna, lying on or buried just below the ground. These radials help to reflect the radio waves and improve the antenna's performance.

With the antenna and ground plane set up, Tom connects the antenna to his transceiver using a coaxial cable. He then uses an antenna tuner to match the impedance of the antenna to his transceiver, minimizing the loss of power and ensuring efficient transmission and reception.

Tom's newly built antenna proves to be quite effective. He is able to make contacts over considerable distances, confirming that his efforts in constructing the antenna have paid off. His success also underlines the importance of understanding and applying basic antenna principles.

In addition to building antennas, this chapter also covers various types of antennas commonly used in amateur radio, each with its specific applications and characteristics. These include:

1. Dipole Antennas: The most basic and widely used antenna, consisting of two pieces of wire or metal rods. The dipole is versatile and can be installed in various configurations, such as inverted V, sloper, or as a flat-top.
2. Yagi-Uda Antennas: A directional antenna that provides high gain, commonly used for DXing and contesting. It consists of a driven element, reflector, and one or more directors.
3. Loop Antennas: Known for their compact size and low noise reception, loop antennas are a good choice for operators with limited space.
4. Wire Antennas: Including long wires, random wires, and end-fed wires, these antennas are simple to construct and can be effective for a variety of bands.

Each antenna type has its own set of design considerations, such as length, height, orientation, and materials. The chapter discusses these factors in detail, providing practical tips for construction and installation.

Additionally, the chapter addresses the topic of antenna safety. Safety considerations include ensuring the antenna is well-supported and secure, avoiding power lines, and considering the effects of RF exposure. Proper grounding and lightning protection are also crucial for the safety of the operator and the equipment.

In conclusion, antennas play a vital role in the effectiveness of an amateur radio station. Understanding the basics of antenna theory and design is essential for any amateur radio operator. Whether building an antenna from scratch, like Tom, or choosing a commercial model, the right antenna can make a significant difference in the success and enjoyment of amateur radio activities.

Chapter 6: "Electronics and Components in Amateur Radio"

A fundamental understanding of electronics and components is essential for amateur radio operators, as it enables them to build, maintain, and troubleshoot their equipment effectively. This chapter provides an overview of the basic electronic components used in amateur radio and their roles in various circuits.

The heart of any electronic device is its components. These include resistors, capacitors, inductors, transistors, and integrated circuits, among others. Each component has a specific function and understanding these functions is key to mastering amateur radio electronics.

Let's consider a practical example where an amateur radio operator, Lisa, decides to build a simple low-pass filter for her transmitter. A low-pass filter allows signals below a certain frequency to pass through while blocking higher frequencies, which can be crucial for eliminating unwanted harmonics from a transmitter.

Lisa starts by reviewing the basic components she will need:

1. **Resistors:** Components that resist the flow of electric current. They are used in virtually every electronic circuit and can be used to set the operating point of a transistor, divide voltages, limit current, and much more.
2. **Capacitors:** Devices that store and release electrical energy. In a low-pass filter, capacitors are used in conjunction with inductors to determine the cutoff frequency of the filter.
3. **Inductors:** Components that store energy in a magnetic field when electric current flows through them. Like capacitors, inductors are key to determining the characteristics of filters.
4. **Transistors:** Semiconductor devices used to amplify or switch electronic signals. While not necessarily part of a simple filter, transistors are fundamental in radio transmitters and receivers.

To build her low-pass filter, Lisa follows these steps:

1. **Calculation:** She calculates the values of the capacitors and inductors needed to achieve her desired cutoff frequency. The cutoff frequency is the point where the filter starts to attenuate higher frequencies. Lisa uses the standard formula for a low-pass filter to determine the necessary values.
2. **Schematic Drawing:** Lisa draws a schematic diagram of her filter, showing how the components are connected. Schematics are the standard way to represent electronic circuits and are essential for planning and troubleshooting.
3. **Assembly:** She carefully solders the components onto a circuit board, following the schematic. Proper soldering technique is crucial to ensure reliable connections and prevent damage to the components.
4. **Testing:** Once the filter is assembled, Lisa tests it using a signal generator and an oscilloscope. She verifies that the filter attenuates frequencies above the cutoff frequency.

Lisa's project illustrates the practical application of electronic components in amateur radio. Through this project, she gains a deeper understanding of how capacitors and inductors interact to form a filter, a concept applicable to many areas of radio electronics.

In addition to building circuits, this chapter also covers the basics of reading and interpreting schematic diagrams. Schematics are a universal language in electronics, depicting how components are interconnected in a circuit. Being able to read schematics is crucial for building, troubleshooting, and repairing electronic devices.

The chapter further explores the principles of analog and digital circuits. Analog circuits, like the low-pass filter Lisa built, process continuous signals, while digital circuits work with discrete signals, typically representing binary data. Both types of circuits are fundamental in modern amateur radio equipment.

Moreover, the chapter addresses the importance of understanding signal flow in a circuit. This includes recognizing input and output stages, amplification stages, filtering stages, and how they are interconnected. A solid grasp of signal flow is essential for effective troubleshooting and optimization of radio equipment.

In conclusion, a solid foundation in electronics and an understanding of the various components and their functions is indispensable for any amateur radio operator. Whether building a simple filter, like Lisa, or tackling more complex projects, the knowledge and skills gained from studying electronics are invaluable assets in the world of amateur radio.

Chapter 7: "Digital Modes and Computer Integration in Amateur Radio"

The advent of digital technology and computer integration has revolutionized amateur radio, introducing a range of new modes and capabilities. This chapter explores the various digital modes used in amateur radio, the role of computers in enhancing radio operations, and provides practical guidance for integrating digital technology into an amateur radio setup.

Digital modes in amateur radio refer to methods of communication that use digital data, rather than traditional voice or Morse code, to convey information. These modes have gained popularity due to their efficiency, the ability to make contacts under challenging conditions, and the additional dimensions they bring to the hobby.

To illustrate the practical application of digital modes, let's follow an amateur radio operator, Alex, as he sets up his station for digital mode operation. Alex decides to start with one of the most popular digital modes, FT8, known for its ability to make contacts over long distances even with low power and compromised antenna setups.

The first step for Alex is to equip his station with the necessary hardware and software:

1. **Computer:** A basic laptop or desktop computer with a sound card, which will be used to process the digital signals.
2. **Interface:** A digital interface connects the computer to the transceiver, handling the conversion between the audio signals from the computer and the radio frequencies used by the transceiver.
3. **Software:** Alex chooses a software package designed for FT8, such as WSJT-X, which includes all the necessary tools to operate in this mode, including decoding, transmitting, and logging capabilities.

Once his equipment is ready, Alex proceeds with the setup:

1. **Connection:** He connects his transceiver to the digital interface and then to his computer.

The interface converts the digital signals from the computer into the appropriate form for the transceiver and vice versa.
2. **Configuration:** Alex configures the software, setting the correct audio levels, choosing the appropriate radio frequency, and ensuring his call sign and grid locator are correctly entered.
3. **Operation:** With everything set, Alex tunes to a popular FT8 frequency on the 20-meter band. He starts the software and observes the waterfall display, a visual representation of the radio signals in the band. He sees several FT8 transmissions and decides to attempt a contact.
4. **Making a Contact:** Using the software, Alex selects a CQ call and clicks to respond. The software automatically handles the timing and content of the transmissions. After a few back-and-forth transmissions, Alex successfully completes a contact, which is automatically logged by the software.

Alex's experience with FT8 demonstrates the appeal of digital modes. They allow for efficient communication, often making it possible to establish contacts in conditions where voice or Morse code would fail.

In addition to FT8, the chapter explores other popular digital modes such as PSK31, a low-power mode great for keyboard-to-keyboard chatting, and JT65, another weak-signal mode similar to FT8. Each mode has its unique characteristics and applications, providing a wide range of options for amateur radio operators.

The integration of computers into amateur radio goes beyond digital modes. Software Defined Radios (SDRs) are also discussed in this chapter. SDRs use computer processing power to perform many of the functions traditionally done by hardware in a radio. This allows for a high degree of flexibility and control over the radio operations.

The chapter also covers the topic of software tools available for various amateur radio activities, such as logging, satellite tracking, and antenna design. These tools greatly enhance the capabilities of an amateur radio station and bring a level of convenience and efficiency that was not possible in the pre-digital era.

Furthermore, the chapter addresses the important considerations for setting up a digital station, including interfacing challenges, computer-radio integration, and troubleshooting common issues like RF interference and grounding problems.

In conclusion, digital modes and computer integration have opened up new horizons in amateur radio, allowing operators to explore and communicate in ways that were unimaginable a few decades ago. Whether it's making distant contacts on low power, chatting in text modes, or experimenting with software-defined radios, the digital aspects of amateur radio offer a rich field of opportunities for both new and experienced operators.

Chapter 8: "Emergency Communication and Public Service"

Amateur radio plays a vital role in emergency communication and public service. In times of disaster, when regular communication channels fail or become overloaded, amateur radio operators step in to provide essential communication links for emergency services and affected communities. This chapter focuses on the role of amateur radio in emergency situations, the preparation required to participate effectively in such operations, and the protocols involved.

To bring these concepts to life, let's follow a scenario involving an amateur radio operator, David, who is actively involved in emergency communication. David is a member of ARES (Amateur Radio Emergency Service), a group of licensed amateurs who volunteer to provide emergency communication support.

David's journey in emergency communication begins with preparation:

1. **Training:** He participates in training sessions organized by ARES, which cover various aspects of emergency communication, such as operating under challenging conditions, understanding emergency protocols, and interoperating with public service agencies.
2. **Equipment Preparation:** David ensures his equipment is ready for rapid deployment. This includes a portable transceiver, a reliable power source (like batteries or a portable generator), and a versatile antenna system that can be quickly set up in the field.
3. **Regular Drills:** David takes part in regular drills and exercises organized by ARES. These drills simulate emergency situations and help operators like David stay prepared and efficient.

One day, a severe storm hits David's region, causing widespread power outages and disrupting communication networks. David receives a call to activate:

1. **Activation and Deployment:** David quickly gathers his emergency communication kit and heads to the designated location, a local emergency operations center (EOC).
2. **Setting Up a Station:** Upon arrival, David sets up his portable station, establishing a communication link with other amateur operators in affected areas and with the authorities coordinating the response.
3. **Operational Role:** David's primary role is to relay messages between the emergency services and other operators in the field. He uses a mix of voice and digital modes, ensuring clear and concise communication.
4. **Log Keeping:** Throughout the operation, David keeps a detailed log of all communications, a crucial component in managing emergency communication effectively.

This scenario exemplifies the importance of amateur radio in emergencies. Operators like David provide a critical service, ensuring the flow of information in situations where it can save lives and aid in recovery efforts.

The chapter also discusses the various organizations and networks that amateur radio operators can join to participate in emergency communication, such as ARES, RACES (Radio Amateur Civil Emergency Service), and SATERN (Salvation Army Team Emergency Radio Network). Each organization has its protocols and areas of focus, but all share the common goal of providing emergency communication support.

In addition to voice communication, the chapter explores the role of digital modes in emergency communication. Modes like Winlink, which allows sending and receiving emails over radio frequencies, are particularly useful when internet services are down.

The chapter also covers the legal and ethical aspects of operating in emergency situations, including the importance of adhering to FCC rules and regulations, even in emergencies, and the need to respect the privacy and confidentiality of information transmitted during such operations.

Furthermore, the importance of personal preparedness is emphasized. This includes not only having the right equipment but also ensuring personal safety and readiness in emergency situations. Operators must be prepared to be self-sufficient, often operating in less-than-ideal conditions.

In conclusion, amateur radio's role in emergency communication is both crucial and multifaceted. It requires operators to be well-trained, equipped, and ready to respond at a moment's notice. For operators like David, participating in emergency communication is a way to give back to the community, using their skills and passion for amateur radio to make a real difference in times of need.

Chapter 9: "Satellite Communication and Space Radio"

Amateur radio extends beyond terrestrial communication, reaching into the realm of satellite communication and space radio. This chapter explores how amateur radio operators can communicate via satellites, engage in satellite tracking, and even interact with space missions, providing a comprehensive guide to this advanced aspect of the hobby.

Satellite communication in amateur radio involves using amateur radio satellites, often referred to as OSCARs (Orbiting Satellite Carrying Amateur Radio), as relay stations in space. These satellites receive signals from an Earth-based amateur radio station and retransmit them back to the ground, often covering a much larger area than terrestrial communication.

To understand the practical application of satellite communication in amateur radio, let's follow a scenario with an enthusiast, Grace. Grace is keen to make her first contact through an amateur radio satellite.

Grace's journey into satellite communication involves several steps:

1. **Understanding the Basics:** Grace starts by learning the basics of satellite orbits, types of amateur radio satellites, and the concept of Doppler shift, which affects the frequency of the signals due to the relative movement of the satellite.
2. **Equipment Setup:** The basic equipment required includes a VHF/UHF transceiver capable of operating on the satellite frequencies, a handheld directional antenna, and a computer or smartphone to track satellite passes.
3. **Satellite Tracking:** Grace uses satellite tracking software to determine when a particular satellite, say AO-91, will be passing overhead. The software provides her with the time, azimuth, and elevation of the pass.
4. **Making Contact:** On the day of the satellite pass, Grace sets up her station. As AO-91 approaches, she tunes her transceiver to the satellite's uplink frequency and adjusts her antenna to the correct azimuth and elevation. As the satellite comes within range, she starts hearing signals from other operators. Grace waits for a break in the conversation and then transmits her call sign during her turn, successfully making contact with another operator via the satellite.

Grace's experience highlights the thrill and technical challenge of satellite communication in amateur radio. She not only manages to establish contact through a satellite but also gains a deeper understanding of the principles of satellite communication.

The chapter further delves into different types of amateur radio satellites, such as low Earth orbit (LEO) satellites, which are relatively easy to access, and geostationary satellites, which provide continuous coverage over a specific area but require more sophisticated equipment.

In addition to communication via OSCARs, the chapter explores the exciting world of space radio, including the Amateur Radio on the International Space Station (ARISS) program. ARISS allows amateur radio operators to communicate with astronauts aboard the International Space Station (ISS), an opportunity that combines the technical aspects of satellite communication with the excitement of space exploration.

The chapter also covers the technicalities of setting up a satellite station, including the choice of antennas, such as Yagi-Uda antennas, and the use of automatic tracking systems that can adjust the antenna's direction as the satellite moves across the sky.

Moreover, the chapter addresses the advanced topic of building and launching amateur radio satellites. It discusses the collaboration between amateur radio organizations and educational institutions in satellite development, providing insights into the technical, legal, and logistical aspects of such projects.

In conclusion, satellite communication and space radio open up new dimensions in the field of amateur radio, allowing operators to explore beyond the boundaries of Earth and engage with the wider universe. For operators like Grace, satellite communication is not just about making distant contacts; it's about being part of a global community that extends into space, pushing the limits of what amateur radio can achieve.

Chapter 10: "Radio Wave Propagation and Atmospheric Effects"

Understanding radio wave propagation and the effects of the atmosphere on radio signals is crucial for amateur radio operators. This knowledge enables them to predict how radio waves will behave under different conditions, facilitating more effective communication. This chapter delves into the science of radio wave propagation, explaining how various atmospheric layers and conditions affect radio communications.

Radio waves can travel in various ways: through the ground (ground wave), by reflecting off the ionosphere (skywave), or by direct line of sight, including possible reflection off the Earth's surface or the ionosphere (tropospheric ducting and sporadic E). The method of propagation greatly influences the distance over which communication is possible and the clarity of the received signal.

To illustrate the practical aspects of radio wave propagation, let's follow an amateur radio operator, Ben, as he plans a DX (long-distance) contact using high-frequency (HF) bands. Ben understands that successful DXing relies heavily on understanding and utilizing ionospheric propagation.

Ben starts by researching the current state of the ionosphere, which affects HF propagation. The ionosphere's behavior is influenced by solar activity, and its condition varies with the time of day, season, and the 11-year solar cycle. Ben uses online tools and reports, such as those from the NOAA/NWS Space Weather Prediction Center, to assess the current ionospheric conditions.

Armed with this information, Ben decides to attempt his DX contact in the late afternoon, aiming to take advantage of the F layer of the ionosphere, which is most reflective to HF radio waves at this time. He sets up his station, choosing a frequency in the 20-meter band, which is known for good DX potential in the current conditions.

As the chosen time approaches, Ben tunes his antenna, a multi-band Yagi, for optimal performance on the 20-meter band. He then begins calling CQ and listening for responses. After several attempts, he makes contact with an operator in a distant country. The contact is successful, with clear reception, a testament to Ben's understanding and application of propagation principles.

This scenario demonstrates the importance of understanding propagation in amateur radio, particularly for activities like DXing. By knowing how radio waves behave, operators like Ben can significantly increase their chances of making successful long-distance contacts.

The chapter further explores the various layers of the ionosphere (D, E, F1, and F2) and how they affect radio signals at different times and frequencies. It explains concepts such as critical frequency, maximum usable frequency (MUF), and lowest usable frequency (LUF).

In addition to ionospheric propagation, the chapter covers ground wave and line-of-sight propagation, which are particularly relevant for VHF and UHF frequencies. Tropospheric ducting, a phenomenon that allows VHF/UHF signals to travel over greater distances under specific atmospheric conditions, is also discussed.

Moreover, the chapter addresses sporadic E propagation, a phenomenon that occurs mainly in the summer months and can allow for unexpectedly long-distance communication on VHF bands.

The chapter also introduces tools and techniques for predicting and observing propagation conditions. These include using propagation prediction software, understanding solar and geomagnetic indices, and participating in beacon networks, which provide real-time observations of propagation conditions.

In conclusion, understanding radio wave propagation and atmospheric effects is a key aspect of amateur radio. It allows operators to maximize their communication potential, whether it's making distant contacts on HF bands or taking advantage of unusual conditions on VHF/UHF bands. For operators like Ben, a deep understanding of propagation is not just a technical skill; it's a gateway to exploring the wider world through amateur radio.

Chapter 11: "Advanced Antenna Systems and Design"

For amateur radio enthusiasts, the antenna is more than just a piece of equipment; it's a gateway to the world. Advanced antenna systems and designs can significantly enhance a station's ability to transmit and receive signals, thereby expanding the operator's reach and capabilities. This chapter delves into the intricacies of advanced antenna systems, exploring sophisticated design concepts and techniques for those looking to elevate their amateur radio experience.

Advanced antenna designs offer a variety of benefits, including increased gain, directional capabilities, and optimized performance for specific bands or modes of operation. Understanding these designs and their applications is key for amateur radio operators looking to push the boundaries of their communication capabilities.

To illustrate the practical application of advanced antenna systems, let's follow an amateur radio operator, Sophia, as she embarks on a project to build a beam antenna, specifically a three-element Yagi for the 10-meter band.

Sophia's journey begins with a thorough planning phase:

1. **Design Considerations:** Sophia starts by determining her requirements, including the frequency range, gain, front-to-back ratio, and beamwidth she desires for her antenna. She also considers the physical space available for the antenna and any weight or wind load limitations.
2. **Antenna Modeling Software:** To optimize her design, Sophia uses antenna modeling software. This tool allows her to input her design parameters and simulate the performance of her antenna, including its radiation pattern and impedance.
3. **Component Sourcing:** Once satisfied with her design, Sophia sources the materials needed for her antenna. This includes aluminum tubing for the elements, a boom to mount the elements on, and a balun to match the impedance of the antenna to her transmission line.
4. **Construction:** Sophia carefully constructs her antenna, paying close attention to the dimensions and spacing of the elements, as these are critical to the antenna's performance. She mounts the driven element (the radiator), the reflector, and the director on the boom, ensuring they are securely attached and properly aligned.
5. **Installation and Testing:** With the antenna constructed, Sophia installs it atop a mast on her property. She then connects it to her transceiver using high-quality coaxial cable and tests it. Using an SWR meter, she checks the standing wave ratio across the 10-meter band, making adjustments to the driven element to optimize performance.

Sophia's project is successful. Her new beam antenna offers a significant improvement over her previous wire antennas, especially in terms of gain and directivity. She can now make contacts more consistently and with stations much further away than before.

Sophia's experience exemplifies the potential benefits of advanced antenna systems in amateur radio. With the right knowledge and resources, operators can design and build antennas that are highly optimized for their specific needs and operating conditions.

The chapter further explores various types of advanced antenna designs, including:

1. **Multi-band Antennas:** These antennas are designed to operate efficiently on multiple bands, making them versatile choices for operators who communicate on different frequencies.
2. **Phased Arrays:** A phased array consists of multiple antennas working together, with the phase of the signal at each antenna adjusted to steer the beam in a particular direction.
3. **Quad Antennas:** Similar to Yagi antennas but with loop elements, quad antennas offer certain advantages in terms of bandwidth and gain.
4. **Magnetic Loop Antennas:** Highly efficient, especially in limited space or in locations with high noise levels, magnetic loop antennas are a popular choice for operators in urban environments.

In addition to these designs, the chapter discusses the importance of antenna maintenance and troubleshooting. Regular maintenance ensures that antennas continue to perform optimally and helps prevent unexpected failures.

The chapter also addresses safety considerations when installing and using advanced antenna systems, including proper grounding, electrical safety, and considerations for working at height.

In conclusion, advanced antenna systems represent a significant area of interest and development within amateur radio. They offer operators the chance to experiment with and optimize their signal transmission and reception capabilities. For enthusiasts like Sophia, delving into advanced antenna design and construction is not only a technical challenge but also an immensely rewarding aspect of the hobby.

Chapter 12: "Building and Experimenting with Transceivers"

The heart of any amateur radio station is the transceiver, an apparatus that combines both transmission and reception capabilities. For many enthusiasts, building and experimenting with transceivers is not just a way to understand the inner workings of radio communication but also a deeply satisfying endeavor. This chapter delves into the process of building a transceiver from scratch, covering the selection of components, the assembly process, and the fine-tuning necessary for optimal performance.

Building a transceiver offers a unique opportunity for amateur radio operators to tailor their equipment to specific needs and preferences. It also provides a deeper understanding of radio theory and electronics.

To illustrate this process, let's follow an amateur radio operator, Carlos, as he embarks on a project to build a single-sideband (SSB) transceiver for the 40-meter band.

Carlos's journey in building his transceiver involves several key steps:

1. **Design Planning:** Carlos begins by outlining his project. He decides on a single-sideband (SSB) transceiver for the 40-meter band, as it's popular for DX contacts and local communications. He chooses a design that is within his skill level but also presents some challenges to aid his learning.
2. **Component Sourcing:** Carlos meticulously sources the components needed for his transceiver. This includes an oscillator, mixer, filters, amplifier stages, and various passive components like resistors, capacitors, and inductors. He opts for high-quality components where crucial, like the oscillator and filters, to ensure the best performance.
3. **Circuit Assembly:** Following the design schematics, Carlos begins assembling the transceiver. He starts with the oscillator, the heart of the transceiver, ensuring it's stable and operates at the correct

frequency. He then moves on to assemble the mixer, filters, and amplifier stages, connecting each section and carefully soldering the components onto a circuit board.
4. **Initial Testing:** After assembling the transceiver, Carlos conducts initial tests with a power meter and a dummy load to ensure that the basic functions are working as expected. He checks for any obvious issues like short circuits or components not operating within their expected parameters.
5. **Fine-Tuning:** With the transceiver functioning, Carlos begins the process of fine-tuning. He adjusts the filters for optimal bandwidth and the amplifier for maximum clean output. He pays special attention to the receiver sensitivity and the transmitter's signal clarity.
6. **Final Testing and Use:** Carlos connects the transceiver to an antenna and starts testing it on-air. He makes several contacts, adjusting the controls and noting the performance. Through these real-world tests, he identifies a few areas for improvement, which he addresses in subsequent tweaks.

Carlos's project showcases the technical challenge and satisfaction that comes with building a transceiver. Not only does he end up with a fully functional piece of equipment, but he also gains an in-depth understanding of how each component contributes to the overall operation of the transceiver.

This chapter further explores different types of transceivers that amateur radio operators might consider building, from simple QRP (low power) kits to more complex designs featuring advanced modes and multi-band capabilities.

The chapter also discusses the importance of understanding FCC regulations and ensuring that any home-built transceiver complies with these rules, particularly concerning frequency coverage, power output, and spurious emissions.

Additionally, the chapter covers the troubleshooting process, which is an integral part of building a transceiver. This includes identifying common problems like oscillation, insufficient power output, or poor receiver sensitivity, and provides guidance on how to rectify these issues.

Furthermore, safety considerations are emphasized, especially when working with circuits that involve high voltages or power levels.

In conclusion, building and experimenting with transceivers represent a core aspect of the amateur radio hobby for many enthusiasts. It allows for a level of customization and understanding that is not possible with off-the-shelf equipment. For operators like Carlos, the process of building a transceiver is as rewarding as using it for communication.

Chapter 13: "Regulations and Licensing in Amateur Radio"

Navigating the world of amateur radio regulations and licensing is crucial for every operator. Adherence to legal requirements not only ensures compliance with national and international communication laws but also promotes safety and cooperation within the amateur radio community. This chapter provides a comprehensive guide to understanding and complying with amateur radio regulations, detailing the process of obtaining and maintaining a license.

Amateur radio is regulated to ensure that the radio spectrum, a public resource, is used responsibly and effectively. Each country has its regulatory body and set of rules governing amateur radio operations. In the United States, for instance, the Federal Communications Commission (FCC) is the regulating authority.

To illustrate the licensing process and the importance of understanding regulations, let's follow an individual, Emma, as she pursues her journey to become a licensed amateur radio operator.

Emma's journey involves several key steps:

1. **Research:** Emma starts by researching the licensing requirements in her country. She discovers that there are different license classes, each with its privileges and limitations. She decides to aim for a Technician Class license, which will allow her access to VHF and UHF frequencies and some limited HF frequencies.
2. **Studying:** Emma begins studying for the license exam. She covers topics like basic electronics, operating practices, and, importantly, the legal aspects of amateur radio. Various study materials are available, including books, online courses, and local amateur radio club resources.
3. **Taking the Exam:** Once she feels prepared, Emma registers for the exam. The test comprises multiple-choice questions, covering both technical aspects of radio and relevant regulations. She takes the exam at a designated testing center, supervised by accredited examiners.
4. **Receiving the License:** After passing the exam, Emma submits her application and relevant documentation to the regulatory body. She receives her call sign, which is her unique identifier in the amateur radio world.
5. **Operating Legally:** With her call sign, Emma is now legally able to operate on amateur radio frequencies within the limits of her license. She ensures to follow all the rules, such as identifying herself with her call sign during transmissions and adhering to the frequency limitations of her license class.
6. **Continued Learning and Upgrading:** Emma understands that her learning doesn't stop with obtaining the license. She continues to educate herself on amateur radio practices and regulations and eventually plans to upgrade her license to gain access to more frequencies and modes of operation.

Emma's journey highlights the process of obtaining an amateur radio license and the importance of understanding and following regulations. Adherence to these rules ensures that amateur radio remains a safe and enjoyable hobby for everyone involved.

The chapter further explores the specific regulations that govern different aspects of amateur radio, such as frequency allocations, power limits, and permissible modes of communication. Understanding these regulations is crucial for operators to ensure they do not inadvertently interfere with other services and comply with international agreements on radio usage.

In addition to national regulations, the chapter discusses the role of international regulatory bodies, such as the International Telecommunication Union (ITU), in coordinating and standardizing radio communications worldwide.

The chapter also addresses the ethical aspects of amateur radio operation, emphasizing the importance of responsible operating practices, respect for other users of the radio spectrum, and the role of amateur radio in serving the community, particularly during emergencies.

Moreover, the chapter covers the process of renewing and upgrading licenses, highlighting the importance of staying current with regulatory changes and advancements in radio technology.

In conclusion, understanding regulations and obtaining a license are fundamental aspects of amateur radio. They ensure that operators like Emma can enjoy the hobby legally and responsibly, contributing positively to the amateur radio community and broader society.

Chapter 14: "Signal Processing and Noise Reduction Techniques"

In the world of amateur radio, effective communication often hinges on the operator's ability to process signals and reduce noise. Signal processing and noise reduction are therefore crucial skills for any amateur radio enthusiast. This chapter delves into the various techniques and technologies available to amateur radio operators for enhancing signal clarity and minimizing interference.

Signal processing in amateur radio involves a range of techniques designed to improve the reception and clarity of radio signals. Noise reduction, a key component of signal processing, focuses on minimizing unwanted sounds and interference that can hinder communication.

To illustrate these concepts, let's follow an amateur radio operator, Henry, as he tackles the challenge of signal processing and noise reduction in his home station.

Henry's journey involves several steps:

1. **Understanding Noise Sources:** Henry first identifies the different types of noise affecting his radio communication. These include external noises like electrical interference from nearby appliances and internal noises originating from his radio equipment.
2. **Implementing Noise Reduction Techniques:** Henry uses a combination of hardware and software solutions for noise reduction. He installs a noise reduction filter in his transceiver, which

helps to suppress background noise. He also uses digital signal processing (DSP) techniques available in his transceiver to further clean up the received signal.
3. **Optimizing Antenna Placement:** Henry realizes that the placement of his antenna can significantly impact the amount of noise received. He experiments with different locations and orientations to find the spot that offers the best reception with the least noise.
4. **Fine-Tuning Equipment Settings:** Henry spends time adjusting the settings on his transceiver, such as the squelch control, RF gain, and DSP filter settings. By tweaking these settings, he can further reduce noise and improve the quality of the received signal.
5. **Software-Based Signal Processing:** Henry also explores software-based signal processing options. He uses a computer program that interfaces with his radio to apply advanced noise reduction algorithms. This software also allows him to visualize the signals and noise, making it easier to identify and eliminate interference.
6. **Evaluating Results:** After implementing these techniques, Henry notices a significant improvement in signal clarity. He can now make out callsigns and conversations that were previously lost in the noise.

Henry's experience demonstrates the importance and effectiveness of signal processing and noise reduction in amateur radio. By understanding the sources of noise and applying the right techniques, operators can significantly enhance their communication capabilities.

The chapter further explores various noise reduction technologies, including:

1. **Noise Blankers:** Used to reduce pulse-type noises such as those from ignition systems or power line arcing.
2. **Notch Filters:** Useful for eliminating continuous tones or carriers, like those from nearby transmitters or electronic devices.
3. **Automatic Gain Control (AGC):** Adjusts the receiver's gain to maintain a steady output level, reducing the impact of strong, sudden signals.
4. **Digital Signal Processing (DSP):** A powerful tool that uses algorithms to filter and enhance received signals. Modern transceivers often have built-in DSP capabilities.

In addition to hardware solutions, the chapter discusses software solutions, such as computer-based signal processing programs that offer a wide range of filtering and noise reduction options.

The chapter also addresses the importance of regular maintenance and calibration of equipment to ensure optimal performance and noise reduction. Regular checks and updates can keep equipment functioning at its best, reducing the likelihood of internal noise issues.

Furthermore, the chapter covers the topic of interference tracking. Occasionally, operators may experience interference from external sources. The chapter provides guidance on how to track down and mitigate these interference sources, often in cooperation with neighbors or local authorities.

In conclusion, mastering signal processing and noise reduction techniques is essential for any amateur radio operator seeking clear and effective communication. The ability to minimize noise and enhance signals can make the difference between a successful and a frustrating amateur radio experience. For operators like Henry, these skills are key to enjoying the hobby to its fullest.

Chapter 15: "Power Supplies and Safety Considerations"

The reliability and safety of an amateur radio station are heavily dependent on the choice and maintenance of power supplies, along with strict adherence to safety practices. This chapter addresses the selection of appropriate power supplies for amateur radio equipment, discusses safety considerations in station setup and operation, and provides guidelines for safe and effective station management.

Adequate power supply selection is crucial for the efficient operation of radio equipment. It involves considering factors like voltage, current capacity, stability, and the presence of noise. Moreover, safety considerations are paramount, as improper handling of electrical equipment can lead to hazardous situations.

To illustrate these principles, let's follow an amateur radio operator, Julia, as she sets up her station with an emphasis on power supply selection and safety.

Julia's journey involves several key steps:

1. **Choosing the Right Power Supply:** Julia needs a power supply that can deliver steady 13.8V DC for her transceiver. She opts for a regulated power supply with enough amperage capacity to handle her transceiver's maximum power output plus a margin for potential future additions.
2. **Setting Up the Power Supply:** Julia installs her power supply in a well-ventilated area to prevent overheating. She ensures it's easily accessible in case she needs to turn it off quickly in an emergency.
3. **Electrical Safety Checks:** Before connecting her equipment, Julia inspects all cables and connectors for any sign of wear or damage. She understands that damaged cables can lead to short circuits and potentially cause fires or damage her equipment.
4. **Grounding the Station:** Proper grounding is essential for safety and effective operation. Julia grounds her station to a copper rod driven into the ground outside her shack. This grounding helps protect her equipment from electrical surges and reduces noise levels.
5. **Surge Protection:** To further protect her equipment from voltage spikes and surges, Julia installs surge protectors on both her power supply and antenna lines.
6. **Testing and Monitoring:** After setting everything up, Julia tests her station under various operating conditions. She monitors the voltage and current to ensure they remain within safe limits. She also installs a smoke detector and a fire extinguisher in her shack as additional safety measures.

Julia's meticulous approach to setting up her power supply and implementing safety measures ensures that her station operates efficiently and safely. Her actions highlight the importance of considering both performance and safety in amateur radio operations.

The chapter further explores different types of power supplies used in amateur radio, including linear and switching power supplies. Each type has its advantages and considerations regarding efficiency, noise generation, and cost.

The importance of regular maintenance of power supplies and electrical equipment is also discussed. Regular checks can prevent issues such as overheating, connection failures, or deterioration of components, which could lead to safety hazards.

In addition to power supply considerations, the chapter emphasizes the broader aspects of station safety. This includes:

1. **Fire Safety:** Guidelines for reducing fire risk, such as avoiding overloading outlets and using flame-retardant materials.
2. **Chemical Safety:** Proper handling and storage of batteries and other potentially hazardous materials.
3. **Physical Safety:** Ensuring a clutter-free operating environment to prevent accidents, especially in the presence of cables and equipment.
4. **RF Exposure:** Understanding and adhering to regulations regarding RF exposure to ensure that radiation levels are within safe limits for both the operator and the public.

In conclusion, the selection and management of power supplies, along with comprehensive safety practices, are critical for the efficient and safe operation of an amateur radio station. For operators like Julia, adhering to these principles is not just about following regulations; it's about ensuring the longevity of their equipment and their well-being.

Chapter 16: "DXing and Contesting in Amateur Radio"

DXing, the pursuit of making long-distance contacts, and contesting, participating in competitive amateur radio events, are both highly engaging and rewarding aspects of the hobby. These activities not only test the skills and equipment of amateur radio operators but also foster a sense of community and camaraderie among enthusiasts worldwide. This chapter explores the world of DXing and contesting, offering insights into strategies, equipment setup, and the thrill of these pursuits.

DXing and contesting require a combination of technical skill, knowledge of propagation, efficient station setup, and operating proficiency. They also provide an excellent opportunity for operators to test their capabilities and learn from the experience.

To illustrate the excitement and challenges of DXing and contesting, let's follow an amateur radio operator, Mike, as he prepares for and participates in a major international amateur radio contest.

Mike's journey in contesting involves several key steps:

1. **Preparation:** As the contest approaches, Mike begins by studying the contest rules and objectives. He understands that each contest has its unique set of rules, such as the mode of operation (CW, SSB, digital), band restrictions, and the scoring system.
2. **Equipment Setup:** Mike reviews his station to ensure it's optimized for the contest. He checks his transceiver, antenna system, and ancillary equipment like amplifiers and filters. He also sets up a computer with logging software specifically designed for contesting.
3. **Antenna Strategy:** Knowing that an efficient antenna system is crucial, Mike decides to use a multi-band beam antenna for its directional capabilities and a wire antenna for the lower bands. He ensures that his antennas are correctly tuned and positioned for optimal performance.
4. **Operating Plan:** Mike develops an operating plan, considering factors like propagation trends, his personal schedule, and the times when bands are likely to be most active. He plans to start on the higher frequency bands and move to the lower bands as night falls.
5. **Contest Participation:** When the contest begins, Mike is ready. He starts making contacts, carefully adhering to the contest's exchange format, which typically includes exchanging signal reports and a serial number. He switches bands as conditions change, always seeking to maximize his rate of contacts.
6. **Log Management:** Throughout the contest, Mike meticulously logs each contact. The logging software helps him avoid duplicate contacts and track his progress in the contest.
7. **Post-Contest:** After the contest ends, Mike reviews his log, ensuring that all entries are accurate. He then submits his log to the contest organizers for scoring.

Through participating in the contest, Mike not only enjoys the thrill of competition but also improves his operating skills and gains a deeper understanding of radio propagation and station setup.

The chapter further delves into various aspects of DXing and contesting, including:

1. **DXpeditions:** These are special trips made by amateur radio operators to rare or remote locations to make DX contacts. The chapter discusses the planning and execution of DXpeditions.
2. **Contest Strategies:** Detailed strategies for different types of contests, including single-operator and multi-operator strategies, are explored.
3. **Awards and Recognition:** The chapter covers the various awards and recognitions that can be achieved through DXing and contesting, such as the DX Century Club (DXCC) or the Worked All States (WAS) award.

4. **Ethics and Sportsmanship:** Good sportsmanship and ethical behavior are emphasized as crucial elements of DXing and contesting. This includes fair play, adherence to rules, and respectful communication.
5. **Technology in Contesting:** The use of technology, such as software-defined radios, digital modes, and computerized logging, is discussed, highlighting how advancements in technology have changed the face of contesting.

In conclusion, DXing and contesting in amateur radio are not just about making contacts or winning competitions; they are about personal growth, technical proficiency, and being part of a global community of enthusiasts. For operators like Mike, these activities offer endless opportunities for learning, improvement, and enjoyment.

Chapter 17: "Mobile and Portable Operations"

Mobile and portable amateur radio operations offer the excitement and challenge of operating in various locations, often under less-than-ideal conditions. This mode of operation appeals to those who enjoy combining radio with travel, outdoor activities, or for those who lack space for a permanent station setup. This chapter explores the essentials of mobile and portable operations, including equipment selection, setup strategies, and tips for successful operations in the field.

Mobile operations refer to operating amateur radio equipment from a moving vehicle, whereas portable operations imply setting up a temporary station at a location other than the operator's home QTH (station location). Both have unique challenges and rewards.

To bring these concepts to life, let's follow an amateur radio enthusiast, Sarah, as she prepares for a weekend of portable operation in a remote location.

Sarah's journey involves several key steps:

1. **Equipment Selection:** For portable operation, compactness and efficiency are key. Sarah chooses a lightweight, battery-powered transceiver with multi-band capabilities. She opts for a portable antenna – a collapsible dipole and a compact vertical for different bands.
2. **Power Requirements:** Since access to electricity is limited in remote areas, Sarah packs rechargeable batteries and a solar charger. She calculates her power needs based on her transceiver's consumption and the expected duration of her operation.
3. **Location Scouting:** Sarah selects a location that is not only scenic but also favorable for radio operations. She looks for a spot with higher elevation and minimal obstructions for effective signal propagation.
4. **Transportation and Packing:** Since she has to hike to her operating location, Sarah packs her equipment, tools, and accessories carefully, balancing weight and necessity. She uses a backpack designed for radio equipment, ensuring everything is protected and easily accessible.
5. **Setup and Testing:** Upon arrival, Sarah sets up her station, carefully erecting her antenna and ensuring her transceiver is properly configured. She tests her equipment to check that everything is functioning as expected.
6. **Operating and Logging:** Sarah begins operating, making contacts and logging them. She uses a portable logging device to record her contacts, mindful of the limited power available.
7. **Safety and Etiquette:** Sarah follows safety guidelines, such as keeping her equipment dry and secure. She also adheres to good operating practices, being considerate of other users of the radio spectrum.

Sarah's weekend operation is a success. She enjoys the tranquility of her remote location and makes several satisfying contacts, demonstrating the unique appeal of portable operations.

The chapter further explores various aspects of mobile and portable operations, including:

1. **Mobile Station Setup:** This section covers setting up an amateur radio station in a vehicle, discussing factors like antenna placement, minimizing vehicle noise interference, and safety considerations while operating from a vehicle.
2. **Emergency and Field Day Operations:** Portable operations play a crucial role in emergency communication and field day events. The chapter discusses how to set up and operate in these scenarios effectively.
3. **Antenna Considerations:** The importance of choosing the right antenna for mobile and portable operations is emphasized, with a focus on ease of setup, efficiency, and performance.
4. **Interference Issues:** Managing interference in mobile and portable setups is discussed, along with tips for identifying and mitigating common sources of noise.
5. **Operating Tips and Techniques:** Practical advice for making the most of mobile and portable operations, including band and frequency selection, and strategies for effective communication.

In conclusion, mobile and portable amateur radio operations offer a unique and enjoyable way to experience the hobby. They provide operators like Sarah the flexibility to operate from anywhere, bringing new challenges and opportunities for communication and exploration.

Chapter 18: "The Future of Amateur Radio"

Amateur radio, a hobby that has continually evolved alongside technological advancements, stands on the brink of yet more significant changes in the future. This chapter explores the potential developments in technology, regulation, and the community aspect of amateur radio, offering insights into how these changes might shape the future of the hobby.

From the integration of digital technologies to changes in spectrum management, amateur radio is poised to continue its evolution, adapting to and incorporating new technologies and methods.

To illustrate how these future changes might manifest, let's envision a scenario with an amateur radio enthusiast, Liam, who is actively engaged in exploring and utilizing cutting-edge technologies in amateur radio.

Liam's journey involves several key aspects:

1. **Software-Defined Radio (SDR) Evolution:** Liam is experimenting with the latest SDR technology, which offers greater flexibility and capability than traditional radios. SDRs in the future are even more powerful, with advanced features like enhanced digital signal processing, AI-assisted modulation recognition, and automated band scanning.
2. **Digital Modes and Internet Integration:** Liam explores new digital modes that offer increased efficiency and reliability, particularly in weak signal conditions. He also uses internet-linked amateur radio technologies that blend traditional radio with online capabilities, allowing for seamless global communication.
3. **Satellite and Space Communication:** Liam participates in amateur radio satellite communications, using satellites with enhanced digital payloads. He also engages with projects involving communication with space missions, including amateur radio links to lunar and Mars explorers.
4. **Regulatory Changes:** As spectrum becomes an even more precious resource, Liam stays informed about regulatory changes. He participates in discussions and advocacy efforts to ensure amateur radio maintains access to vital frequency bands.
5. **Community and Education:** Liam is active in his local amateur radio club, which now offers virtual reality (VR) workshops for training and simulation. He mentors new enthusiasts using these

immersive tools, helping them experience different aspects of amateur radio in a controlled, virtual environment.
6. **Emergency and Public Service:** With his expertise in digital communication modes, Liam volunteers in emergency communication networks. These networks increasingly use mesh networking and other decentralized communication systems, which amateur radio operators help to build and maintain.

Liam's experience showcases the potential future of amateur radio, where traditional aspects of the hobby blend with new technologies and approaches. This future promises even more opportunities for innovation, learning, and community involvement.

The chapter further delves into several areas of potential development, including:

1. **Technological Innovations:** Continued advancements in areas like quantum communication, low-earth-orbit satellite constellations, and even integration with IoT (Internet of Things) devices.
2. **Spectrum Management:** How new technologies and increased demands might change spectrum management and what it means for amateur radio.
3. **Youth Engagement:** Strategies to engage younger generations in amateur radio, leveraging modern technology and aligning with contemporary interests in STEM fields.
4. **Globalization of the Hobby:** Increased collaboration and communication among amateur radio enthusiasts worldwide, facilitated by digital platforms and enhanced communication modes.
5. **Public Service and Disaster Relief:** The evolving role of amateur radio in public service, particularly in disaster relief efforts with the advent of more robust and versatile communication tools.

In conclusion, the future of amateur radio looks bright and promising, offering a blend of traditional radio practices with cutting-edge technologies. For enthusiasts like Liam, these advancements open up new frontiers for exploration, experimentation, and contribution, both within the amateur radio community and beyond.

Chapter 19: "Case Studies and Real-World Applications"

Amateur radio extends far beyond being just a hobby; it has real-world applications and has made significant contributions in various fields. This chapter presents a series of case studies that illustrate the practical and sometimes critical role amateur radio plays in communication, technology development, emergency services, and community engagement. These case studies provide insights into the diverse ways amateur radio operators apply their skills and knowledge.

To effectively demonstrate the impact of amateur radio, let's delve into a case study involving an amateur radio operator, Nora, and her involvement in a disaster response scenario.

Case Study: Emergency Communication During Natural Disaster

Nora, an experienced amateur radio operator and member of the Amateur Radio Emergency Service (ARES), plays a crucial role in emergency communication during a natural disaster:

1. **Pre-Disaster Preparation:** Aware of the impending hurricane, Nora prepares her emergency communication kit, including a portable transceiver, power supplies, and various antennas. She verifies the functionality of all her equipment and reviews emergency communication protocols.
2. **Activation and Deployment:** As the hurricane makes landfall, causing widespread power outages and disrupting communication networks, Nora is activated by ARES. She promptly moves to a local emergency operations center (EOC), where she sets up her station.

3. **Emergency Communication:** Nora's station becomes a crucial link in the disaster response effort. She facilitates communication between the EOC, various shelters, and other amateur radio operators in affected areas. She relays critical information about rescue operations, medical emergencies, and resource needs.
4. **Coordination with Agencies:** Nora works closely with public service agencies, including the Red Cross and FEMA, providing them with real-time information from her network of amateur radio contacts. Her efforts help streamline the response and resource allocation.
5. **Post-Disaster Efforts:** After the initial emergency phase, Nora continues to provide communication support, helping coordinate recovery efforts and relay information to families seeking news about their loved ones.

Nora's involvement in disaster response highlights the invaluable service amateur radio operators provide during emergencies. Her skills, along with her ability to operate under challenging conditions, make a significant difference in the community's response to the disaster.

The chapter presents additional case studies, each highlighting a different aspect of amateur radio:

1. **International Space Station (ISS) Contact:** A case study of a school where students use amateur radio to communicate with astronauts aboard the ISS, inspiring interest in science and technology.
2. **Wildlife Tracking and Conservation:** How amateur radio operators assist in tracking wildlife for conservation efforts, using radio telemetry techniques.
3. **Technical Innovation in Equipment Design:** A case study on how amateur radio enthusiasts contribute to the development of new radio technologies and equipment.
4. **Community Events and Public Demonstrations:** Examples of how amateur radio clubs organize field days and public demonstrations, showcasing the hobby and educating the public about radio communication.
5. **DXpeditions to Remote Locations:** Documenting the challenges and achievements of amateur radio operators who set up stations in remote or rare locations, contributing to the global amateur radio community.

In conclusion, these case studies underscore the versatility and real-world impact of amateur radio. For operators like Nora and many others, amateur radio is not just a pastime but a platform for learning, innovation, and community service.

Chapter 20: "Building a Community: Clubs and Organizations"

The sense of community is a cornerstone of the amateur radio hobby. Clubs and organizations play a vital role in fostering this community spirit, offering opportunities for learning, collaboration, and camaraderie. This chapter delves into the importance of amateur radio clubs and organizations, detailing how they contribute to the hobby, support their members, and engage with the broader community.

To illustrate the significance of clubs and organizations in amateur radio, let's follow the story of an amateur radio club and its impact on its members and the local community, focusing on the experiences of one of its members, Tom.

Tom's Journey with an Amateur Radio Club:

1. **Joining the Club:** Tom, a relatively new amateur radio enthusiast, joins a local amateur radio club to learn more about the hobby and connect with other operators. He finds a welcoming community eager to share knowledge and experiences.
2. **Club Meetings and Activities:** The club holds regular meetings where members discuss various aspects of amateur radio, from technical topics to operating practices. Guest speakers are often invited to share their expertise on specific subjects.

3. **Education and Training:** Tom benefits from the educational programs offered by the club, including licensing classes and workshops on topics like antenna building, digital modes, and emergency communication.
4. **Field Days and Contests:** The club participates in annual field days and contests, providing Tom with hands-on experience in setting up temporary stations, operating under different conditions, and honing his skills in radio communication.
5. **Public Service Events:** The club is actively involved in public service, providing communication support for local events like marathons and parades. Tom volunteers in these events, using his radio skills to serve the community.
6. **Outreach and Advocacy:** The club engages in outreach activities, promoting amateur radio in schools and at public events. They also advocate for amateur radio interests at the local and national levels, ensuring the hobby's continued vitality.
7. **Club Projects:** Tom participates in club projects, such as building a club station and developing a mesh network for local amateur radio operators. These projects foster teamwork and technical innovation within the club.

Tom's involvement in the amateur radio club enriches his experience of the hobby. He not only develops his skills and knowledge but also forms lasting friendships and contributes to his community.

The chapter further explores the roles and functions of amateur radio clubs and organizations, including:

1. **Mentorship and Elmering:** How experienced members (Elmers) mentor new operators, providing guidance and encouragement.
2. **Special Interest Groups:** The formation of groups within clubs focused on specific aspects of amateur radio, such as satellite communication, digital modes, or QRP operation.
3. **Club Stations and Repeaters:** The establishment and maintenance of club stations and repeaters that enhance the capabilities and reach of club members.
4. **Disaster Preparedness and Emergency Communication:** The role of clubs in organizing and training members for participation in emergency communication networks.
5. **Partnerships and Collaboration:** Collaboration between clubs and other organizations, both within and outside the amateur radio community, to promote the hobby and engage in community service.

In conclusion, amateur radio clubs and organizations are much more than social groups; they are hubs of learning, collaboration, and service. For operators like Tom and countless others, these entities provide essential support and opportunities for growth, making the amateur radio hobby a rich and rewarding experience.

Conclusion:

"Amateur Radio: A Journey of Continuous Learning and Innovation"

Amateur radio, a blend of technology, community, and communication, represents a unique and enduring hobby that continually adapts and evolves with the changing technological landscape. This conclusion synthesizes the themes explored in the preceding chapters, reflecting on the past, present, and future of amateur radio, and reaffirming its relevance and appeal in the modern world.

At its core, amateur radio is about connection—connecting people across continents, cultures, and communities. It's a journey that starts with the basic curiosity about radio waves and extends to a lifelong pursuit of knowledge, skill, and service.

Let's encapsulate this journey through the experiences of an amateur radio operator, Jane, who embodies the spirit of amateur radio throughout her years in the hobby:

1. **Discovery and Learning:** Jane's journey began as a teenager, fascinated by the magic of radio waves. Her early experiences with a simple receiver, listening to distant stations, sparked a passion that led her to obtain her amateur radio license.
2. **Exploration and Growth:** Over the years, Jane explored various aspects of the hobby—DXing, contesting, building antennas, and experimenting with digital modes. Each activity offered new challenges and opportunities for learning.
3. **Community and Mentorship:** Jane became an active member of her local amateur radio club, finding mentors who guided her and friends who shared her passion. She later became an 'Elmer' herself, mentoring newcomers to the hobby.
4. **Innovation and Adaptation:** Embracing technological changes, Jane incorporated software-defined radios and digital communication modes into her station. She stayed abreast of the latest trends, continually adapting her skills.
5. **Service and Contribution:** Recognizing the value of amateur radio in emergencies, Jane trained in emergency communication, participating in drills and real-life responses to natural disasters. She contributed her skills to serve her community when it mattered most.
6. **Reflection and Continuity:** Now, with decades of experience, Jane reflects on her journey, seeing a hobby that has not only given her immense personal satisfaction but also allowed her to contribute meaningfully to society. She looks forward to continuing her journey, embracing new technologies and encouraging the next generation of amateur radio enthusiasts.

Jane's story is a microcosm of the amateur radio world—a world that thrives on curiosity, innovation, and community. Her journey exemplifies the spirit of amateur radio operators worldwide, who share a common bond regardless of their diverse backgrounds.

The conclusion reiterates the versatility of amateur radio, which transcends mere communication. It's a tool for education, a platform for technological experimentation, a means of public service, and a window to the world.

Looking to the future, the conclusion highlights the ongoing relevance of amateur radio. Despite the proliferation of digital communication, amateur radio holds its ground, offering unique opportunities that modern technologies cannot replicate. It's a hobby that constantly evolves, integrating new technologies while preserving its core values of communication, experimentation, and community.

In sum, amateur radio is not just a pastime; it's a journey of continuous learning and innovation. For enthusiasts like Jane and countless others, it's a lifelong adventure that offers endless possibilities for personal growth, technological exploration, and meaningful contribution to society.

BOOK 4
Embracing the World of Ham Radio:

A Journey from Novice to Expert

Introduction

The realm of ham radio, an intriguing and continuously evolving field, offers a unique blend of technology, communication, and community. This book, unlike a traditional operator's guide, delves into the multifaceted world of amateur radio, providing a comprehensive resource for both the novice enthusiast and the seasoned operator. The journey into ham radio is not merely about learning how to operate a radio; it's about understanding the science behind it, integrating into a global community, and embracing a hobby that has significant implications in both our daily lives and in times of crisis.

Ham radio, or amateur radio, has a storied history that dates back to the early 20th century. What began as an experimental pursuit in wireless telegraphy quickly blossomed into a global phenomenon, connecting people across continents and cultures. It's a history marked by constant innovation and adaptation, a trait that continues to define the hobby today. This book aims to provide a window into this fascinating world, offering insights into the technical aspects of radio operation while also highlighting the human element that makes ham radio enduringly popular.

The first step for any aspiring ham radio operator is understanding the basics: what is ham radio, and what does it entail? This book begins by exploring these fundamental questions, offering a clear definition and overview of the hobby. It's important to recognize that ham radio is more than just a means of communication; it's a scientific hobby, a tool for emergency communication, a means of technical experimentation, and a path to forming worldwide friendships.

The technical aspects of ham radio cannot be understated. Understanding radio waves, the science of how they travel, and the way they can be manipulated to carry information is at the core of being an effective operator. This book delves into these topics with clarity and depth, ensuring that even those with no prior knowledge of radio science can grasp these concepts. From the basic principles of frequency and modulation to the more advanced theories of radio wave propagation, the reader will gain a comprehensive understanding of what makes radio communication possible.

Another critical aspect of ham radio is the equipment. Choosing the right equipment is essential, whether it's for setting up a home station or for portable operation. This guide provides detailed advice on selecting and setting up radios, antennas, and other necessary equipment, tailored both to beginners making their initial purchases and to experienced operators looking to upgrade their stations. Building and modifying equipment is also a significant aspect of the hobby, and this book offers practical guidance and project ideas for those who wish to delve into this more technical side of ham radio.

The heart of ham radio is communication, and this book places a strong emphasis on operating procedures and etiquette. Good operating practices are essential for effective communication and for maintaining the spirit of camaraderie and respect that characterizes the ham radio community. The reader will learn about the various modes of communication available to ham operators, from traditional voice communication to digital modes and even satellite communication. The book also covers the exciting world of DXing – making long-distance contacts – and offers tips and strategies for making these challenging connections.

In addition to being a rewarding hobby, ham radio plays a crucial role in emergency communication. In times of disaster, when conventional communication systems fail, ham radio operators have repeatedly proven invaluable in facilitating emergency communication. This book discusses the role of ham radio in crisis situations and provides guidance on how to prepare and operate in these circumstances.

Becoming a licensed ham radio operator is an important step, and this guide offers comprehensive advice on obtaining a license. It covers the various license classes, what to expect in the examination, and how to prepare effectively. The book also discusses the legal aspects and regulations that govern ham radio, ensuring that readers understand how to operate within these guidelines.

The future of ham radio is as exciting as its past. New technologies like Software-Defined Radio (SDR) are revolutionizing the hobby, and this book explores these advancements, offering a glimpse into the future of amateur radio. The integration of computer technology with traditional radio practices is opening up new possibilities and making the hobby more accessible than ever.

Finally, this book acknowledges that ham radio is not just a solitary pursuit but a gateway into a vibrant global community. Ham radio operators share a unique bond, a shared passion for communication and technology that transcends geographical and cultural boundaries. This book encourages readers to join this community, participate in clubs and events, and experience the full richness of the ham radio world.

In sum, this book is a comprehensive guide, designed to take readers on a journey from the basic concepts of ham radio to the complexities of advanced operation. It is both a technical manual and a celebration of a hobby that brings people together, fosters innovation, and serves the greater good in times of need. Whether you are taking your first steps into the world of amateur radio or seeking to deepen your existing knowledge and skills, this book is an invaluable companion on your ham radio journey.

Chapter 1: The Basics of Ham Radio – Understanding the Fundamentals

Amateur radio, commonly known as ham radio, is a hobby that connects people through the use of radio communication equipment. This chapter is dedicated to unraveling the fundamentals of ham radio, providing a foundational understanding for those who are new to this exciting and technical field.

Ham radio operates on various frequencies and modes, allowing operators to communicate locally, nationally, and even internationally without the reliance on the internet or cellular networks. This form of communication is facilitated by radio waves, which are electromagnetic waves that can travel through the air and space.

Understanding Radio Waves

To comprehend the essence of ham radio, it is crucial to first understand radio waves. Radio waves are a type of electromagnetic radiation with wavelengths that are longer than infrared light. These waves can travel vast distances, depending on their frequency and the conditions of the atmosphere.

There are various bands, or ranges of frequencies, that ham radio operators are permitted to use. These bands are regulated by government entities like the Federal Communications Commission (FCC) in the United States. The most commonly used bands in ham radio include:

- **High Frequency (HF) Bands (3-30 MHz):** Ideal for long-distance communications, these frequencies can travel around the world.
- **Very High Frequency (VHF) Bands (30-300 MHz):** Primarily used for local and regional communication.
- **Ultra High Frequency (UHF) Bands (300 MHz-3 GHz):** Often used for local contacts and can penetrate urban environments more effectively.

Setting Up Your First Radio Station

As a practical example, let's consider setting up a basic ham radio station. The essential components you will need are:

1. **Transceiver:** A transceiver is a device that combines both a transmitter and a receiver. For beginners, a simple VHF/UHF transceiver is a good start.

2. **Antenna:** The antenna is crucial for sending and receiving signals. A simple vertical or dipole antenna is sufficient for starters.
3. **Power Supply:** This provides power to your transceiver. A basic 12-volt power supply is adequate for most beginner setups.
4. **Coaxial Cable:** This cable connects your transceiver to the antenna.

Practical Setup Example:

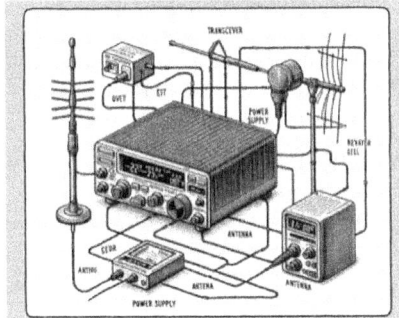

1. **Choose a Location:** Select a location for your station. It should be a quiet space with minimal electrical interference.
2. **Assemble the Transceiver:** Place your transceiver on a stable surface and connect it to the power supply.
3. **Install the Antenna:** If using a vertical antenna, it should be placed as high as possible, ideally on the roof or an elevated structure. For a dipole antenna, it should be hung in an open space, clear from obstructions.
4. **Connect the Antenna to the Transceiver:** Use the coaxial cable to connect the antenna to the transceiver. Ensure the connections are secure and weatherproofed if outdoors.
5. **Test the Setup:** Power on the transceiver and tune into a known frequency or a local repeater to test your setup.

The Importance of Licensing

Before you can start transmitting, it's important to obtain a ham radio license. The licensing process ensures that operators are knowledgeable about radio operation, safety, and the legal aspects of ham radio. In the United States, there are three classes of licenses: Technician, General, and Extra. Each level grants different privileges in terms of frequency bands and modes of operation.

The Technician class license is the entry-level license. It primarily allows you to operate on VHF and UHF frequencies, which are ideal for local and regional communication. To obtain this license, you must pass an examination that covers basic regulations, operating practices, and electronics theory.

Joining the Ham Radio Community

Once you have your station set up and your license in hand, you can start communicating with other ham radio operators. One of the best ways to begin is by joining a local club. Ham radio clubs are invaluable resources for beginners. They provide mentoring, equipment access, and organize events like field days and contests.

Conclusion of Chapter 1

In conclusion, the basics of ham radio encompass understanding radio waves, setting up a basic station, obtaining a license, and becoming part of the ham radio community. This chapter serves as a stepping stone into the world of amateur radio, laying the groundwork for the exciting journey ahead. As you progress through this book, you will delve deeper into each of these areas, expanding your knowledge and skills in the fascinating world of ham radio.

Chapter 2: Choosing Your Equipment – A Beginner's Guide

Embarking on the journey of ham radio is an exhilarating experience, and choosing the right equipment is a pivotal step. This chapter is designed to guide you through the process of selecting the appropriate gear for your station, tailored to your interests, budget, and the type of communication you wish to engage in.

Understanding Your Needs

Before diving into the vast sea of equipment choices, it's important to understand your own needs and objectives. Are you interested in local, regional, or worldwide communication? Do you prefer voice communication, digital modes, or perhaps morse code? The answers to these questions will influence the type of equipment you should consider.

Types of Radios

1. **Handheld Transceivers (HTs):** These are portable, battery-operated radios, ideal for on-the-go communication and local contacts via repeaters. They are perfect for beginners due to their ease of use and affordability.
2. **Mobile Transceivers:** Designed for vehicle installation, these offer more power and range than HTs. They are suitable for operators who want to communicate while traveling.
3. **Base Station Transceivers:** These are high-powered units designed for home use. They offer the widest range of frequencies and modes, ideal for making long-distance contacts.

Practical Example: Setting Up a VHF/UHF Base Station

For a beginner interested in local and regional communication, setting up a VHF/UHF base station is an excellent starting point. Here's a step-by-step guide:

1. **Select a Transceiver:** Choose a dual-band VHF/UHF transceiver with a power output of 50-100 watts. Ensure it has the features you need, such as memory channels and scanning functions.
2. **Choose an Antenna:** A dual-band vertical antenna is a good choice for VHF/UHF operation. It should be mounted as high as possible to maximize its range.
3. **Select a Power Supply:** A 12-volt power supply with at least 20 amperes capacity will ensure your transceiver has sufficient power.
4. **Install the Equipment:** Install the transceiver in a well-ventilated area to prevent overheating. Connect it to the power supply and the antenna using the appropriate cables.
5. **Test Your Setup:** Turn on the transceiver and tune into a local repeater or a known frequency. Check if you can receive and transmit clearly.

Antennas: The Key to Successful Communication

The antenna is arguably the most important part of your ham radio setup. It's the component that radiates and receives radio waves. There are various types of antennas, each with its own set of characteristics:

1. **Dipoles:** Simple and effective, these are great for beginners and can be easily made at home.
2. **Verticals:** These are omnidirectional and ideal for VHF/UHF operation.
3. **Yagis:** Directional antennas that provide significant gain, excellent for making long-distance contacts on HF bands.

When choosing an antenna, consider factors like the available space, the frequencies you plan to operate on, and the type of communication you're interested in.

Coaxial Cables and Connectors

The quality of your coaxial cable and connectors can significantly impact your station's performance. Coaxial cables carry the radio signals between your transceiver and antenna. It's crucial to choose a cable with low loss, especially for higher frequencies. Connectors must be properly installed to ensure good electrical contact and to prevent water ingress.

Additional Accessories

1. **SWR Meter:** Standing Wave Ratio (SWR) meters are essential for checking that your antenna is properly tuned to the frequencies you're using.
2. **Power Meter:** This measures the power output from your transceiver, ensuring that you're transmitting effectively.
3. **Filters and Preamps:** These can improve reception and transmission by filtering out unwanted noise and boosting weak signals.

Conclusion of Chapter 2

Choosing the right equipment is a critical step in setting up your ham radio station. It involves understanding your needs, selecting the appropriate radio, antenna, and accessories, and ensuring everything is properly installed and configured. With the right setup, you'll be well on your way to exploring the fascinating world of amateur radio communication. As you gain experience, you may find yourself delving into more advanced equipment and modes of operation, but the foundation laid by your initial choices will be indispensable throughout your ham radio journey.

Chapter 3: Setting Up Your Ham Radio Station – Step-by-Step Instructions

Creating a functional and efficient ham radio station is a rewarding endeavor that combines technical skill with personal creativity. This chapter will guide you through the process of setting up your station, considering factors like location, equipment arrangement, and station ergonomics.

Choosing the Right Location

The first step in setting up your ham radio station is choosing an optimal location. This decision can significantly impact your station's performance and your overall experience as a ham radio operator. Factors to consider include:

1. **Interference:** Select a location with minimal electrical noise. Avoid areas close to large electronic appliances or heavy wiring.
2. **Space:** Ensure enough space for your equipment, including radios, antennas, power supplies, and additional accessories.
3. **Antenna Placement:** Your location should allow for proper antenna installation, considering height and surrounding obstacles.
4. **Safety:** Ensure the area is safe, particularly from electrical hazards and well-ventilated to prevent equipment overheating.

Practical Example: Setting Up a Home Station

Let's consider setting up a basic home station for a beginner. This setup will include a VHF/UHF base station transceiver, a power supply, and a vertical antenna.

1. **Select a Room:** Choose a quiet room with enough space for your equipment and easy access to the roof or an outdoor area for the antenna.
2. **Desk and Chair:** Set up a sturdy desk and a comfortable chair. Organize the desk to have the transceiver, power supply, and any other equipment within easy reach.
3. **Install the Antenna:** If using a vertical antenna for VHF/UHF, install it on the roof or a high structure. Ensure it's securely mounted and grounded.
4. **Run Coaxial Cable:** Run the coaxial cable from the antenna to your transceiver. Use proper cable management to avoid tangles and reduce trip hazards.

5. **Set Up the Transceiver and Power Supply:** Place the transceiver on the desk and connect it to the power supply. Ensure all connections are secure and well-organized.
6. **Test the Station:** Power on the equipment and perform a test transmission. Check that all components are functioning correctly.

Equipment Configuration

Configuring your equipment correctly is vital for optimal performance. This involves setting up your transceiver's basic functions, such as frequency, mode, and power settings. It's also important to configure any additional devices like SWR meters or external speakers for maximum effectiveness.

Ergonomics and Station Layout

Ergonomics plays a crucial role in station setup. Your operating position should be comfortable for long periods. The transceiver, microphone, key (for Morse code), and other controls should be within easy reach. Good lighting and a clutter-free environment can greatly enhance your operating experience.

Grounding and Electrical Safety

Grounding is a critical aspect of any ham radio station. It serves two primary purposes: safety and reducing interference. Proper grounding can protect against electrical surges and improve the overall performance of your equipment. Ensure all equipment is grounded to a common ground point, and if possible, use a grounding rod driven into the earth.

Antenna Tuning

Tuning your antenna is crucial for efficient transmission and to protect your radio from damage. An SWR meter is used to measure the antenna's standing wave ratio, indicating how well the antenna is matched to the transceiver's frequency. Adjustments may be needed to optimize the SWR for the bands you intend to operate on.

Managing Interference

Interference can be a significant challenge in ham radio. It can come from various sources, both within your home and outside. Using filters, choosing the right location, and proper station grounding can help mitigate interference. Be prepared to troubleshoot and identify sources of noise that may impact your station's performance.

Regular Maintenance

Maintaining your station is essential for long-term operation. This includes regular checks of all cables and connections, ensuring that the antenna remains securely mounted and in good condition, and keeping the equipment clean and dust-free. Regular maintenance will prevent many common issues and prolong the life of your equipment.

Conclusion of Chapter 3

Setting up your ham radio station is a process that combines technical knowledge with personal preferences. From choosing the right location to configuring your equipment and ensuring operational safety, each step plays a crucial role in creating an effective and enjoyable operating environment. With your station properly set up, you're now ready to delve into the world of amateur radio communication, exploring the airwaves and connecting with other enthusiasts worldwide. As you gain experience, you may find new ways to optimize and expand your station, reflecting the dynamic and evolving nature of ham radio.

Chapter 4: Understanding Radio Waves – The Science Behind the Signals

Radio waves are the fundamental medium through which ham radio operators communicate. This chapter delves into the science of radio waves, explaining how they are generated, how they propagate, and how they are received. A comprehensive understanding of these concepts is crucial for any ham radio enthusiast.

The Nature of Radio Waves

Radio waves are a form of electromagnetic radiation, similar to light waves, but with longer wavelengths and lower frequencies. These waves are generated by alternating current (AC) in a conductor, such as an antenna. When AC flows through an antenna, it creates an electromagnetic field that radiates away from the antenna in the form of radio waves.

Frequency and Wavelength

The frequency of a radio wave is the number of times the wave oscillates per second, measured in Hertz (Hz). Wavelength is the physical length of one cycle of the wave, inversely related to frequency. Understanding the relationship between frequency and wavelength is critical in designing antennas and tuning them to specific frequencies.

The Radio Spectrum

The radio spectrum is divided into bands, each characterized by its frequency range. These bands are designated for different uses, including commercial broadcasting, aviation, and amateur radio. Ham radio operators are allocated specific bands across the spectrum, ranging from low-frequency (LF) bands to ultra-high-frequency (UHF) bands.

Propagation of Radio Waves

Radio waves can travel in several ways, depending on their frequency and atmospheric conditions:

1. **Ground Wave Propagation:** Low-frequency waves travel along the surface of the Earth, ideal for local communications.
2. **Skywave Propagation:** High-frequency waves can be reflected by the ionosphere, allowing them to travel over long distances.
3. **Line-of-Sight Propagation:** VHF and UHF waves travel in straight lines, making them suitable for local and regional communication.

Practical Example: Skywave Propagation

To understand skywave propagation, consider a ham radio operator using a high-frequency band to make an international contact. The operator transmits a signal that is directed upwards into the sky. When the signal reaches the ionosphere, it is refracted back towards the Earth, allowing it to cover distances far beyond the horizon.

Modulation of Radio Waves

Modulation is the process of encoding information onto a radio wave. There are several types of modulation, each suited to different types of communication:

1. **Amplitude Modulation (AM):** The amplitude (strength) of the wave is varied to encode information.
2. **Frequency Modulation (FM):** The frequency of the wave is varied.
3. **Phase Modulation (PM):** The phase of the wave is varied.
4. **Digital Modes:** Information is encoded as digital data, often using techniques like phase-shift keying (PSK) or frequency-shift keying (FSK).

Antennas and Wave Radiation

The antenna is a crucial component in both transmitting and receiving radio waves. Different types of antennas are designed to radiate and receive waves efficiently at specific frequencies. The design and placement of the antenna significantly impact the quality and range of communication.

Types of Antennas

1. **Dipole Antennas:** Simple antennas consisting of two conductive elements, ideal for beginners.
2. **Yagi Antennas:** Directional antennas that provide gain in one direction, excellent for long-distance communication.
3. **Vertical Antennas:** Omnidirectional antennas, best for VHF and UHF communications.

Radio Wave Reception

Receiving radio waves is the reverse process of transmitting them. The antenna captures the electromagnetic field of the wave, generating a small AC in the antenna. This signal is then amplified and demodulated in the receiver to retrieve the original information.

Interactions with the Environment

Radio waves interact with various environmental factors, including terrain, buildings, and weather. These interactions can cause effects like reflection, refraction, diffraction, and absorption, which can either enhance or hinder radio communication.

Safety Considerations

While operating with radio waves, safety is paramount. High power transmissions can create strong electromagnetic fields, which can be harmful if not properly managed. It's important to adhere to safety guidelines and regulatory limits on power and antenna placement.

Conclusion of Chapter 4

Understanding the science of radio waves is essential for effective and efficient ham radio operation. This knowledge not only enhances the operator's ability to communicate over various distances and conditions but also informs the choices made in equipment and operating practices. With a firm grasp of how radio waves work, ham radio operators can fully appreciate and utilize the remarkable capabilities of their equipment, opening up a world of communication possibilities.

Chapter 5: Getting Licensed – Your Path to Becoming a Ham Radio Operator

A ham radio license is the key to unlocking the full potential of amateur radio. This chapter guides you through the licensing process, providing insights into the various license classes, the examination process, and tips for successful preparation. Understanding and navigating this process is crucial for anyone aspiring to become a part of the ham radio community.

Understanding the Licensing Structure

In many countries, the ham radio licensing system is structured into different levels, each granting varying degrees of privileges. In the United States, for example, the Federal Communications Commission (FCC) issues three classes of licenses: Technician, General, and Extra. Each class offers progressively greater access to radio frequencies and modes of operation.

1. **Technician License:** This entry-level license allows access to all amateur radio frequencies above 30 MHz, which includes the popular 2-meter and 70-centimeter bands. It's ideal for local and regional communication.
2. **General License:** This license opens up access to most amateur radio HF bands, enabling worldwide communication.
3. **Extra License:** The most advanced level, offering full access to all amateur radio bands and frequencies.

The Examination Process

The path to obtaining a ham radio license involves passing an examination that tests your knowledge of radio theory, regulations, and operating practices. The exam is multiple-choice and is administered by volunteer examiners.

Practical Example: Preparing for the Technician License Exam

To demonstrate the process, let's consider preparing for the Technician class license exam in the U.S.:

1. **Study the Material:** Begin by studying the materials for the Technician license. Resources include study guides, online courses, and practice exams. Focus on topics like basic electronics theory, FCC rules, operating practices, and safety.
2. **Join a Study Group:** Consider joining a local or online study group. Interacting with others can enhance your understanding and provide motivation.
3. **Take Practice Exams:** Regularly take practice exams to assess your progress. These exams are available online and mimic the format of the actual test.
4. **Register for the Exam:** Once you're consistently scoring well on practice exams, register for an actual exam. Exams are conducted by accredited Volunteer Examiner Coordinators (VECs) and are often held at ham radio conventions, clubs, or dedicated testing centers.
5. **Exam Day:** On the day of the exam, bring a government-issued photo ID, your Social Security Number (SSN) or FCC Registration Number (FRN), and any applicable fee. The exam typically consists of 35 questions, and a passing score is 74%.

Study Tips and Resources

Effective preparation is crucial for passing the ham radio license exam. Utilize various study resources like books, online tutorials, and practice exams. Engaging with the ham radio community through clubs or online forums can also provide valuable insights and tips.

Understanding Regulations and Operating Procedures

A significant portion of the exam covers regulations and operating procedures. Familiarity with these topics ensures that licensed operators conduct themselves responsibly and legally on the airwaves.

The Role of Ethics and Etiquette in Ham Radio

While not always a formal part of the exam, understanding the ethics and etiquette of ham radio is important for integrating into the community. This includes aspects like respecting frequency allocations, maintaining civility in communications, and offering assistance to fellow operators.

Post-Examination: Obtaining Your Call Sign

After passing the exam, you will be issued a call sign by the licensing authority. This unique identifier is used to identify you on the air and is a badge of honor for many ham radio operators.

Continuing Education and Upgrading Your License

Obtaining your license is just the beginning. Many operators choose to continue their education and eventually upgrade to higher license classes. Each upgrade brings new privileges and opportunities for exploration in the world of amateur radio.

Conclusion of Chapter 5

Becoming a licensed ham radio operator is a journey of learning and personal development. Passing the licensing exam opens up a world of communication possibilities and embeds you into a global community of enthusiasts. Whether you aim for local communication or global outreach, obtaining your ham radio license is the first significant step toward achieving your amateur radio goals.

Chapter 6: Operating Procedures – Best Practices and Etiquette

Once you have obtained your ham radio license, understanding and adhering to proper operating procedures and etiquette is paramount. This chapter focuses on the best practices for operating a ham radio, covering the key aspects of communication, protocol, and interaction within the amateur radio community.

Understanding the Basics of Communication

Effective communication is the cornerstone of ham radio operations. This involves not only the technical aspect of transmitting and receiving messages but also the human element of interaction.

Calling and Responding

1. **Making a Call:** When initiating a call, you typically start with the word "CQ" (seeking you), followed by your call sign. For example, "CQ CQ CQ, this is [Your Call Sign]."
2. **Responding to a Call:** To respond, first, ensure the frequency is clear. Then, transmit the call sign of the station you're responding to, followed by your own call sign.

Practical Example: Making a Contact

Imagine you're trying to make a local contact on a 2-meter band. You would:

1. Tune into a clear frequency.
2. Transmit, "CQ CQ CQ, this is [Your Call Sign], calling CQ and standing by."
3. Wait for a response. If someone responds, they will say your call sign followed by theirs.
4. Engage in a conversation, ensuring to periodically identify both stations by call signs.

Radio Etiquette

Good radio etiquette is crucial for maintaining order and respect on the airwaves. This includes:

1. **Listening Before Transmitting:** Always listen to ensure the frequency is not in use before transmitting.
2. **Speaking Clearly and Slowly:** Articulate your words and speak at a moderate pace to ensure clarity.
3. **Using Standard Phonetics:** When spelling out call signs or important information, use the standard NATO phonetic alphabet.
4. **Respecting Others:** Be polite and respectful in all communications. Avoid controversial topics and heated discussions.

Signal Reports

Signal reports are a common part of ham radio communication. They provide feedback on the quality of the received signal, using the "R-S-T" system (Readability, Signal Strength, Tone).

Managing Interference

Interference is a common challenge in ham radio. If you encounter or cause interference, handle it politely and professionally. Try to resolve the issue by adjusting your frequency or equipment settings.

Emergency and Priority Traffic

Amateur radio plays a crucial role in emergency communications. If you hear a station announcing emergency or priority traffic, clear the frequency immediately.

Digital Modes and Net Operations

Digital modes of communication, like FT8 or PSK31, and participation in nets (scheduled on-air meetings) have their own set of operating procedures and etiquettes. Familiarize yourself with these before participating.

Record Keeping

Keeping a log of your contacts is not only a good practice but also a requirement in some countries. Logs should include details like date, time, frequency, mode, and call signs.

Community Involvement and Mentorship

Engaging with the ham radio community is a great way to learn and grow as an operator. Seek mentorship from experienced operators and, in turn, mentor newcomers as you gain experience.

Conclusion of Chapter 6

Understanding and following proper operating procedures and etiquette is essential for a rewarding ham radio experience. These practices ensure effective communication, foster a respectful community, and enable operators to fully enjoy the hobby. By adhering to these guidelines, you contribute to the rich tradition of amateur radio, characterized by mutual respect, cooperation, and a shared passion for communication.

Chapter 7: Emergency Communication – Ham Radio in Crisis Situations

Amateur radio plays a pivotal role in emergency communication, often stepping in when traditional communication systems fail. This chapter explores the importance of ham radio in emergencies, detailing the protocols, equipment, and strategies necessary for effective crisis communication.

Understanding the Role of Ham Radio in Emergencies

During emergencies, standard communication infrastructures like telephones and the internet can become overloaded or non-functional. Ham radio operators, with their independent and versatile setups, are often able to fill these communication gaps, providing critical links between affected areas and emergency services.

Preparing for Emergency Communication

1. **Equipment Readiness:** Ensure your equipment is in good working condition. This includes having a reliable power source, such as batteries or a generator.
2. **Antenna Systems:** Antennas should be robust and, if possible, have the capability to operate on multiple bands.
3. **Emergency Frequencies:** Be familiar with designated emergency frequencies and nets in your area.
4. **Skills Practice:** Regularly practice emergency communication skills, such as net operation and message handling.

Practical Example: Participating in a Simulated Emergency Test (SET)

Imagine participating in an SET organized by your local amateur radio club:

1. **Preparation:** Before the test, check your equipment, ensuring all components are functioning correctly. Charge batteries and set up your station to be able to operate off-grid.
2. **Test Participation:** During the SET, follow the instructions of the net control station. This may include passing simulated emergency traffic, checking into emergency nets, and testing various communication modes.
3. **Debriefing:** After the SET, participate in a debriefing session to discuss what went well and what could be improved.

Joining Emergency Communication Groups

Many countries have organized amateur radio groups dedicated to emergency communication, such as the Amateur Radio Emergency Service (ARES) in the United States. Joining these groups can provide training, resources, and a structured approach to emergency communications.

Protocols for Emergency Communication

In an emergency, clear and efficient communication is key. This includes:

1. **Using Standardized Message Formats:** Learn and use standardized formats like the Radiogram or ICS-213 for message handling.
2. **Net Operations:** Understand how to participate in a directed net, including net check-ins, handling traffic, and following net control directives.
3. **Priority and Health & Welfare Traffic:** Learn to prioritize emergency traffic and understand the protocols for handling health and welfare inquiries.

Legal Considerations

During emergencies, certain regulatory exceptions may apply to amateur radio operations, such as increased power limits or expanded frequency privileges. Be aware of these exceptions and the legal framework governing emergency communications.

Building a Go-Kit

A "Go-Kit" is a portable collection of equipment and supplies that can be quickly deployed for emergency operations. This kit should include:

1. **Portable Radio and Antennas:** A multi-band transceiver and portable antennas.
2. **Power Supplies:** Batteries, solar chargers, and power adapters.
3. **Accessories:** Headphones, microphones, key for Morse code, and necessary cables.
4. **Other Essentials:** First aid kit, food, water, and clothing appropriate for the conditions.

Conclusion of Chapter 7

Ham radio's role in emergency communication cannot be overstated. Through preparation, training, and participation in emergency communication networks, amateur radio operators can provide invaluable services during crises. This chapter not only underscores the importance of being prepared for emergency scenarios but also highlights the profound impact that amateur radio can have in supporting communities during times of need.

Chapter 8: Joining the Community – Clubs, Contests, and Events

The ham radio community is vibrant and diverse, offering a range of activities and groups for enthusiasts of all levels. This chapter focuses on how to engage with this community through clubs, contests, and various ham radio events, enhancing your experience and knowledge in the field.

The Benefits of Joining a Ham Radio Club

Joining a local ham radio club is one of the best ways to immerse yourself in the amateur radio culture. Clubs provide a platform for learning, mentorship, and sharing experiences. They often conduct regular meetings, training sessions, and special events.

Practical Example: Becoming a Club Member

Imagine you're interested in joining a local ham radio club. Here's how you might go about it:

1. **Research:** Find local clubs through online directories or ham radio websites.
2. **Attend a Meeting:** Most clubs welcome visitors to their meetings. Attend a meeting to get a feel for the club's activities and membership.
3. **Participate in Events:** Many clubs host field days, educational sessions, or operate special event stations. Participating in these events can provide hands-on experience and networking opportunities.
4. **Become a Member:** If the club feels like a good fit, apply for membership. This may involve paying dues and filling out a membership form.

Participating in Contests

Contests, or "radiosport," are a popular aspect of ham radio. These events challenge operators to make as many contacts as possible within a set period. Contests vary in their rules and objectives, and they can be a fun way to improve your operating skills.

Types of Contests

1. **DX Contests:** Focus on making long-distance contacts.
2. **VHF/UHF Contests:** Aimed at contacts on the VHF and UHF bands.
3. **Field Day:** An annual event that combines a contest with emergency preparedness.

Attending Hamfests and Conventions

Hamfests and conventions are gatherings where hams can buy equipment, attend workshops, and meet other enthusiasts. These events are excellent opportunities to learn about the latest trends and technologies in amateur radio.

Practical Example: Visiting a Hamfest

When planning to visit a hamfest:

1. **Research the Event:** Look for information about the vendors, workshops, and presentations.
2. **Prepare a List:** Make a list of items or information you are interested in.
3. **Engage with Exhibitors:** Talk to vendors and exhibitors about their products and services.
4. **Attend Workshops:** Participate in workshops or forums to gain new knowledge and skills.

Volunteering and Community Service

Many amateur radio operators find fulfillment in using their skills for community service. This can include participating in emergency communication networks, providing communication support for public events, or engaging in educational outreach.

Online Communities and Resources

In addition to physical clubs and events, the online ham radio community is thriving. Online forums, social media groups, and websites offer platforms for discussion, advice, and sharing experiences.

Conclusion of Chapter 8

The ham radio community is dynamic and welcoming, offering a wealth of opportunities for growth, learning, and contribution. Whether through local clubs, contests, hamfests, or online forums, engaging with the community enhances the amateur radio experience. It provides a sense of camaraderie, a network of support, and endless opportunities for personal and technical development. This chapter emphasizes the importance of community involvement in the amateur radio journey, encouraging readers to explore and participate in the myriad of activities available.

Chapter 9: Digital Modes and Technologies – Modernizing Ham Radio

In recent years, the advent of digital technologies has revolutionized the world of amateur radio, introducing a range of new modes and capabilities. This chapter delves into these modern digital modes, explaining their operation, benefits, and how to integrate them into your ham radio activities.

Understanding Digital Modes

Digital modes in ham radio involve the use of digital data, such as text or binary code, instead of voice or Morse code. These modes are known for their efficiency, particularly in weak signal conditions, and their ability to facilitate various forms of communication, from text messaging to image transmission.

Common Digital Modes

1. **RTTY (Radio Teletype):** One of the earliest digital modes, transmitting text using a 5-bit code.
2. **PSK31 (Phase Shift Keying, 31 Baud):** A popular low-bandwidth mode used for real-time text communication.
3. **FT8:** A fast mode designed for weak-signal HF band communication.
4. **D-STAR (Digital Smart Technologies for Amateur Radio):** A digital voice and data protocol developed for amateur radio.
5. **WSJT-X Modes (including JT65, JT9):** Designed for weak-signal communication on shortwave bands.

Setting Up for Digital Modes

To operate in digital modes, you will need:

1. **A Computer with Suitable Software:** Many digital modes require specific software. For instance, WSJT-X is commonly used for FT8.
2. **An Interface Between Your Radio and Computer:** This can be a commercially available interface or a simple home-built one.
3. **A Sound Card:** Most modern computers have a suitable sound card built-in.

Practical Example: Setting Up for FT8

Here's a step-by-step guide to setting up an FT8 station:

1. **Install the Software:** Download and install WSJT-X software on your computer.
2. **Connect the Radio to the Computer:** Use an interface to connect the audio output of your radio to the sound input of your computer, and vice versa.
3. **Configure the Software:** Set up the WSJT-X software with your call sign, grid square, and interface settings.
4. **Tune to an FT8 Frequency:** Using your transceiver, tune to a known FT8 frequency, such as 14.074 MHz for the 20m band.
5. **Start Transmitting and Receiving:** Use the software to monitor incoming signals and to transmit.

The Benefits of Digital Modes

Digital modes offer several advantages:

1. **Efficiency in Weak Signal Conditions:** Digital modes can make effective communication possible even with very weak signals.
2. **Low Bandwidth Use:** Many digital modes require less bandwidth than voice communication.
3. **Error Correction:** Digital modes often include error correction algorithms to ensure message accuracy.
4. **Diverse Communication Forms:** Digital modes enable various forms of communication, including text, data, and images.

Operating Protocols for Digital Modes

Each digital mode has its own set of operating protocols. For instance, FT8 follows a strict timing sequence for transmission and receiving. Familiarize yourself with the protocols of the modes you choose to use.

Digital Mode Contests and Awards

There are contests and award programs specifically for digital modes, which can be an exciting way to challenge your skills and engage with the community.

Integrating Digital and Traditional Modes

While digital modes offer exciting possibilities, they complement rather than replace traditional modes like voice and Morse code. Many hams enjoy using a combination of digital and traditional modes.

Conclusion of Chapter 9

Digital modes are an exciting aspect of modern ham radio, offering new ways to communicate and experiment. Whether you're interested in text-based communication, weak signal work, or digital voice modes, the world of digital amateur radio has something to offer. This chapter provides the foundation to start exploring these modes, encouraging readers to embrace the evolving nature of ham radio technology.

Chapter 10: Building and Modifying Equipment – A DIY Guide

For many ham radio enthusiasts, the ability to build and modify equipment is a rewarding aspect of the hobby. This chapter provides guidance on DIY projects, from simple antenna constructions to more complex transceiver modifications, catering to a range of skill levels.

The Appeal of DIY in Ham Radio

Building and modifying equipment allows for a deeper understanding of how radio components work. It also provides the satisfaction of tailoring equipment to specific needs and preferences. Whether it's constructing a simple antenna or designing a complete transceiver, DIY projects can significantly enhance your ham radio experience.

Getting Started with DIY Projects

1. **Educate Yourself:** A solid understanding of basic electronics and radio theory is crucial. Resources include books, online courses, and club workshops.
2. **Gather the Right Tools:** Basic tools like soldering irons, wire cutters, and multimeters are essential.
3. **Start Small:** Begin with simple projects to build your skills and confidence.

Practical Example: Building a Simple Dipole Antenna

A great starting project is constructing a basic half-wave dipole antenna for the 20-meter band.

1. **Calculate the Length:** The formula for a half-wave dipole is Length (in meters) =468Frequency (in MHz) Length (in meters) = Frequency (in MHz)468. For a 20-meter band (14 MHz), the length of each leg of the antenna would be approximately 16.8 feet.
2. **Gather Materials:** You'll need wire for the antenna, insulators for the ends, a balun, and coaxial cable.

3. **Cut the Wire:** Cut two pieces of wire, each 16.8 feet long.
4. **Attach to Insulators:** Secure each wire to an insulator at one end.
5. **Install the Balun:** Attach the center of the antenna to a balun, which in turn connects to the coaxial cable.
6. **Mount the Antenna:** Hang the antenna as high as possible, ensuring it's clear of obstructions and metallic objects.

Intermediate Projects

Once you're comfortable with basic projects, you can move on to intermediate ones like building tuners, power meters, or even simple transceivers. Kits are available that provide all the necessary components along with instructions.

Advanced DIY: Transceiver Modifications and Custom Builds

For the more experienced, modifying existing transceivers or building them from scratch can be a challenging and rewarding project. This could involve adding features, improving performance, or even designing a new circuit.

Learning from Mistakes

DIY projects often involve a trial-and-error approach.

Mistakes are part of the learning process and can lead to a deeper understanding of electronics and radio operations.

The Importance of Safety

Safety is paramount in any DIY project. Always follow safety guidelines, especially when working with electricity, soldering, or antennas at height.

Sharing Your Projects and Learning from Others

The ham radio community is an excellent resource for sharing and learning. Participate in online forums, attend club meetings, and engage with other DIY enthusiasts to exchange ideas and get advice.

Conclusion of Chapter 10

DIY projects in ham radio not only enhance your technical skills but also bring a unique sense of accomplishment. Whether you're building a simple antenna or designing complex circuits, these projects deepen your understanding of radio technology and provide a customizable approach to your ham radio journey. This chapter encourages readers to explore the rewarding world of ham radio DIY, offering practical examples and highlighting the community's collaborative spirit.

Chapter 11: Antenna Design and Theory – Maximizing Your Signal

An effective antenna is crucial for successful ham radio communication. This chapter delves into the principles of antenna design and theory, offering guidance on choosing, constructing, and optimizing antennas for various applications.

Understanding Antenna Basics

An antenna is a transducer that converts electrical power into radio waves and vice versa. The performance of a ham radio station is often more dependent on the antenna system than on the radio itself. Understanding the basic properties of antennas is key to selecting or designing the right one for your needs.

Key Antenna Parameters

1. **Gain:** A measure of how well the antenna focuses energy in a particular direction.
2. **Bandwidth:** The range of frequencies over which the antenna can operate effectively.
3. **Polarization:** The orientation of the electric field of the radio wave (horizontal or vertical).
4. **Impedance:** The antenna's resistance to electrical current, which should match the transmitter for maximum power transfer.

Types of Antennas

1. **Dipoles:** Simple and effective, suitable for beginners.
2. **Verticals:** Good for omnidirectional communication, especially on VHF and UHF bands.
3. **Yagi-Uda Antennas:** Directional antennas providing significant gain, ideal for DX communication.
4. **Loop Antennas:** Compact and efficient, particularly for limited spaces.
5. **Wire Antennas:** Versatile and can be configured in various ways to suit different frequencies and conditions.

Practical Example: Constructing a Multiband Wire Antenna

A multiband wire antenna can be an excellent project, allowing operation on multiple HF bands.

1. **Design Considerations:** Decide on the type (e.g., fan dipole, G5RV) and the bands you wish to operate on.
2. **Calculate Lengths:** Use antenna theory formulas to calculate the length of the wire for each band.
3. **Gather Materials:** Obtain wire, insulators, a balun, and necessary hardware.
4. **Construction:** Cut the wires to the required lengths, attach them to the central insulator, and connect them to the balun.
5. **Installation:** Erect the antenna as high as possible, ensuring it's clear from obstructions and potential hazards.

Antenna Tuning and SWR

Tuning an antenna to the desired frequency band is crucial for efficient operation. The Standing Wave Ratio (SWR) is a critical parameter indicating how well the antenna is matched to the transmitter. An SWR meter can be used to adjust the antenna for the lowest SWR.

Antenna Safety Considerations

Safety is paramount in antenna construction and installation.

Considerations include electrical safety (especially when near power lines), mechanical stability, and legal/regulatory compliance regarding structure height and placement.

Advanced Antenna Theory

For those interested in delving deeper, topics like antenna radiation patterns, antenna theory mathematics, and the effects of ground and nearby structures are worth exploring.

Experimentation and Optimization

Experimentation is a key part of antenna design. Try different configurations and adjustments to see how they affect performance. Tools like antenna analyzers can be invaluable in this process.

Conclusion of Chapter 11

Antennas are a fascinating and crucial aspect of ham radio. Whether you're constructing a simple dipole or a complex beam antenna, the right antenna can significantly enhance your station's capabilities. This chapter provides the knowledge and practical guidance to embark on the journey of antenna experimentation and optimization, encouraging readers to not only understand but also to apply antenna theory in real-world scenarios.

Chapter 12: Advanced Operating Techniques – Honing Your Skills

After mastering the basics of ham radio, many operators seek to enhance their skills and knowledge. This chapter explores advanced operating techniques, providing insights into sophisticated methods and practices that can elevate your ham radio experience.

Exploring Different Operating Modes

Ham radio offers various operating modes, each with unique challenges and opportunities. Beyond the popular voice and CW (Morse code) modes, there are numerous digital modes, satellite communication, and even moonbounce (EME) communications. Understanding and mastering these modes can greatly expand your ham radio capabilities.

Practical Example: Satellite Communication

Setting up a station for amateur radio satellite communication is an exciting advanced project:

1. **Equipment Needs:** You will need a dual-band VHF/UHF transceiver capable of full-duplex operation, a suitable antenna (like a handheld Yagi), and a means of tracking satellites.
2. **Satellite Tracking:** Use software to track the pass times of amateur radio satellites.
3. **Making Contact:** During a satellite pass, adjust your antenna to follow the satellite's path while transmitting and listening on the designated frequencies.

Advanced Digital Communication

Digital modes like JT65, FT8, and PSK31 offer unique operating experiences. Exploring these modes requires understanding of software settings, proper timing, and efficient use of bandwidth. Engaging in these modes can lead to successful contacts under challenging conditions.

Contesting and DXing

For many hams, contesting and DXing (making long-distance contacts) are the pinnacle of operating achievement. These activities require not only good technical skills but also an understanding of propagation, efficient station setup, and operating strategy.

Specialized Antenna and Propagation Techniques

Advanced operators often experiment with specialized antennas and study propagation to enhance their ability to make distant contacts. Techniques like using directional antennas, understanding ionospheric conditions, and leveraging low-noise receiving setups are critical for success.

Morse Code Proficiency

Despite the advent of modern technologies, Morse code remains a highly respected and efficient mode of communication in ham radio. Improving your speed and accuracy can open up new avenues for DXing and contesting.

Traffic Handling and Message Relay

Traffic handling, the practice of passing written messages via radio, is an art in itself.

Participating in traffic nets and learning the precise format for message handling can be a rewarding challenge.

Building and Using Amplifiers

For those interested in technical projects, building or optimizing amplifiers can enhance your station's performance. This involves an understanding of electronics, safety considerations, and regulatory compliance regarding power output.

Emergency and Public Service Communication

Advanced operators often contribute their skills to emergency and public service communication efforts. This includes participating in drills, providing communication support during events, and engaging with emergency communication organizations.

Teaching and Mentoring

Many advanced ham radio operators find satisfaction in teaching and mentoring newer hams. Sharing your knowledge and experience can be immensely rewarding and helps sustain the amateur radio community.

Conclusion of Chapter 12

Advancing your operating skills in ham radio is a journey of continuous learning and experimentation. From exploring new modes and techniques to contributing to public service, there are numerous ways to deepen your engagement with the hobby. This chapter provides the guidance and inspiration to explore these advanced aspects, encouraging a deeper understanding and greater enjoyment of the world of amateur radio.

Chapter 13: Radio Wave Propagation – Understanding How Signals Travel

Effective communication in ham radio is deeply influenced by how radio waves propagate. This chapter explores the science of radio wave propagation, helping operators understand and utilize various atmospheric conditions to enhance their communication reach.

The Basics of Radio Wave Propagation

Radio waves can travel through different layers of the Earth's atmosphere, each affecting the signals in unique ways. Understanding these effects is crucial for predicting signal strength and reach.

Layers of the Atmosphere

1. **Troposphere:** The lowest layer, where weather phenomena occur. Tropospheric ducting can enhance VHF and UHF signal range.
2. **Ionosphere:** Extends from about 50 km to 600 km above the Earth. The ionosphere plays a vital role in HF radio wave propagation, enabling long-distance communication.

Types of Propagation

1. **Ground Wave Propagation:** Follows the curvature of the Earth, useful for local communications on lower frequencies.
2. **Skywave Propagation:** Involves the reflection or refraction of radio waves off the ionosphere, enabling long-distance communications on HF bands.
3. **Line-of-Sight Propagation:** Straight-line propagation used in VHF and UHF communications, essential for satellite and terrestrial microwave links.

Practical Example: Experiencing Skywave Propagation

A practical exercise in understanding skywave propagation can be conducted by monitoring the signals on HF bands:

1. **Select a Frequency:** Choose a frequency in the HF band, ideally in the late afternoon or early evening.
2. **Listen for Changes:** Over time, observe how the reception of distant stations changes, noting the times when signals are strongest.
3. **Record Observations:** Keep a log of your observations, correlating them with the time of day and atmospheric conditions.

Understanding Solar Activity and Its Effects

Solar activity, such as sunspots and solar flares, significantly impacts radio wave propagation, especially on HF bands. Learning to monitor solar indices (like the sunspot number and solar flux index) can help predict propagation conditions.

Maximizing Propagation Conditions

Different frequencies work better at different times of the day and under various atmospheric conditions:

1. **Low Bands (160m, 80m, 40m):** Best used during nighttime for long-distance communication.
2. **High Bands (20m, 15m, 10m):** Generally, more effective during the daytime, especially during periods of high solar activity.

Antenna Strategies for Optimal Propagation

Adjusting your antenna setup based on desired propagation can enhance communication:

1. **Height:** Higher antennas are better for line-of-sight and some skywave communications.
2. **Orientation:** The direction your antenna faces can affect its reception and transmission, particularly with directional antennas like Yagis.

3. **Polarization:** Matching the polarization of your antenna to the intended mode of propagation can improve signal strength.

Utilizing Propagation Prediction Tools

There are various tools and software available for predicting radio wave propagation. These tools can help in planning communication activities, contests, and DX expeditions.

Conclusion of Chapter 13

Radio wave propagation is a complex but fascinating subject that significantly impacts the ham radio experience. By understanding the principles of how radio waves travel and are affected by the Earth's atmosphere and solar activity, operators can optimize their communication strategies. This chapter empowers readers to embrace the science of propagation, applying it practically to enhance their ham radio endeavors.

Chapter 14: Mobile and Portable Operations – Ham Radio on the Go

Mobile and portable ham radio operations offer the flexibility to communicate from almost anywhere. This chapter covers the essentials of setting up and operating a mobile or portable ham radio station, addressing the unique challenges and opportunities of operating outside a traditional home setup.

Understanding Mobile and Portable Operations

Mobile operations typically involve operating a ham radio station from a vehicle, while portable operations refer to setting up a station that can be easily transported and operated from temporary locations like parks or hillsides.

Mobile Operations

Mobile ham radio involves installing equipment in a vehicle. This setup allows for communication while on the move, which can be especially useful for public service events or just for the enjoyment of operating from different locations.

1. **Equipment Selection:** Mobile transceivers are compact and designed to be powered by a vehicle's electrical system. Antenna selection is crucial, with options including mag-mount antennas, screwdriver antennas, and hamsticks.
2. **Installation:** Key considerations include secure mounting of the radio, proper antenna placement, and minimizing interference from the vehicle's electrical systems.

Portable Operations

Portable operations involve carrying equipment to a location and temporarily setting up a station. This mode is popular for activities like Summits on the Air (SOTA) or Parks on the Air (POTA).

1. **Equipment Selection:** Portable equipment includes lightweight transceivers, battery packs, and portable antennas like wire antennas or compact verticals.
2. **Setup:** The setup should be quick to assemble and disassemble, and easy to transport.

Practical Example: Setting Up a Portable Station for a POTA Activation

Imagine setting up a portable station in a local park for a POTA activation:

1. **Plan Your Equipment:** Choose a lightweight transceiver, a battery pack, and a portable antenna. Pack necessary accessories like coaxial cables, headphones, and a logbook.
2. **Transportation:** Pack all equipment in a backpack or a suitable carrying case.
3. **On-Site Setup:** Once at the park, find a suitable location to set up. Erect the antenna (a simple wire antenna or a telescopic pole can be used) and connect it to the transceiver.
4. **Operating:** Operate the station, making as many contacts as possible. Be sure to adhere to park rules and respect the environment.

Power Considerations

Power is a critical aspect of mobile and portable operations. In mobile setups, the vehicle's battery is the primary power source. For portable operations, options include rechargeable battery packs, solar panels, or small generators.

Antenna Challenges and Solutions

Mobile and portable operations often require compromise antennas due to space and setup time constraints. Understanding the trade-offs and how to maximize antenna efficiency is key.

Operating Techniques and Best Practices

Operating from a mobile or portable station presents unique challenges, such as dealing with variable signal conditions and power limitations. Adapting operating techniques to these conditions is vital for successful communication.

Safety and Legal Considerations

Safety is paramount in mobile and portable operations. This includes safe driving practices for mobile operation, ensuring your setup is secure and won't cause a hazard, and adhering to regulations concerning operation from public or private lands.

The Joy of Exploration and Experimentation

Mobile and portable operations open up a world of exploration. They provide the opportunity to operate from new and exciting locations, offering unique propagation conditions and the chance to make rare contacts.

Conclusion of Chapter 14

Mobile and portable ham radio operations add a dynamic aspect to the hobby, combining radio communications with adventure and exploration. This chapter provides the foundation for successful and enjoyable mobile and portable operations, encouraging operators to step out of the shack and explore the world of ham radio on the go.

Chapter 15: Satellite Communication and Ham Radio – Reaching Beyond Earth

Amateur radio satellite communication is a thrilling aspect of the hobby that combines traditional ham radio skills with the excitement of communicating via satellites orbiting the Earth. This chapter will guide you through the basics of satellite communication, including equipment, operating techniques, and how to make your first satellite contact.

Introduction to Amateur Radio Satellites

Amateur radio satellites, often built and operated by ham radio organizations, orbit the Earth and serve as repeaters or transponders in space. They receive signals from Earth and retransmit them back, allowing hams to communicate over long distances.

Types of Amateur Radio Satellites

1. **Low Earth Orbit (LEO) Satellites:** Orbit close to the Earth and are the most accessible for amateur radio operators.
2. **Geostationary Satellites:** Remain in a fixed position relative to the Earth's surface, offering continuous coverage over a specific area but are more challenging to access.

Equipment for Satellite Communication

To communicate via satellites, you'll need:

1. **A Dual-Band Transceiver:** Capable of transmitting on one band (usually VHF) and receiving on another (usually UHF).
2. **Antennas:** Directional antennas like Yagis are preferred for tracking satellites. Portable setups often use handheld Arrow or Elk antennas.
3. **Satellite Tracking Software:** Software to track satellite orbits and predict passes.

Practical Example: Making a QSO via an Amateur Satellite

Setting up and making a contact (QSO) via a LEO satellite involves several steps:

1. **Select a Satellite:** Choose a suitable amateur satellite. Websites and apps can provide pass predictions based on your location.
2. **Setup Your Equipment:** Set up your transceiver and antenna. Ensure your transceiver is programmed with the satellite's uplink and downlink frequencies, and account for Doppler shift.
3. **Track the Satellite:** As the satellite approaches, use your antenna to track its movement across the sky. This might require manual adjustment throughout the pass.
4. **Make Contact:** Listen for activity and when you hear a clear opportunity, call out your call sign and location. Once you make contact, exchange signal reports, then clear the frequency for others.

Understanding Satellite Orbits and Passes

The orbit of a satellite determines its pass over a particular location. Understanding how to read pass predictions and the concept of satellite footprint is crucial for successful communication.

Doppler Shift in Satellite Communication

Doppler shift is a phenomenon where the frequency of the satellite signal changes as it moves relative to the Earth. Compensating for this shift is essential for clear communication, especially on higher frequency bands.

Operating Etiquette on Satellites

Satellite bandwidth is limited, and operators must follow specific protocols to ensure fair access. This includes keeping transmissions short, waiting for your turn to speak, and not transmitting during satellite telemetry downlinks.

Advanced Satellite Operations

For the more advanced operator, there are opportunities to engage in digital modes via satellite, work through geostationary satellites, or even bounce signals off the Moon's surface (EME).

Conclusion of Chapter 15

Amateur radio satellite communication offers a unique and exciting way to explore the hobby, extending the reach of traditional ham radio to a global scale. This chapter provides the knowledge and practical steps to get started with satellite communication, opening up a world of opportunities to communicate in new and innovative ways.

Chapter 16: Interference and Troubleshooting – Solving Common Problems

In the world of amateur radio, interference is an inevitable challenge that every operator must learn to manage. This chapter addresses the common types of interference that ham radio operators encounter and offers strategies for identifying, troubleshooting, and resolving these issues.

Understanding Types of Interference

Interference in ham radio can come from a variety of sources and can manifest in different forms. It's crucial to understand these types to effectively tackle them.

Common Types of Interference

1. **RFI (Radio Frequency Interference):** Unwanted signals or noise that interfere with desired radio communications.
2. **EMI (Electromagnetic Interference):** Disturbance generated by external sources that affect electrical circuits.
3. **Intermodulation:** Occurs when two or more signals mix in a non-linear device, producing additional unwanted signals.
4. **Atmospheric Noise:** Caused by natural phenomena like thunderstorms.

Practical Example: Identifying and Resolving RFI

Imagine you're experiencing RFI in your home station:

1. **Identify the Source:** Start by turning off all electronic devices in your home one by one to see if the interference stops. This can help pinpoint the offending device.
2. **Use a Portable Radio:** Walk around with a portable AM/FM radio. The intensity of the interference on the radio can help locate the source.
3. **Implement Solutions:** Once identified, solutions may include adding ferrite chokes to cables, improving grounding, or moving the ham radio equipment away from the interference source.

Techniques for Troubleshooting Interference

1. **Isolation:** Isolate the radio equipment from potential internal and external RFI sources.
2. **Filtering:** Use filters to block or reduce unwanted signals.
3. **Antenna Positioning:** Sometimes, simply repositioning or changing the orientation of the antenna can reduce interference.
4. **Consultation:** Consult with fellow hams or local clubs for advice, as they may have encountered similar issues.

Preventing Interference in Your Station

Prevention is often the best approach to handling interference:

1. **Good Station Design:** Proper layout and grounding of your station can minimize the potential for interference.
2. **Quality Equipment:** Using good quality cables, connectors, and filters can help avoid many common interference issues.

Dealing with Interference from Neighbors

Sometimes, your ham radio operations might cause interference to neighbors' electronic equipment. Handling these situations diplomatically is key:

1. **Verify the Claim:** First, ensure that your station is indeed the source of the interference.
2. **Offer Solutions:** Propose solutions such as filters or changes in your operating times or frequencies.
3. **Maintain Good Relations:** Keeping a friendly and cooperative relationship with your neighbors can go a long way in resolving such issues.

Legal Aspects of Interference

Understand the legal aspects of interference, especially regulations set by bodies like the FCC. Know your rights and responsibilities as a ham radio operator regarding interference.

Advanced Troubleshooting Techniques

For more complex interference issues, advanced techniques like using a spectrum analyzer or consulting with an experienced RF engineer might be necessary.

Conclusion of Chapter 16

Dealing with interference is a skill that all ham radio operators need to develop. This chapter provides the foundational knowledge and practical steps to identify and resolve common interference issues, ensuring a more enjoyable and uninterrupted ham radio experience. By understanding and applying these strategies, operators can minimize the impact of interference on their communications and coexist harmoniously with other electronic devices and users in their environment.

Chapter 17: The Future of Ham Radio – Trends and Emerging Technologies

As technology evolves, so does the world of amateur radio. This chapter explores emerging trends and technologies in ham radio, offering insights into how these advancements are shaping the future of the hobby.

Digital and Software-Driven Technologies

The integration of digital technologies is profoundly transforming ham radio. Digital modes, software-defined radios (SDRs), and network-linked repeaters are just a few examples of how digital advancements are expanding the capabilities of amateur radio operators.

Software-Defined Radios (SDRs)

SDRs represent a significant shift in radio technology. Unlike traditional radios, SDRs use software for most radio functions, offering greater flexibility and the ability to update and upgrade via software changes.

Practical Example: Setting Up an SDR Station

To set up a basic SDR station:

1. **Select an SDR:** Choose an SDR device that suits your needs and budget. Options range from inexpensive dongles to high-end units.
2. **Install Software:** Install the necessary software on your computer. Programs like SDR# or GNU Radio are popular choices.
3. **Connect Antenna and Computer:** Connect your SDR to an antenna and your computer.
4. **Configure and Explore:** Configure the software settings for your desired frequencies and modes. Explore the wide range of frequencies and signals that your SDR can receive.

Remote Operation and Internet Linking

Remote operation, where operators control their station equipment from a distant location via the internet, is becoming increasingly popular. Internet-linked repeaters and networks like Echolink and D-STAR also allow for worldwide communication without the need for high-powered antennas.

Satellites and Space Communication

The involvement of amateur radio in space exploration is growing. With initiatives like CubeSats and the Amateur Radio on the International Space Station (ARISS) program, hams have opportunities to engage in space communications and satellite development.

Emergence of AI and Machine Learning

Artificial intelligence and machine learning are beginning to find applications in amateur radio. These technologies can be used for signal identification, propagation prediction, and even automated QSOs (contacts).

The Internet of Things (IoT) and Ham Radio

The IoT revolution is opening new frontiers for amateur radio, with possibilities for integrating radio

communication into a network of connected devices. This integration can lead to innovative applications in areas like remote sensing and automated station control.

Ham Radio's Role in Emergency Communication

The role of amateur radio in emergency communication continues to evolve with technology. Digital modes, improved portable equipment, and enhanced global connectivity are making ham radio an even more vital tool in disaster response and public service.

Conclusion of Chapter 17

The future of ham radio is vibrant and full of potential. Emerging technologies are not only enhancing traditional aspects of the hobby but also opening new avenues for exploration and innovation. This chapter provides a glimpse into the exciting developments on the horizon, encouraging operators to embrace change and continue learning in the ever-evolving world of amateur radio.

Chapter 18: Global Communication and DXing – Connecting Worldwide

One of the most exhilarating aspects of ham radio is the ability to communicate across the globe. This chapter delves into the art and science of DXing – making long-distance contacts – and offers strategies for successful global communication.

The Thrill of DXing

DXing, or making contact with distant stations, is a popular aspect of ham radio that offers a unique challenge. It combines technical skills, knowledge of propagation, and often a bit of luck to make contact with someone in a far-off land.

Understanding DX Awards and Entities

Many organizations offer awards for confirming contacts with a certain number of countries or specific entities. Understanding the criteria for these awards can add an exciting goal to your DXing pursuits.

Equipment for Effective DXing

While you can make DX contacts with basic equipment, certain gear can enhance your chances:

1. **High-Frequency (HF) Transceivers:** A good quality HF transceiver is essential for DXing.
2. **Effective Antennas:** Directional antennas like Yagi or beam antennas are preferred for their ability to focus signals in a particular direction.
3. **Low-Noise Amplifiers (LNAs):** LNAs can enhance the reception of weak signals.
4. **Antenna Tuners:** These devices can help match the antenna system to the transceiver for optimal performance.

Practical Example: Setting Up a Station for DXing

Imagine setting up a ham radio station optimized for DXing:

1. **Choose a Transceiver:** Select an HF transceiver with good sensitivity and selectivity.
2. **Install a Beam Antenna:** Erect a Yagi antenna, aimed in the direction you wish to make contact.
3. **Set Up a Low-Noise Environment:** Minimize electronic noise in and around your station.
4. **Use a Logging Program:** Use software to log contacts and to identify potential DX opportunities.

Strategies for Successful DXing

1. **Understanding Propagation:** Knowing how radio waves travel at different times of the day and during various solar conditions can help in planning your DX attempts.
2. **Listening Skills:** Often, successful DXing is more about listening than transmitting. Identifying the right moment to make your call is crucial.
3. **Operating Practices:** Good DX operating practices include clear and concise transmissions and patience in waiting for the right opportunity to make a contact.

Participating in DX Contests

DX contests are events where operators try to make as many DX contacts as possible in a set period. These contests can be a fun and intense way to improve your DXing skills.

Building a DX Network

Networking with other DXers can provide valuable tips and information. Joining DX clubs or online groups can enhance your knowledge and inform you about rare DX opportunities.

The Role of QSL Cards

Exchanging QSL cards, which are confirmation cards for radio contacts, is a long-standing tradition in DXing. These cards can serve as a physical record of your DX achievements.

The Ethics of DXing

Ethical behavior is paramount in DXing. This includes respecting other operators, correctly following band plans, and adhering to regulations.

Conclusion of Chapter 18

DXing offers a unique way to explore the world through radio waves. It challenges operators to continuously improve their technical skills, understand complex propagation phenomena, and practice patience and precision in their operations. This chapter not only equips readers with the knowledge to begin or enhance their DX journey but also inspires the pursuit of those exciting, long-distance contacts that embody the spirit of global communication in ham radio.

Chapter 19: Software-Defined Radio (SDR) – The New Frontier

Software-Defined Radio (SDR) represents a significant evolution in radio technology, offering unparalleled flexibility and new capabilities for amateur radio operators. This chapter delves into the world of SDR, explaining its principles, how to set up an SDR station, and the possibilities it unlocks for the modern ham.

Introduction to Software-Defined Radio

SDR technology shifts much of the signal processing in a radio from hardware to software. This allows for a wide range of frequencies to be received and transmitted and for the radio's characteristics to be easily modified through software updates.

Core Concepts of SDR

1. **Flexibility:** SDRs can be reconfigured for different frequencies and modes through software changes.
2. **Wide Frequency Range:** Many SDRs offer a broad receiving range, from LF to GHz frequencies.
3. **Digital Signal Processing (DSP):** SDRs use DSP to provide enhanced filtering, noise reduction, and modulation capabilities.

Setting Up an SDR Station

Setting up an SDR station involves both hardware and software components. The hardware is typically a small box connected to a computer, while the software is what defines the radio's capabilities.

Practical Example: Creating a Basic SDR Setup

To start with SDR:

1. **Select an SDR Receiver:** Choose an SDR receiver that fits your needs and budget. Options range from entry-level RTL-SDR dongles to more advanced SDR transceivers.
2. **Install SDR Software:** Install SDR software on your computer. Popular choices include SDR#, HDSDR, and GNU Radio.
3. **Connect to an Antenna:** Connect your SDR receiver to an appropriate antenna. The choice of antenna will depend on the frequencies you wish to explore.
4. **Configure Your Software:** Tune the SDR software to the desired frequencies and adjust settings like filters and gains to optimize reception.

Exploring the Radio Spectrum with SDR

One of the joys of SDR is the ability to visually scan a wide range of frequencies and quickly tune into different signals. This capability makes it easier to find interesting transmissions and explore parts of the spectrum that are not accessible with traditional radios.

The Advantages of DSP in SDR

DSP allows for advanced filtering and noise reduction techniques that can significantly improve signal clarity and reception quality. These features are particularly useful in challenging signal conditions.

SDR in Ham Radio Operations

SDRs are not just for receiving; they can also be used for transmitting on amateur bands, provided they are compliant with regulations. SDRs bring new dimensions to ham radio, including digital modes, spectrum monitoring, and even developing custom communication protocols.

Building Your Own SDR

For the technically inclined, building your own SDR from scratch or from a kit can be a rewarding project. This can provide a deeper understanding of both radio and software principles.

The Future of SDR in Amateur Radio

SDR technology is continually evolving, with new software and hardware being developed that push the boundaries of what's possible in amateur radio. As the technology becomes more accessible, it is likely to play an increasingly central role in the hobby.

Conclusion of Chapter 19

Software-Defined Radio is transforming the landscape of amateur radio, offering unprecedented flexibility and new capabilities. From exploring wide swaths of the radio spectrum to customizing radios through software, SDR opens up a world of possibilities for innovation and exploration. This chapter provides a comprehensive introduction to SDR, guiding readers through setting up their own SDR station and exploring the exciting opportunities this technology brings to the amateur radio community.

Chapter 20: Legal Aspects and Regulations – Staying Compliant

Navigating the legal landscape of amateur radio is essential for every operator. This chapter provides an overview of the key legal aspects and regulations governing ham radio, helping operators stay compliant and informed.

Understanding Amateur Radio Licensing

The foundation of legal ham radio operation is the license issued by national regulatory bodies, such as the Federal Communications Commission (FCC) in the United States. This license grants the operator the privilege to use specific frequency bands under certain conditions.

License Classes and Privileges

Each class of license comes with its own set of privileges and restrictions. Operators must be aware of the bands and modes they are authorized to use based on their license class.

Frequency Allocations and Band Plans

Frequency allocations are determined internationally by organizations like the International Telecommunication Union (ITU) and are implemented nationally by local regulatory bodies. Band plans further organize these allocations into specific segments for different modes and activities.

Practical Example: Understanding Band Plans

A new amateur radio operator with a technician class license wants to ensure compliance:

1. **Consult the Band Plan:** The operator checks the current FCC band plan for Technician licensees, identifying the frequencies they are allowed to use.
2. **Adhere to Restrictions:** The operator notes the specific modes and power limits allowed on these bands and adheres to these restrictions during operation.

Rules on Emissions and Power

Operators must comply with rules regarding the type of emissions (modes) they can use and the maximum power levels permitted. Exceeding these limits can cause interference and lead to legal issues.

Antenna and Tower Regulations

Local zoning laws and regulations often govern the erection of antennas and towers. Operators must be aware of and comply with these regulations, which may include height restrictions and permit requirements.

Interference Issues and Resolution

Interference with other radio services or electronic devices can lead to complaints and regulatory scrutiny. Operators should strive to minimize interference and address any issues promptly and cooperatively.

Operating Across Borders

When operating in or communicating with stations in other countries, international regulations and

agreements, such as those set by the ITU, must be observed. Special permissions may be required to operate in some countries.

Ethical Practices in Amateur Radio

Beyond legal requirements, ethical practices play a crucial role in the amateur radio community. This includes respecting other operators, operating with integrity, and contributing positively to the hobby.

Keeping Up with Changes in Regulations

Regulations and laws governing amateur radio can change. Staying informed through resources like national amateur radio organizations or regulatory bodies is essential for ongoing compliance.

Conclusion of Chapter 20

Understanding and adhering to the legal aspects and regulations of amateur radio ensures that operators can enjoy their hobby without legal complications. This chapter provides the necessary information to navigate the regulatory environment, promoting responsible and lawful amateur radio operation. By staying informed and compliant, operators contribute to the positive reputation and sustainability of the amateur radio community.

Conclusion:

The Endless Horizon of Ham Radio – Continuing Your Journey

As we reach the conclusion of this comprehensive guide to amateur radio, it's clear that the journey into ham radio is as vast and varied as the airwaves themselves. Ham radio is not just a hobby; it's a continuous adventure, a path of learning, and a gateway to a global community. This concluding chapter encapsulates the essence of ham radio and looks forward to the endless opportunities it offers.

The Ever-Evolving World of Ham Radio

Ham radio is a dynamic hobby, constantly shaped by technological advancements, changing regulations, and the evolving interests of its practitioners. From the early days of Morse code to the modern era of digital modes and software-defined radios, ham radio has continually reinvented itself.

Embracing Change and Innovation

The key to enjoying ham radio to its fullest is to embrace change and innovation. This means being open to new technologies, experimenting with different modes and equipment, and continually seeking to expand your knowledge and skills.

The Community: Ham Radio's Greatest Asset

Perhaps the most enduring aspect of ham radio is the community it fosters. This global network of enthusiasts shares not only a passion for radio but also a spirit of camaraderie, support, and mutual respect.

Practical Example: Engaging with the Community

An operator decides to deepen their engagement with the ham radio community:

1. **Join a Club:** They become active in a local ham radio club, participating in meetings and events.
2. **Volunteer:** They volunteer for public service events and emergency communication drills, using their skills to benefit others.
3. **Mentorship:** As they gain experience, they mentor new hams, sharing their knowledge and helping others grow in the hobby.

Lifelong Learning and Exploration

Ham radio is a journey of lifelong learning. Whether it's delving into advanced technical topics, exploring new modes of communication, or simply improving your operating skills, there's always something new to learn and explore.

The Role of Ham Radio in Society

Ham radio continues to play a significant role in society, from providing emergency communications during disasters to advancing our understanding of electronics and communication technologies. As a ham radio operator, you are part of this legacy.

Looking to the Future

The future of ham radio is as bright as ever. Emerging technologies like satellite communication and SDR are opening new frontiers, while the core values of the hobby – communication, innovation, and community – remain strong.

Conclusion

In conclusion, this guide has traversed the wide-ranging landscape of amateur radio, from the basics of setting up a station and making your first contacts to exploring advanced technologies and legal considerations. The journey in ham radio is ongoing, filled with opportunities for personal growth, community involvement, and endless exploration. As you continue on this path, remember that each contact, each experiment, and each challenge add to the rich tapestry of the amateur radio experience. The horizon of ham radio is indeed endless, and your journey through this fascinating world is only just beginning.

BOOK 5
The Radio Communication Handbook:

A Comprehensive Guide to the Art and Science of Radio

Introduction

The realm of radio communication presents a fascinating and ever-evolving landscape where the seamless blend of technology, physics, and innovation come together. This book, titled "The Radio Communication Handbook: A Comprehensive Guide to the Art and Science of Radio," aims to delve into the intricate world of radio communication, offering a detailed and technical exploration suitable for both novices and seasoned enthusiasts. As we embark on this journey through the various facets of radio theory and practice, it is essential to lay a solid foundation that not only introduces the basic principles but also sets the stage for more advanced topics.

Radio communication, at its core, is the art and science of transmitting information over distances without the need for physical connections, using electromagnetic waves as the medium. This form of communication has revolutionized the way we connect across vast distances, influencing numerous aspects of our daily lives, from broadcast media to critical emergency services. The history of radio dates back to the late 19th and early 20th centuries, with pioneers like Guglielmo Marconi and Nikola Tesla making significant contributions to the development of wireless communication technologies. Since those early days, the field of radio communication has witnessed a remarkable evolution, embracing new technologies, adapting to changing needs, and expanding into diverse applications.

The first chapter of this book introduces the fundamental concept of radio waves, a type of electromagnetic radiation with frequencies that fall within the radio frequency (RF) portion of the electromagnetic spectrum. Understanding radio waves is crucial as they form the backbone of all radio communication systems. This chapter will delve into the physics of radio wave propagation, explaining how these waves travel through different mediums, the factors that affect their transmission, and the principles behind their generation and reception.

Subsequent chapters will focus on the practical aspects of setting up and operating a radio station. This includes a detailed look at the various components of a radio system, such as transmitters, receivers, and antennas. Each component plays a critical role in the overall functionality and efficiency of a radio system. We will explore how these components work individually and in unison, discussing the principles of their operation and the technical considerations involved in their design and selection.

Antenna design and theory form another crucial aspect of radio communication. The antenna is the point of interface between the radio system and the space through which the radio waves travel. An efficient antenna is essential for effective communication, as it determines the range and quality of the signal transmission and reception. This book will guide readers through the principles of antenna design, including the various types of antennas, their radiation patterns, and the factors influencing their performance.

As we delve deeper into the technical aspects of radio communication, we will explore the various modulation techniques used to encode information onto radio waves. Modulation is a critical process that allows the transmission of voice, data, and video signals over radio frequencies. Understanding the different types of modulation – such as amplitude modulation (AM), frequency modulation (FM), single-sideband (SSB) modulation, and digital modulation techniques – is vital for anyone keen on grasping the intricacies of radio communication.

A comprehensive discussion on radio wave propagation is also crucial. This chapter will explain how radio waves travel through different environments, such as the earth's atmosphere and space. Factors like ionospheric reflection, tropospheric ducting, and line-of-sight propagation significantly affect the transmission of radio waves and, by extension, the quality and reliability of radio communication.

Moving forward, the book delves into the practical aspects of building and operating radio equipment. This includes detailed chapters on designing and constructing receivers and transmitters, selecting and maintaining power supplies and batteries, and understanding the operating procedures and protocols for efficient communication. These chapters are designed to provide hands-on knowledge and practical tips, making them invaluable for hobbyists and professionals alike.

Another significant aspect of radio communication is the understanding of the radio spectrum and frequency allocation. This involves a comprehensive look at the legal and technical considerations surrounding the allocation and use of different frequency bands. Given the finite nature of the radio spectrum and its critical importance in various sectors, effective management and understanding of frequency allocation are essential for anyone involved in radio communication.

As we progress towards more advanced topics, the book will introduce readers to the role of digital signal processing (DSP) in modern radio communications. DSP has revolutionized the field by enabling more efficient and sophisticated processing of radio signals. This chapter will cover the basics of DSP and its applications in enhancing signal quality, filtering, and modulation.

In the realm of emergency and mobile radio communications, we will explore the specific techniques and equipment used in critical and on-the-move communication scenarios. This includes an overview of the different types of mobile and portable radio systems, their applications in emergency services, and the challenges faced in such environments.

Additionally, the book will touch upon the intriguing topic of radio communication in space. This includes the unique challenges and technologies involved in extraterrestrial communication, such as satellite communication and deep-space radio links.

The later chapters will delve into advanced antenna systems, exploring directional and beamforming antennas, which are crucial for applications requiring focused signal transmission and reception. This is followed by an in-depth look at software-defined radio (SDR), a technology that represents the future of radio communication. SDR offers unprecedented flexibility and capabilities, allowing software to perform many functions traditionally handled by hardware components.

Security in radio communication is another critical topic. In an age where information security is paramount, this chapter will address the methods and technologies used to encrypt and secure radio communications, ensuring privacy and preventing unauthorized access.

The book also includes a comprehensive guide on troubleshooting and maintaining radio equipment. This is essential for ensuring the longevity and optimal performance of radio systems, covering common issues and their solutions, routine maintenance practices, and tips for diagnosing and fixing problems.

In conclusion, the final chapter reflects on the evolving landscape of radio communication. It offers insights into emerging trends and technologies that are shaping the future of radio, discussing potential developments and their implications for both hobbyists and professionals in the field.

By the end of this book, readers will have gained a thorough understanding of the art and science of radio communication. From the basic principles to advanced technologies, this comprehensive guide aims to equip readers with the knowledge and skills needed to explore and excel in this dynamic field. Whether you are a beginner taking your first steps into the world of radio or a seasoned expert seeking to deepen your understanding, this book offers a wealth of information and insights into the fascinating world of radio communication.

Chapter 1: The Basics of Radio Waves

Radio waves, a type of electromagnetic radiation, are at the heart of all forms of radio communication. This chapter delves into the fundamental concepts of radio waves, offering a comprehensive understanding of their nature, behavior, and how they are used in communication systems.

Electromagnetic radiation consists of waves of electric and magnetic fields oscillating at right angles to each other and to the direction of wave propagation. Radio waves are electromagnetic waves with wavelengths longer than infrared light, and they occupy a specific portion of the electromagnetic spectrum. To comprehend radio waves fully, it is essential to grasp two fundamental properties: frequency and wavelength.

Frequency, measured in Hertz (Hz), represents the number of cycles of the wave that pass a point in one second. Wavelength, on the other hand, is the distance between two consecutive peaks (or troughs) of a wave. There is an inverse relationship between frequency and wavelength, as described by the formula: speed of light (c) = frequency (f) × wavelength (λ). Since the speed of light is a constant (approximately 300,000 kilometers per second in a vacuum), as the frequency increases, the wavelength decreases, and vice versa.

The radio spectrum is divided into various bands, each characterized by its frequency range. These include the Low Frequency (LF), Medium Frequency (MF), High Frequency (HF), Very High Frequency (VHF), Ultra High Frequency (UHF), and others. Each band has unique propagation characteristics and is suited for different types of communication.

For a practical example, let's consider the setup of a simple radio communication system, such as an amateur radio station. This station consists of basic components: a transmitter, an antenna, and a receiver. The transmitter converts sound or data into radio waves, the antenna transmits these waves into space, and the receiver at the other end captures these waves and converts them back into sound or data.

Let's say our amateur radio operator wants to communicate using the High Frequency (HF) band, particularly in the 20-meter band (14.000 to 14.350 MHz). This band is chosen for its ability to support long-distance communication, making use of a phenomenon known as skywave propagation. At these frequencies, radio waves can bounce off the ionosphere and return to Earth, covering distances much greater than the line of sight.

The operator sets up a dipole antenna, a simple and effective type of antenna for HF bands. The length of this antenna is critical and is directly related to the wavelength of the radio waves it is designed to transmit and receive. To calculate the length of each leg of the dipole antenna for the 20-meter band, the formula λ/2 is used, where λ is the wavelength. Given that the speed of light is 300,000,000 meters per second, and the frequency is 14,200,000 Hz (in the middle of the 20-meter band), the wavelength λ can be calculated as follows:

Wavelength(λ)=Speed of LightFrequencyWavelength(λ)=FrequencySpeed of Light

λ=300,000,000 m/s14,200,000 Hzλ=14,200,000 Hz300,000,000 m/s

λ≈21.13 metersλ≈21.13 meters

Thus, each leg of the dipole should be approximately λ/2, which is about 10.56 meters.

After setting up the antenna, the operator tunes the transmitter to the desired frequency within the 20-meter band. The transmitter generates radio waves by rapidly varying the current through the antenna. These variations in current create oscillating electric and magnetic fields, which propagate away from the antenna as radio waves.

Once the radio waves are transmitted, they travel through the atmosphere. When they reach the ionosphere, they are refracted back towards the Earth, allowing them to cover significant distances beyond the horizon. This is particularly effective during the day when the ionosphere is more ionized by the sun's radiation.

At the receiving end, another amateur radio operator with a similar setup captures these waves using their antenna. The receiver is tuned to the same frequency as the transmitter. It captures the incoming radio waves and converts them back into electrical signals that can be processed to retrieve the original sound or data.

This entire process is governed by the principles of radio wave propagation and antenna theory. Factors like the time of day, solar activity, and atmospheric conditions can significantly impact the effectiveness of HF radio communication. Additionally, the choice of frequency and antenna design plays a critical role in ensuring successful transmission and reception of radio signals.

In conclusion, understanding the basics of radio waves is fundamental for anyone involved in radio communication. From the simple setup of an amateur radio station to more complex communication systems, the principles of frequency, wavelength, and wave propagation are central to the effective use of radio waves for communication. The example provided illustrates these principles in action, demonstrating the practical application of theory in real-world scenarios. As we proceed through this book, we will explore these concepts in greater depth, along with more advanced topics in radio communication.

Chapter 2: Radio Hardware Components

In the realm of radio communication, the hardware components form the backbone of any operational system. This chapter delves into the essential elements that constitute a radio communication setup, namely transmitters, receivers, and antennas. A deep understanding of these components is vital for anyone aspiring to build, operate, or enhance a radio communication system.

Transmitters

The transmitter is a crucial component in a radio communication system. Its primary function is to convert information (such as voice, data, or video) into an electromagnetic signal capable of being sent over distances. This process involves various stages, including modulation, amplification, and transmission.

For a practical example, consider a simple FM (Frequency Modulation) radio transmitter. In FM transmission, the frequency of the carrier wave is varied in accordance with the amplitude of the input signal, which could be a voice or music. The basic components of an FM transmitter include an oscillator, a modulator, an amplifier, and an antenna.

The oscillator generates a steady carrier wave at a specific frequency. This wave is then fed into the modulator, where the input audio signal modulates it. The modulated signal is then amplified to increase its strength before being sent to the antenna for transmission.

Simple FM Transmitter

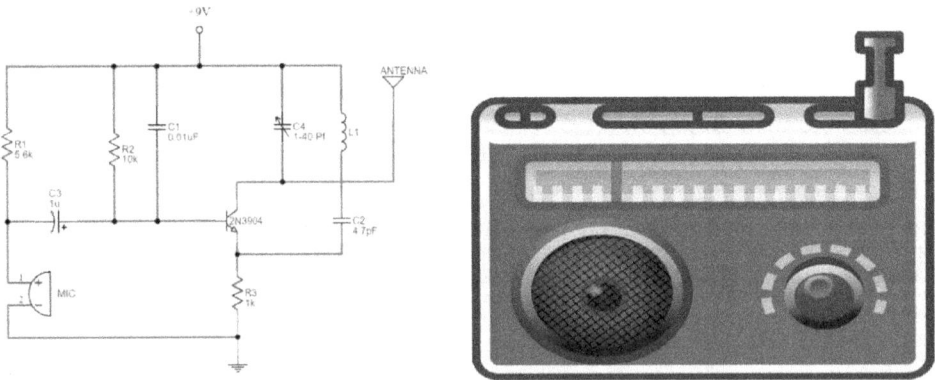

Receivers

The receiver's role is to capture the transmitted electromagnetic waves, extract the encoded information, and convert it back into a usable form. A basic radio receiver consists of an antenna, tuner, demodulator, amplifier, and output device (like speakers or a display).

Continuing with the FM radio example, an FM receiver would be designed to receive the specific frequency range in which the transmitter operates. The receiver uses its antenna to capture the incoming FM signal and passes it to the tuner. The tuner filters and selects the desired frequency from all the signals received by the antenna. The selected signal is then demodulated, where the frequency variations are converted back into the original audio signal. This signal is then amplified and sent to the output device.

Antennas

Antennas are critical in both transmitting and receiving radio waves. They come in various designs and sizes, depending on their intended use and the frequency of operation. In simple terms, an antenna in a transmitting system converts electrical signals into electromagnetic waves, while in a receiving system, it does the reverse.

For instance, in our FM radio example, a simple dipole antenna can be used for both transmitting and receiving. The length of the antenna is crucial and is typically proportional to the wavelength of the radio frequency it is designed to operate at.

To illustrate, for an FM radio station transmitting at 100 MHz (wavelength approximately 3 meters), the length of each leg of a half-wave dipole antenna would be approximately 1.5 meters.

Putting It All Together: A Practical Example

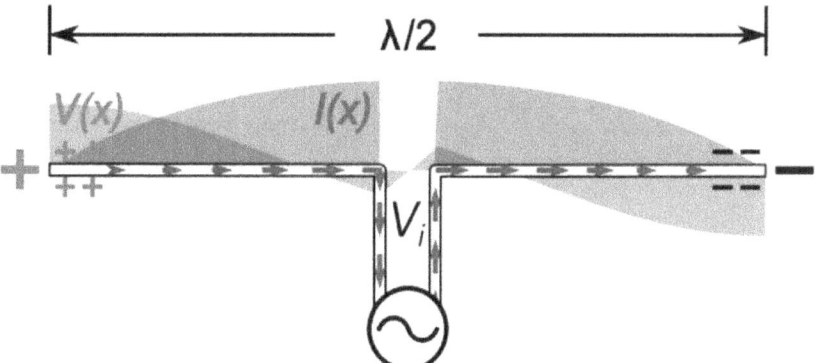

Let's put these components together in a real-world scenario. Imagine setting up a small community FM radio station. The first step is to design and assemble the transmitter. This involves creating an FM transmitter circuit that includes an oscillator, modulator, and amplifier. The oscillator sets the carrier frequency (say 100 MHz), and the modulator is configured to vary this frequency in response to the audio input.

The next step is to construct the antenna. Based on the chosen frequency, a half-wave dipole antenna with each leg measuring approximately 1.5 meters is constructed. This antenna is then connected to the transmitter.

On the receiving end, individuals in the community would use FM radios to tune into the station's frequency. Each radio consists of a receiver circuit capable of capturing the 100 MHz signal, demodulating it to retrieve the audio, and then playing it through the speakers.

This simple example demonstrates the interplay between transmitters, receivers, and antennas in a basic FM radio communication system. Understanding and mastering these components lays the foundation for more complex and sophisticated radio communication setups. As we progress through the book, we will delve deeper into each of these components, exploring their intricacies and advanced functionalities in various communication scenarios.

Chapter 3: Setting Up Your Radio Station

Establishing a radio station, whether for amateur radio, community broadcasting, or emergency communication, requires careful planning and a comprehensive understanding of the components involved. This chapter will guide you through the process of setting up a radio station, covering the essential equipment and setup procedures.

Understanding Your Requirements

The first step in setting up a radio station is to understand your specific needs and objectives. Are you setting up an amateur radio station for personal communication and experimentation? Or is it a community radio station intended for public broadcasting? The purpose of your station will dictate the type of equipment, power requirements, and regulatory compliance needed.

Selecting the Right Equipment

The core equipment for any radio station includes a transmitter, receiver, antenna, power supply, and various ancillary components like cables, connectors, and possibly a tuner or an amplifier. The choice of equipment is influenced by factors like the desired range of communication, frequency bands of operation, and budget.

Transmitter and Receiver

For our practical example, let's consider setting up an amateur radio station for HF (High Frequency) band communication. The transmitter and receiver can be separate units, or a transceiver can be used, which combines both functions into a single device. Modern transceivers come with various features like digital signal processing, multiple band capabilities, and built-in tuners.

Antenna

The antenna is a critical component of the setup. For HF bands, common choices include dipole antennas, vertical antennas, or more complex beam antennas for directional communication. The antenna choice depends on factors like the available space, the bands you plan to operate on, and whether you need omnidirectional or directional communication.

Power Supply

A stable and reliable power supply is crucial. For most amateur radio setups, a 12-volt DC power supply is standard. It's essential to ensure that the power supply can deliver sufficient current for your transmitter, especially during peak transmission periods.

Setting Up the Station

Once you have all the equipment, the next step is setting up the station. This involves finding a suitable location, ensuring proper grounding and safety measures, and configuring the equipment.

1. **Location**: Choose a location that is free from obstructions for your antenna. For HF communication, height and clear surroundings are beneficial for effective signal propagation.
2. **Grounding**: Proper grounding is essential for safety and to reduce interference. All equipment should be grounded to a common point.
3. **Antenna Installation**: Install your antenna as per the manufacturer's guidelines. For a dipole antenna, ensure it is mounted high and clear of obstructions. The orientation of the antenna will affect its radiation pattern and reception.
4. **Connecting Equipment**: Connect your transceiver to the antenna using appropriate coaxial cables. Ensure all connections are secure and waterproofed, especially for outdoor installations.
5. **Power Supply Connection**: Connect the transceiver to the power supply, ensuring that all connections are correctly made to avoid any power surges or short circuits.
6. **Testing and Tuning**: Once everything is connected, power up the station and test the reception and transmission. Use the built-in tuner of the transceiver or an external tuner to ensure that the antenna is properly tuned to the desired frequency.

Practical Example: Setting Up an Amateur HF Station

Imagine setting up a simple amateur HF station. The operator selects a transceiver capable of covering various HF bands (e.g., 3.5 – 30 MHz). A multi-band dipole antenna is chosen for its simplicity and effectiveness. The antenna is installed at a height of about 10 meters above ground, ensuring it's clear from surrounding obstructions.

The transceiver is connected to a 12-volt power supply, capable of handling up to 20 amps of current. The antenna is connected to the transceiver using a 50-ohm coaxial cable. The operator ensures all equipment is grounded to a common ground point.

After setting up, the operator tunes the transceiver to a specific HF band, say 14 MHz (20-meter band), and adjusts the antenna tuner for optimal SWR (Standing Wave Ratio). Initial tests are conducted to check the clarity of reception and transmission quality.

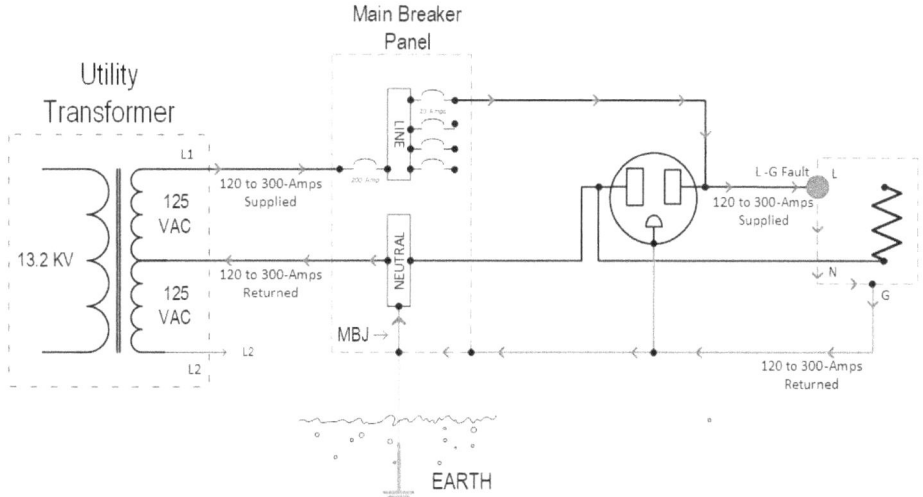

Fig 2. NEC Compliant Dedicated 120 VAC 20-Amp Branch Circuit with Line to Ground Dead Short Circuit Ground Fault

Conclusion

Setting up a radio station is a rewarding experience that combines technical skills with the thrill of communication. Whether it's for hobby, community service, or emergency communication, understanding and following the correct setup procedures ensures a functional and efficient station. This chapter provides a foundational guide for beginners and enthusiasts alike, paving the way for more advanced exploration in subsequent chapters.

Chapter 4: Antenna Design and Theory

The antenna is a pivotal component in radio communication, acting as the interface between the radio waves traveling through space and the electrical signals in the radio equipment. A well-designed antenna can significantly enhance the performance of any radio communication system. This chapter focuses on the principles of antenna design and theory, exploring how antennas work, the different types of antennas, and how to design an antenna for specific applications.

Understanding Antennas

An antenna is a transducer that converts electrical signals into electromagnetic waves and vice versa. The performance of an antenna is defined by several parameters, including gain, bandwidth, radiation pattern, and polarization. The gain of an antenna indicates how well it can direct radio energy in a particular direction. Bandwidth refers to the range of frequencies over which the antenna can operate effectively. The radiation pattern describes how the antenna radiates energy in space, and polarization refers to the orientation of the electric field of the radiated waves.

Basic Antenna Theory

The basic theory behind antennas is rooted in the principles of electromagnetic radiation. When an electric current oscillates in an antenna, it creates an electromagnetic field that propagates away from the antenna. The design of the antenna determines the characteristics of this radiation. For instance, the length of the antenna is typically related to the wavelength of the frequency it is intended to transmit or receive. A common rule of thumb is that the length of a resonant antenna is half the wavelength ($\lambda/2$) of the frequency of operation.

Types of Antennas

There are various types of antennas, each suited for specific applications:

1. **Dipole Antennas**: The simplest form of antenna, typically $\lambda/2$ long.
2. **Yagi-Uda Antennas**: Directional antennas commonly used for TV reception and amateur radio.
3. **Parabolic Antennas**: High-gain antennas used for satellite communication and radar systems.
4. **Loop Antennas**: Small antennas used for receiving at lower frequencies.
5. **Vertical Antennas**: Omnidirectional antennas often used in mobile and maritime communication.

Designing a Simple Dipole Antenna

For a practical example, let's design a simple dipole antenna for the 20-meter amateur radio band (around 14 MHz). The wavelength (λ) at 14 MHz is approximately 21.4 meters, so each leg of the dipole should be about $\lambda/4$, or roughly 5.35 meters.

1. **Calculating the Length**: The length of each leg of the dipole is given by:

   Length per leg=$\lambda 4$=300/Frequency (MHz)4Length per leg=4λ=4300/Frequency (MHz)

   For a frequency of 14 MHz, the length per leg = 5.35 meters.

2. **Materials**: You will need a wire for the antenna, insulators for the ends, a balun (to balance the unbalanced coaxial feed line), and coaxial cable for connection to the radio.
3. **Construction**: Cut two pieces of wire, each 5.35 meters long. Attach each wire to the balun at the center. Secure the ends of the wires with insulators.

4. **Mounting**: The dipole can be mounted horizontally between two supports (like trees or poles). The center (where the balun is located) should be the highest point.
5. **Connecting to the Radio**: Connect the coaxial cable from the balun to the radio. Ensure the connections are weatherproof if the antenna is outdoors.

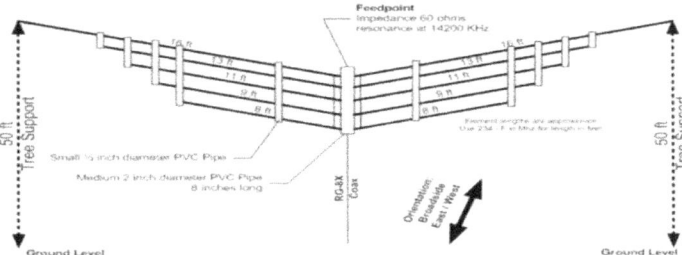

Testing and Adjustments

After setting up the antenna, it's crucial to test and adjust it:

1. **SWR Measurement**: Use an SWR meter to measure the standing wave ratio. This indicates how well the antenna is matched to the transmission line and the radio.
2. **Adjustments**: If the SWR is too high, adjust the length of the antenna wires slightly and retest. The goal is to achieve the lowest SWR at the desired operating frequency.

Conclusion

Antenna design is both an art and a science. It requires a good understanding of basic principles and practical skills. By designing and building a simple dipole antenna, as demonstrated in this example, one can gain valuable insights into the workings of antennas. This chapter provides a foundation for further exploration into more complex antenna designs and applications, which will be covered in subsequent chapters. An effective antenna not only improves the performance of a radio station but also enhances the overall experience of radio communication.

Chapter 5: Transmission Lines and Feeders

Transmission lines and feeders are essential components of any radio communication system, serving as the critical link between the transmitter (or receiver) and the antenna. This chapter delves into the types, characteristics, and practical considerations of transmission lines and feeders, providing insights into their role in ensuring efficient signal transmission.

Understanding Transmission Lines

A transmission line is a specialized cable or other structure designed to carry alternating current of radio frequency, that is, currents with a frequency high enough to radiate off a conductor. The primary purpose of these lines is to transport RF energy from the transmitter to the antenna with minimal losses. Key parameters defining a transmission line's performance include impedance, attenuation, and SWR (Standing Wave Ratio).

Types of Transmission Lines

There are several types of transmission lines used in radio communication:

1. **Coaxial Cable**: A common type, consisting of a central conductor, insulating spacer, outer conductor (shield), and insulating sheath.

2. **Parallel Wire or Ladder Line**: Consists of two parallel conductors with consistent spacing, offering low loss but susceptible to external interference.
3. **Waveguides**: Structures that guide waves, typically used at microwave frequencies.

Coaxial Cable: The Common Choice

For most radio applications, especially in amateur radio, coaxial cable is the preferred transmission line due to its availability, ease of use, and immunity to external interference. Coaxial cables come in various sizes and specifications, each suitable for different applications and power levels.

Characteristics of Coaxial Cables

- **Impedance**: Typically, 50 ohms for radio applications, matching the impedance of most antennas and radio equipment.
- **Attenuation**: Represents signal loss over distance, varying with frequency and cable quality.
- **Capacity**: Higher power handling cables are required for high-power transmissions.

Practical Example: Installing a Coaxial Cable for a Dipole Antenna

Let's consider the installation of a coaxial cable for a dipole antenna in an amateur radio setup:

1. **Cable Selection**: Choose a 50-ohm coaxial cable, like RG-8 or RG-213, for a balance of low loss and physical manageability.
2. **Length Calculation**: Calculate the required length of the cable from the radio equipment to the antenna. It's essential to consider the route the cable will take and any additional length needed for strain relief and connections.
3. **Connectors**: Install appropriate connectors on both ends of the coaxial cable. Typically, PL-259 connectors are used in amateur radio setups.
4. **Connection**: Connect one end of the coaxial cable to the radio transceiver and the other end to the antenna's balun.
5. **Routing and Securing**: Route the cable from the transceiver to the antenna, avoiding sharp bends and keeping the cable away from electrical noise sources. Secure the cable using cable ties or clamps.
6. **Weatherproofing**: If the cable runs outdoors, use weatherproofing tape or sealant at the connectors to prevent moisture ingress.

Testing and Troubleshooting

After installation, testing the transmission line is crucial:

1. **SWR Testing**: Use an SWR meter to check the standing wave ratio at the frequency of operation. A low SWR indicates a well-matched system.
2. **Loss Measurement**: If possible, measure the attenuation of the line to ensure it is within acceptable limits for your transmission power and frequency.

Conclusion

Transmission lines and feeders play a crucial role in the effectiveness of a radio communication system. Understanding their characteristics, proper selection, and correct installation are fundamental to achieving optimal performance. This chapter offers a foundational understanding of transmission lines, particularly coaxial cables, and their practical application in radio setups. As we progress into more advanced topics, the knowledge gained here will be invaluable in designing and troubleshooting more complex radio communication systems.

Chapter 6: Modulation Techniques

Modulation is a fundamental concept in radio communication, essential for transmitting information over varying distances and through different mediums. This chapter explores various modulation techniques, their principles, applications, and a practical example of how modulation is used in a radio communication system.

Understanding Modulation

Modulation involves altering a carrier wave in accordance with the information or message signal to be transmitted. This process allows the effective transmission of the signal over long distances and makes it possible to share the frequency spectrum with multiple users. The key properties of a carrier wave that can be modulated are amplitude, frequency, and phase.

Types of Modulation

The main types of modulation used in radio communication are:

1. **Amplitude Modulation (AM)**: Varies the amplitude of the carrier wave.
2. **Frequency Modulation (FM)**: Varies the frequency of the carrier wave.
3. **Phase Modulation (PM)**: Varies the phase of the carrier wave.
4. **Digital Modulation**: Includes various techniques like Quadrature Amplitude Modulation (QAM), Phase-Shift Keying (PSK), and Frequency-Shift Keying (FSK).

Amplitude Modulation (AM)

In AM, the amplitude of the carrier wave is varied in proportion to the message signal while keeping the frequency and phase constant. AM is simple but less efficient and more susceptible to noise.

Frequency Modulation (FM)

FM varies the frequency of the carrier wave in accordance with the amplitude of the message signal. FM is more complex than AM but offers better noise immunity and is widely used in VHF broadcasting.

Phase Modulation (PM)

In PM, the phase of the carrier wave is changed according to the message signal. PM is often used in digital communication systems.

Digital Modulation Techniques

Digital modulation involves converting the message signal into a digital format and then modulating the carrier wave. Techniques like QAM, PSK, and FSK are more efficient and robust against interference and noise.

Practical Example: Setting Up an FM Transmitter

Let's consider the setup of a basic FM transmitter for a local radio station:

1. **Message Signal**: Assume the message signal is audio content from a microphone or a mixer.
2. **Carrier Wave Generation**: The FM transmitter generates a carrier wave at a specific frequency, say 100 MHz.

3. **Modulation Process**: The audio signal modulates the frequency of the carrier wave. This means the frequency of the carrier wave changes in accordance with the amplitude of the audio signal.
4. **Amplification**: The modulated signal is then amplified to a suitable power level for transmission.
5. **Antenna Transmission**: The amplified signal is fed into an antenna, which broadcasts the signal over the air.

Testing and Adjustment

After setting up the transmitter:

1. **Fine-Tuning**: Adjust the modulator to ensure proper frequency deviation based on the amplitude of the audio signal.
2. **SWR Check**: Use an SWR meter to check the antenna's standing wave ratio, ensuring efficient transmission.
3. **Broadcast Test**: Conduct a test broadcast and adjust the modulation settings for optimal sound quality.

Conclusion

Modulation is a critical aspect of radio communication, enabling the transmission of information through radio waves. Understanding different modulation techniques and their applications is essential for anyone involved in radio communication. This chapter provides a foundational understanding of modulation, with a focus on practical implementation in an FM broadcasting scenario. As we delve deeper into radio communication theory and practice in subsequent chapters, this knowledge will be integral to understanding more complex systems and technologies.

Chapter 7: Radio Wave Propagation

Radio wave propagation is the study of how radio waves travel from a transmitter to a receiver in a radio communication system. This chapter delves into the principles and phenomena affecting radio wave propagation, offering a comprehensive understanding vital for efficient radio communication.

Understanding Radio Wave Propagation

Radio waves can travel through different paths from the transmitter to the receiver. The behavior of these waves is influenced by various factors, including frequency, atmospheric conditions, and the physical environment. The main propagation modes are ground wave, skywave, and line-of-sight.

Ground Wave Propagation

Ground wave propagation involves radio waves traveling along the surface of the Earth. It is predominant at lower frequencies (LF and MF bands) and is used in AM broadcasting, maritime communication, and other applications where long-distance communication is required without relying on the ionosphere.

Skywave Propagation

Skywave propagation occurs when radio waves are reflected or refracted back to Earth by the ionosphere. This mode allows for long-distance communication over the horizon and is commonly used in HF band communications, such as shortwave broadcasting and amateur radio.

Line-of-Sight Propagation

Line-of-sight propagation is where radio waves travel directly from the transmitter to the receiver. This mode is typical in VHF and UHF bands and is used in FM broadcasting, television, and satellite communication.

Factors Affecting Propagation

1. **The Ionosphere**: The ionosphere plays a crucial role in skywave propagation, particularly for HF bands. The ionosphere's reflective properties vary with solar activity, time of day, and frequency.
2. **Atmospheric Conditions**: Weather conditions, humidity, and temperature can affect the propagation of radio waves, especially at higher frequencies.
3. **Terrain**: The physical landscape, including mountains, buildings, and other structures, can obstruct or reflect radio waves, affecting signal reception.

Practical Example: Establishing an HF Amateur Radio Link

Let's consider setting up a long-distance communication link using HF skywave propagation:

1. **Frequency Selection**: Choose a frequency in the HF band, say 14 MHz (20-meter band), which is known for good daytime skywave propagation.
2. **Antenna Setup**: Install a dipole antenna oriented in the direction of the intended communication. The antenna should be elevated, at least a half-wavelength above the ground, to enhance signal strength.
3. **Propagation Analysis**: Use propagation prediction software or tools to determine the best time and frequency for communication, considering the ionospheric conditions and the distance between the transmitter and receiver.
4. **Communication Test**: Conduct a test transmission and adjust the frequency if necessary based on propagation conditions and the reception quality.

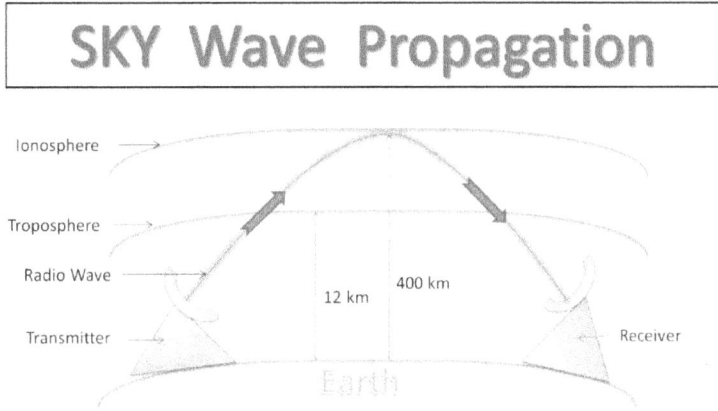

Testing and Adjustments

After setting up the system:

1. **Monitor Reception**: Regularly monitor the quality of reception and adjust the frequency or antenna orientation as needed, considering changes in ionospheric conditions.
2. **Record Observations**: Keep a log of propagation conditions, frequency adjustments, and communication quality to develop a better understanding of propagation behavior.

Conclusion

Radio wave propagation is a dynamic and complex aspect of radio communication, influenced by various natural and man-made factors. Understanding propagation modes and their influencing factors is crucial for effective communication, especially in amateur radio and broadcasting. This chapter provides foundational knowledge on propagation, with a focus on practical implementation in an HF communication scenario. As we advance through the book, this knowledge will be crucial for exploring more sophisticated communication strategies and technologies.

Chapter 8: Building a Receiver

Building a radio receiver is a fascinating project that combines theoretical knowledge with practical skills. This chapter focuses on the basics of receiver design, outlining the steps to construct a simple but effective radio receiver. We will also touch upon the principles underlying each component's function in the receiver.

Understanding Radio Receivers

A radio receiver's primary function is to capture radio waves transmitted by a radio station and convert them into audible sound or other forms of data. The basic stages of a radio receiver include the antenna, RF amplifier, mixer, IF (Intermediate Frequency) amplifier, demodulator, and the audio amplifier.

Types of Receivers

There are various types of radio receivers, including:

1. **Crystal Set**: The simplest form of a receiver, requiring no external power source.
2. **Regenerative Receiver**: Offers better amplification and selectivity using feedback.
3. **Superheterodyne Receiver**: The most common type, offering excellent sensitivity and selectivity.

Designing a Simple AM Radio Receiver

For a practical example, let's design a basic AM (Amplitude Modulation) superheterodyne receiver. This type of receiver is known for its ability to efficiently convert radio waves to audio signals and is widely used due to its superior performance.

Components and Their Functions

1. **Antenna**: Captures the AM radio waves.
2. **RF Amplifier**: Amplifies the weak radio signals received by the antenna.
3. **Mixer**: Mixes the amplified signal with a local oscillator frequency to produce an IF.
4. **IF Amplifier**: Amplifies the IF while improving selectivity and sensitivity.
5. **Demodulator**: Extracts the audio signal from the modulated carrier wave.
6. **Audio Amplifier**: Amplifies the audio signal for output to speakers or headphones.

Constructing the Receiver

1. **Gather Components**: Obtain all necessary components, including transistors, resistors, capacitors, a local oscillator, an IF transformer, a demodulator, and an audio amplifier IC.
2. **Circuit Assembly**: Assemble the circuit on a breadboard or PCB (Printed Circuit Board), following a superheterodyne receiver schematic.
3. **Antenna and Grounding**: Connect a wire antenna and ensure proper grounding for the receiver.

4. **Testing and Calibration**: Power up the receiver and tune the local oscillator to receive an AM station. Adjust the IF transformer for optimal signal clarity.

Practical Example: Building and Using the Receiver

Let's say you decide to build this AM receiver to listen to local AM radio stations:

1. **Component Soldering**: Carefully solder the components onto the PCB, following the circuit diagram.
2. **Initial Testing**: Once assembled, connect the receiver to a power source and attach a pair of headphones or a speaker.
3. **Tuning and Listening**: Use the tuning control (connected to the local oscillator) to select different AM stations. Fine-tune the IF transformer for the clearest sound.
4. **Experimentation**: Experiment with different antenna lengths and positions to study their effect on reception quality.

Troubleshooting and Enhancements

- If reception is poor, check all soldered connections, component values, and the alignment of the IF transformer.
- Enhancements like adding a more sophisticated audio amplifier or using a better antenna can significantly improve the receiver's performance.

Conclusion

Building a radio receiver is a rewarding experience that offers practical insights into the workings of radio communication. This chapter presents a foundational approach to constructing a simple AM radio receiver, suitable for beginners and hobbyists. The knowledge and skills gained here pave the way for more advanced projects and a deeper understanding of radio technology. As we progress through the book, these concepts will be invaluable in exploring more complex receiver designs and applications.

Chapter 9: Transmitter Design and Construction

Building a radio transmitter is an advanced project that requires a solid understanding of electronic circuit design and radio frequency (RF) engineering principles. This chapter will guide you through the process of designing and constructing a basic radio transmitter, focusing on a simple frequency modulation (FM) transmitter suitable for hobbyist applications.

Understanding Radio Transmitters

A radio transmitter's primary purpose is to generate a radio frequency signal, modulate it with information (like voice or data), and emit it through an antenna. The core components of a transmitter include the oscillator, modulator, RF amplifier, and antenna.

Key Components of a Transmitter

1. **Oscillator**: Generates the carrier frequency.
2. **Modulator**: Imposes information onto the carrier frequency.
3. **RF Amplifier**: Increases the power of the modulated signal.
4. **Antenna**: Radiates the signal into the air.

Designing a Simple FM Transmitter

For our practical example, we will design a basic FM transmitter for broadcasting within a short range, such as within a home or a small building.

Components and Their Functions

1. **Voltage-Controlled Oscillator (VCO)**: Generates the carrier frequency and allows frequency variation for FM modulation.
2. **Microphone and Pre-Amplifier**: Captures and amplifies the audio signal for modulation.
3. **Varactor Diode**: Used for modulating the VCO frequency in response to the audio signal.
4. **RF Amplifier**: Boosts the power of the FM signal for transmission.
5. **Transmitting Antenna**: A simple wire or dipole antenna for radiating the FM signal.

Constructing the FM Transmitter

1. **Gather Components**: Obtain a VCO, varactor diode, transistors for the RF amplifier, capacitors, resistors, a microphone, and an antenna.
2. **Circuit Assembly**: Assemble the components on a breadboard or PCB according to an FM transmitter circuit diagram.
3. **Connecting the Antenna**: Attach a wire or dipole antenna to the RF amplifier output.
4. **Powering the Circuit**: Connect the transmitter to a suitable power source, ensuring the voltage matches the requirements of your circuit.
5. **Testing and Calibration**: Start by testing the transmitter with no modulation to ensure the VCO is generating the correct carrier frequency. Then, connect the microphone and adjust the varactor diode circuit for clear FM modulation.

Practical Example: Using the FM Transmitter

Imagine you have built the FM transmitter and now want to test its broadcasting capabilities:

1. **Initial Testing**: Tune an FM radio receiver to the transmitter's frequency. You should hear static if the transmitter is working but not yet modulated.
2. **Modulation Testing**: Speak into the microphone. Your voice should modulate the carrier frequency, and you should hear it on the FM radio receiver.
3. **Range Testing**: Experiment with the transmitter's range by moving the FM radio receiver away from the transmitter. Note the distance at which the signal starts to degrade.

Troubleshooting and Enhancements

- If there's no transmission, check all connections, the power supply, and the oscillator circuit.
- Enhancements can include adding a more sophisticated RF amplifier for greater range or implementing a more stable VCO for better frequency stability.

Conclusion

Designing and building a radio transmitter is a complex but highly rewarding endeavor that deepens your understanding of radio communication technology. This chapter provides a foundational approach to creating a simple FM transmitter, suitable for amateur radio enthusiasts and electronics hobbyists. The skills and knowledge gained in this project are essential stepping stones to more advanced transmitter designs and applications in radio communication.

Chapter 10: Power Supplies and Batteries

In radio communication systems, having a reliable and efficient power source is crucial. This chapter explores the different types of power supplies and batteries used in radio equipment, focusing on their characteristics, applications, and a practical example involving setting up a power supply for a radio station.

Understanding Power Supplies in Radio Systems

A power supply in radio communication converts electrical energy from a source (like mains electricity or a battery) into a form usable by radio equipment, typically delivering a steady DC (Direct Current) voltage. The primary considerations for a power supply are its voltage output, current capacity, and stability.

Types of Power Supplies

1. **Linear Power Supplies**: Known for their simplicity and low noise output, but less efficient.
2. **Switching Power Supplies**: More efficient and lighter but can introduce RF noise.
3. **Battery Power Supplies**: Essential for portable or backup power, with varying capacities and voltages.

Selecting the Right Power Supply

The choice of power supply depends on factors such as the required voltage and current, the type of radio equipment, and the operational environment (e.g., stationary, mobile, or remote).

Voltage and Current Requirements

- The voltage output must match the radio equipment's requirements.
- The current capacity should exceed the maximum current draw of the radio equipment to ensure reliable operation and accommodate future expansions.

Noise Considerations

- Power supply noise can interfere with radio communication, especially in sensitive receivers. Therefore, selecting a power supply with low RF noise emission is essential.

Practical Example: Setting Up a Power Supply for an Amateur Radio Station

Consider setting up a power supply for an amateur radio station that includes a transceiver, an antenna tuner, and some peripheral devices.

1. **Determining Power Requirements**: If the transceiver requires 13.8V DC and draws a maximum of 20A during transmission, choose a power supply that can deliver at least this voltage and current.
2. **Choosing the Power Supply**: A switching power supply with a 13.8V DC output and a 30A current capacity would be appropriate, providing sufficient power and allowing for additional equipment.
3. **Setting Up the Power Supply**: Connect the power supply to the mains electricity, ensuring it is grounded correctly.
4. **Connecting the Radio Equipment**: Use appropriate cables to connect the power supply to the transceiver and other devices. Ensure that connections are secure and correctly polarized.
5. **Testing**: Power up the station and check all equipment for proper operation. Monitor the power supply during use to ensure it maintains a stable output voltage under load.

Using Batteries for Portable Operation

Batteries are essential for portable radio operations or as a backup power source.

1. **Battery Types**: Common types include lead-acid, lithium-ion, and nickel-metal hydride, each with different capacities, voltages, and discharge characteristics.
2. **Capacity Selection**: Choose a battery with sufficient capacity (measured in ampere-hours, Ah) to power the radio equipment for the intended duration.

Maintaining Power Supplies and Batteries

- Regularly check the power supply for signs of overheating or voltage fluctuations.
- For battery maintenance, ensure proper charging and storage, and regularly check for capacity degradation or physical damage.

Conclusion

Adequate power supply and battery management are critical for the effective and reliable operation of radio communication systems. This chapter provides essential knowledge for setting up and maintaining power supplies and batteries for various radio systems. Understanding these concepts is fundamental for both stationary and mobile radio operations, ensuring uninterrupted communication under different circumstances. As we progress, this knowledge becomes invaluable in dealing with more complex systems and scenarios in the field of radio communication.

Chapter 11: Operating Procedures and Protocols

Effective communication over radio requires more than just technical knowledge; it also involves understanding and adhering to specific operating procedures and protocols. This chapter will explore the essential procedures and protocols that govern the use of radio communication systems, particularly in amateur radio.

Understanding Operating Procedures

Operating procedures in radio communication are a set of guidelines and practices designed to ensure efficient, effective, and courteous use of radio frequencies. These procedures cover a range of activities, from initiating contact with other stations to signing off after a communication session.

Key Elements of Radio Communication Procedures

1. **Call Signs**: The unique identifier assigned to each licensed radio station.
2. **Frequency Management**: Selecting and using frequencies without causing interference.
3. **Communication Protocol**: The standardized way of initiating, conducting, and ending a communication.

Standard Communication Protocol

The typical protocol for a radio communication includes:

1. **Calling**: Identifying the station you wish to contact and your station.
2. **Exchanging Information**: Sharing the intended message clearly and concisely.
3. **Signing Off**: Concluding the communication with an appropriate sign-off.

Practical Example: Amateur Radio QSO (Contact)

Let's consider a practical example of a QSO (a two-way radio contact) between two amateur radio operators:

1. **Initiating Contact**:
    - Operator A tunes to a clear frequency and listens to ensure it's not in use.
    - Operator A calls, "CQ CQ CQ, this is [Operator A's call sign], calling CQ and standing by."
    - Operator B responds with, "This is [Operator B's call sign], responding to [Operator A's call sign]."
2. **Exchanging Information**:
    - Both operators exchange information such as their location, signal report, and any other relevant details.

3. **Signing Off**:
    - After the conversation, Operator A says, "Thanks for the QSO, [Operator B's call sign], this is [Operator A's call sign], signing off and clear."
    - Operator B responds similarly and both operators clear the frequency.

Frequency Management and Etiquette

- Always ensure the frequency is clear before transmitting.
- Avoid "kerchunking" (keying the transmitter briefly without identifying) and lengthy transmissions that tie up the frequency.
- Be mindful of others waiting to use the frequency.

Emergency Communication Protocols

In emergencies, different procedures may apply:

1. **Priority for Emergency Traffic**: Regular communication should yield to emergency traffic.
2. **Use of Standard Emergency Phrases**: Phrases like "MAYDAY" or "PAN-PAN" indicate emergencies.

Logging and Documentation

Keeping a log of radio communications is essential for tracking contacts, managing frequencies, and recording any important incidents.

Conclusion

Adhering to established operating procedures and protocols is essential for effective and responsible radio communication. This chapter outlines the fundamental procedures for conducting a standard amateur radio QSO, managing frequency use, and handling emergency communications. Understanding and practicing these guidelines will ensure that radio operators can communicate effectively while respecting the shared use of radio frequencies. As we delve further into specific aspects of radio operation in subsequent chapters, this foundational knowledge will be crucial for more advanced and specialized communication scenarios.

Chapter 12: Radio Spectrum and Frequency Allocation

In radio communication, efficient use of the radio spectrum is vital. This chapter discusses the radio spectrum, frequency allocation, and the considerations and regulations that guide its usage. Understanding these concepts is crucial for anyone involved in radio communication, from amateur radio operators to professional broadcasters.

Understanding the Radio Spectrum

The radio spectrum is the range of electromagnetic frequencies used for wireless communication. It spans from about 3 kHz to 300 GHz and is divided into bands, each with unique propagation characteristics and designated uses.

Frequency Allocation

Frequency allocation is the process of dividing the radio spectrum into different bands and assigning these bands for specific purposes, such as broadcasting, mobile communication, satellite, amateur radio, and so forth. This allocation is regulated by national and international bodies to prevent interference and ensure effective use of the spectrum.

International Regulation Bodies

1. **ITU (International Telecommunication Union)**: Manages global radio spectrum and satellite orbits.
2. **Regional Telecommunications Organizations**: Such as CEPT (Europe), CITEL (Americas), APT (Asia-Pacific), and ATU (Africa).

National Regulatory Bodies

Each country has its regulatory body, like the FCC (Federal Communications Commission) in the United States, which manages the domestic allocation of the spectrum and enforces regulations.

Radio Spectrum Bands

- **LF (Low Frequency), MF (Medium Frequency), and HF (High Frequency)**: Used for AM broadcasting, maritime, and amateur radio.
- **VHF (Very High Frequency) and UHF (Ultra High Frequency)**: Used for FM broadcasting, television, mobile phones, and amateur radio.
- **SHF (Super High Frequency) and EHF (Extremely High Frequency)**: Used for satellite communication, radar, and certain wireless systems.

Practical Example: Setting Up an Amateur Radio Station

Consider the setup of an amateur radio station with a focus on HF bands:

1. **Frequency Selection**: The operator chooses a frequency within the allocated amateur bands, say

14.200 MHz within the 20-meter band.
2. **Equipment Setup**: The operator sets up a transceiver, antenna, and other necessary equipment, ensuring they are capable of operating on the chosen frequency.
3. **License and Regulations Compliance**: The operator holds a valid amateur radio license and adheres to the power limits and operational guidelines for the 20-meter band.
4. **Operating the Station**: The operator uses the station for making contacts with other amateur radio operators, participating in contests, and experimenting with different communication modes within the band's allocation.

Frequency Allocation Challenges

- **Spectrum Congestion**: As demand for wireless services increases, managing spectrum congestion becomes crucial.
- **Interference Management**: Avoiding interference between different services within the same or adjacent bands.

Conclusion

The radio spectrum is a limited and valuable resource that requires careful management and regulation. Understanding frequency allocation and adhering to the regulations set by international and national bodies is essential for all radio communication users. This chapter provides a foundational understanding of the radio spectrum and frequency allocation, emphasizing the importance of compliance and responsible usage. As we explore more advanced topics in radio communication, this knowledge will be instrumental in navigating the complexities of spectrum management and operation within allocated bands.

Chapter 13: Digital Signal Processing in Radio

Digital Signal Processing (DSP) represents a significant advancement in radio communication technology. DSP involves the use of digital techniques to process radio signals, offering enhanced performance, flexibility, and capabilities over traditional analog methods. This chapter will explore the principles of DSP in radio, its applications, and a practical example of DSP implementation in a radio communication system.

Understanding Digital Signal Processing

DSP in radio involves the conversion of analog radio signals into digital format and the use of algorithms to process these signals. This process can improve signal clarity, filter unwanted noise, and enable advanced features like digital modulation and error correction.

Key Components of DSP in Radio Systems

1. **Analog-to-Digital Converter (ADC)**: Converts the received analog signal into a digital format.
2. **Digital Signal Processor**: A microprocessor specifically designed to carry out DSP algorithms.
3. **Digital-to-Analog Converter (DAC)**: Converts the processed digital signal back into an analog format for transmission or audio output.

Applications of DSP in Radio

- **Signal Filtering**: Removing unwanted noise and interference from the signal.
- **Modulation and Demodulation**: Facilitating various digital modulation techniques.
- **Signal Enhancement**: Improving the quality of weak or distorted signals.
- **Data Compression**: Reducing the bandwidth required for transmitting digital data.

Advantages of DSP

- **Improved Signal Quality**: DSP can significantly enhance signal clarity and reduce noise.
- **Flexibility**: Software-based processing allows for easy updates and modifications.
- **Advanced Features**: Enables sophisticated functions like digital modulation, automatic gain control, and adaptive filtering.

Practical Example: Implementing DSP in a Software-Defined Radio (SDR)

Let's consider an example of using DSP in a Software-Defined Radio setup, a type of radio where many of the physical components are replaced by software:

1. **SDR Setup**: The operator sets up an SDR system, which includes an SDR receiver, a computer, and the necessary software.
2. **Signal Reception**: The SDR receiver captures radio signals, which are then converted into digital format by the ADC.
3. **DSP Processing**: The digital signal is processed using DSP software on the computer. This may include filtering out noise, demodulating digital signals, or enhancing weak signals.
4. **Output**: The processed signal is either converted back to analog for listening or further processed for digital modes of communication.

Developing a DSP Algorithm for Noise Reduction

Imagine developing a simple DSP algorithm to reduce noise in received radio signals:

1. **Algorithm Design**: The operator designs an algorithm to filter out specific types of noise, such as static or hum, using digital filtering techniques.
2. **Software Implementation**: The algorithm is implemented in software that can be run on the SDR's computer system.
3. **Testing and Optimization**: The operator tests the algorithm on various received signals, adjusting parameters to optimize noise reduction without losing important signal details.

Conclusion

Digital Signal Processing is revolutionizing the field of radio communication, offering enhanced performance and new capabilities. By incorporating DSP into radio systems, operators can achieve better signal quality, flexibility, and advanced features that were not possible with traditional analog methods. This chapter provides an introduction to DSP in radio communication, illustrating its applications and advantages through the example of Software-Defined Radio. As the field of radio communication continues to evolve, the role of DSP becomes increasingly significant, paving the way for more sophisticated and efficient communication systems.

Chapter 14: Emergency and Mobile Radio Communications

Effective communication is crucial in emergency situations, and mobile radio systems play a vital role in ensuring timely and reliable communication. This chapter explores the intricacies of emergency and mobile radio communications, discussing the equipment, protocols, and best practices essential for successful operation in dynamic and sometimes critical environments.

Importance of Emergency and Mobile Radio Communications

In emergencies, traditional communication networks may be unreliable or unavailable. Mobile radio systems provide an essential alternative, offering robust and flexible communication channels for first responders, disaster relief agencies, and individuals in crisis situations.

Key Elements of Emergency and Mobile Radio Systems

1. **Portability and Durability**: Equipment must be compact, robust, and capable of operating in harsh conditions.
2. **Reliability**: Systems must function consistently, with minimal failure.
3. **Ease of Use**: In high-stress situations, simplicity and intuitiveness are crucial for operation.
4. **Interoperability**: Ability to communicate across different systems and agencies.

Types of Mobile Radio Systems

1. **Handheld Radios (Walkie-Talkies)**: Portable and used for short-range communication.
2. **Mobile Radios**: Installed in vehicles, offering greater power and range.
3. **Base Stations**: Fixed stations that coordinate communication between mobile units.
4. **Repeaters**: Devices that extend the range of radio signals.

Practical Example: Setting Up a Mobile Radio System for a Community Emergency Response Team (CERT)

Let's consider a scenario where a Community Emergency Response Team (CERT) sets up a mobile radio system:

1. **Equipment Selection**: The team selects VHF handheld radios for individual members and a mobile radio with a higher power output for the command vehicle.
2. **Frequency and Channel Planning**: The team obtains a dedicated frequency for emergency communication and establishes a channel plan for different operations.
3. **Training**: Members receive training on radio operation, communication protocols, and emergency procedures.
4. **System Test**: The team conducts a drill to test the radio system, ensuring clear communication between handheld units, the mobile radio in the command vehicle, and the local base station.

Communication Protocols in Emergencies

- **Priority of Communication**: Emergency traffic always has priority over regular communication.
- **Use of Standardized Codes**: Using codes (like the NATO phonetic alphabet) for clarity and brevity.
- **Emergency Signals**: Understanding and using signals like SOS or MAYDAY.

Integrating with Other Emergency Services

Effective coordination with other emergency services (like fire, police, and medical) often requires interoperable communication systems and adherence to shared protocols.

Maintenance and Preparedness

Regular maintenance of equipment and continuous training are vital to ensure readiness for emergency situations.

Conclusion

Emergency and mobile radio communications are pivotal in ensuring effective response and coordination in crisis situations. This chapter provides an overview of the essential components, setup, and protocols involved in emergency radio communication, illustrated through the example of a CERT's mobile radio system. The principles and practices discussed here are critical not only for emergency responders but also for anyone responsible for communication in high-stakes environments. As we delve further into radio communication, understanding the nuances of emergency and mobile communications becomes increasingly important, enabling effective response in times of need.

Chapter 15: Radio Communication in Space

Radio communication in space represents one of the most challenging and fascinating aspects of radio science. This chapter explores the principles, technologies, and practical applications of space-based radio communication, which is crucial for satellite communication, deep space exploration, and astronomical observations.

Understanding Space Radio Communication

Space radio communication involves transmitting and receiving radio waves over vast distances in space, often spanning millions or even billions of kilometers. This type of communication faces unique challenges, including signal attenuation, long delay times, and interference from cosmic sources.

Key Challenges in Space Radio Communication

1. **Signal Attenuation**: The weakening of signals over long distances.
2. **Propagation Delay**: The time it takes for signals to travel between Earth and spacecraft.
3. **Doppler Effect**: The change in frequency or wavelength of a signal due to relative motion.
4. **Interference**: Cosmic noise and interference from natural celestial sources.

Technologies in Space Radio Systems

1. **High-Gain Antennas**: Used to focus radio beams for long-distance communication.
2. **Powerful Transmitters**: Required to send signals across vast distances in space.
3. **Sensitive Receivers**: Capable of detecting extremely weak signals.
4. **Error Correction Techniques**: Essential to recover information from distorted or partial signals.

Practical Example: Communication with a Mars Rover

Consider the scenario of communicating with a rover on Mars:

1. **Earth Station Setup**: A ground station on Earth equipped with a high-gain directional antenna, a powerful transmitter, and a sensitive receiver.
2. **Rover Equipment**: The rover on Mars is equipped with a radio transceiver, a moderately sized antenna, and signal processing units.
3. **Communication Process**:
    - The ground station transmits signals to the rover. Given the distance to Mars (which varies between 54.6 million and 401 million kilometers), there's a significant propagation delay (ranging from 3 to 22 minutes).
    - The rover receives the signals, performs necessary actions, and transmits data back to Earth.
    - The ground station processes the received data, accounting for the Doppler effect and signal attenuation.

4. **Data Handling**: The data sent from the rover includes scientific measurements, images, and rover status information, which are processed and analyzed by scientists on Earth.

Deep Space Network (DSN)

The DSN is a worldwide network of large antennas and communication facilities that support interplanetary spacecraft missions. It plays a crucial role in maintaining communication with space missions like the Mars rover.

Conclusion

Radio communication in space is a testament to the advancements in radio and space technology. It enables not only the exploration of other planets and celestial bodies but also enhances our understanding of the universe. This chapter provides an insight into the complex world of space radio communication, illustrated through the example of a Mars rover mission. As radio technology continues to evolve, its application in space exploration and communication will undoubtedly yield more groundbreaking discoveries and advancements.

Chapter 16: Advanced Antenna Systems

Advancements in antenna technology have led to the development of sophisticated antenna systems that offer improved performance, directional capabilities, and adaptability. This chapter will delve into advanced antenna systems, focusing on their design, applications, and a practical example of setting up a directional antenna system.

Understanding Advanced Antenna Systems

Advanced antenna systems include a range of designs from beamforming arrays to steerable parabolic dishes, offering enhanced capabilities like directivity, gain, and bandwidth optimization. These systems are crucial in applications requiring focused signal transmission and reception, such as satellite communication, radar systems, and high-frequency trading.

Types of Advanced Antenna Systems

1. **Directional Antennas**: Designed to focus energy in a particular direction. Examples include Yagi-Uda and log-periodic antennas.
2. **Phased Arrays**: Consist of multiple antenna elements whose phase and amplitude are controlled to steer the beam direction electronically.
3. **Parabolic Antennas**: Used for high-gain requirements, such as in satellite dishes and radio telescopes.
4. **Adaptive Antennas**: Automatically adjust their pattern in response to the signal environment to optimize performance.

Design Considerations for Advanced Antenna Systems

- **Directivity and Gain**: High directivity and gain are essential for long-distance and weak-signal applications.
- **Bandwidth**: The range of frequencies over which the antenna can operate effectively.
- **Size and Form Factor**: Depending on the application, the physical size of the antenna can be a critical factor.

Practical Example: Setting Up a Yagi-Uda Antenna for Amateur Radio

Let's consider an amateur radio enthusiast setting up a Yagi-Uda antenna for DXing (long-distance communication):

1. **Antenna Selection**: The operator chooses a Yagi-Uda antenna designed for the 14 MHz (20-meter) band, offering high gain and directivity.
2. **Installation**: The antenna is mounted on a mast at a significant height above the ground for optimal performance. Orientation is carefully considered for targeting specific geographical areas.
3. **Alignment and Tuning**: The antenna is aligned for the desired direction, and the driven element is tuned for the center of the 20-meter band.
4. **Testing and Operation**: The operator tests the antenna by making contacts with distant stations, adjusting the antenna's orientation as needed for optimal reception and transmission.

Benefits and Applications

- **Improved Signal Quality**: Focused reception and transmission lead to clearer signals.
- **Interference Reduction**: Directionality helps in reducing interference from unwanted sources.
- **Specialized Communication Needs**: Ideal for applications like satellite tracking and earth-moon-earth (EME) communication.

Conclusion

Advanced antenna systems represent a significant leap in radio communication technology, offering enhanced capabilities for a wide range of applications. This chapter provides a comprehensive overview of these systems, emphasizing their design, functionality, and practical implementation in scenarios like amateur radio DXing. As we continue to explore the vast field of radio communication, the knowledge of advanced antenna systems becomes increasingly important, enabling users to tailor their setups for specific requirements and achieve optimal performance.

Chapter 17: Software-Defined Radio (SDR)

Software-Defined Radio (SDR) represents a paradigm shift in radio technology, moving much of the signal processing from hardware to software. This chapter delves into the concept, capabilities, and applications of SDR, as well as providing a practical example of setting up an SDR system.

Understanding Software-Defined Radio

SDR is a type of radio communication system where components that have traditionally been implemented in hardware (e.g., mixers, filters, amplifiers, modulators/demodulators) are instead implemented by means of software on a personal computer or embedded system. This approach offers significant flexibility, allowing the same hardware to be used for different radio applications.

Key Components of SDR

1. **SDR Hardware**: Includes a wide-band RF transceiver and an analog-to-digital converter (ADC).
2. **Computer or Processing Unit**: Runs software that processes the radio signals.
3. **Software Applications**: Perform various functions such as modulation, demodulation, filtering, and frequency control.

Advantages of SDR

- **Flexibility**: Can be reconfigured for different frequencies and protocols through software.
- **Cost-Effectiveness**: Reduces the need for multiple pieces of hardware for different radio functions.
- **Upgradeability**: Software updates can introduce new features and capabilities.

Practical Example: Setting Up an SDR for Amateur Radio

Consider an amateur radio enthusiast setting up an SDR system for various radio operations:

1. **SDR Hardware Selection**: The operator chooses an SDR receiver capable of covering frequencies from HF to UHF.
2. **Computer and Software**: A personal computer is equipped with SDR software capable of handling various modulation types and offering features like spectrum analysis and recording.
3. **Antenna Connection**: The operator connects a multi-band antenna to the SDR hardware to receive a wide range of signals.
4. **Software Configuration**: The software is configured to tune into different amateur radio bands, demodulate various signal types, and filter out unwanted noise.
5. **Operation**: The operator uses the SDR system to listen to different amateur radio transmissions, experiment with digital modes, and even transmit if the SDR hardware supports it.

Applications of SDR

- **Amateur Radio**: Accessing a wide range of frequencies and modes.
- **Research and Development**: Experimenting with new communication protocols and signal processing techniques.
- **Commercial and Military Use**: Customizable communication systems that can be adapted to various needs.

SDR in Signal Analysis and Spectrum Monitoring

SDR can be effectively used for spectrum analysis, enabling the user to visualize and monitor a broad range of frequencies to detect, analyze, and troubleshoot transmissions.

Challenges and Considerations

- **Software Complexity**: Requires a good understanding of both radio principles and software.
- **Computational Requirements**: High-performance computing may be required for complex processing tasks.

Conclusion

Software-Defined Radio offers an incredibly versatile and powerful platform for radio communication, blending traditional RF technology with modern computing power and software flexibility. This chapter provides an introduction to SDR, highlighting its capabilities and practical application in amateur radio. The future of SDR is promising, with potential advancements and innovations poised to further transform the radio communication landscape.

Chapter 18: Radio Communication Security

In an age where information is a valuable commodity, securing radio communications becomes imperative. This chapter delves into the various aspects of radio communication security, focusing on encryption techniques, secure transmission protocols, and best practices for maintaining confidentiality and integrity in radio communications.

Understanding Radio Communication Security

Security in radio communication involves protecting transmitted information from interception and unauthorized access. This includes safeguarding the content of the messages and ensuring the authenticity of the communication parties.

Key Aspects of Radio Communication Security

1. **Encryption**: Encoding messages to prevent unauthorized access.
2. **Authentication**: Verifying the identity of communication parties.
3. **Frequency Hopping**: Changing frequencies at regular intervals to prevent interception.
4. **Secure Protocols**: Implementing protocols designed to enhance security.

Encryption Techniques

- **Symmetric Encryption**: Uses the same key for encryption and decryption. Easier to implement but requires secure key distribution.
- **Asymmetric Encryption**: Uses a pair of keys (public and private) for encryption and decryption. Provides enhanced security but is computationally more intensive.

Practical Example: Setting Up a Secure Amateur Radio Communication System

Consider an amateur radio operator setting up a secure communication link:

1. **Encryption Module Installation**: The operator installs an encryption module in the radio equipment, capable of encrypting the transmitted signal.
2. **Key Distribution**: The operator securely distributes the encryption keys to the intended communication parties.
3. **Secure Communication Setup**: The operator sets up the radio system, ensuring the encryption module is activated and functioning correctly.
4. **Test Communication**: A test transmission is conducted to ensure that the encrypted communication is operational and only accessible by parties with the correct decryption key.

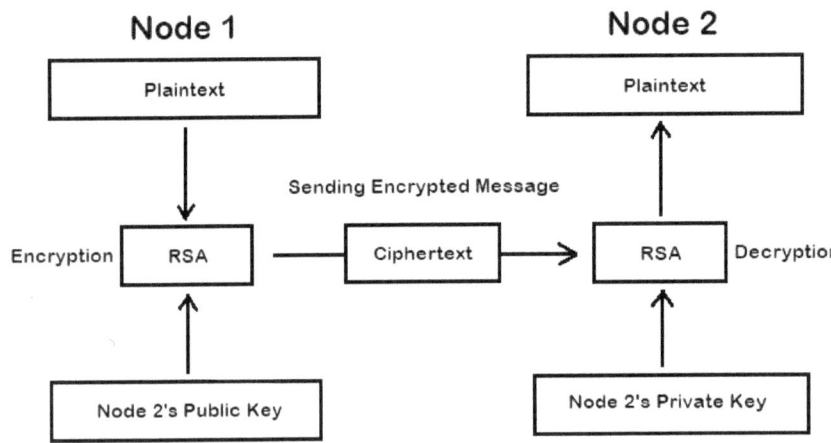

Authentication Protocols

- **Challenge-Response Mechanism**: A method where one party presents a challenge, and the other must provide a valid response to be authenticated.
- **Digital Certificates**: Utilize public key infrastructure (PKI) for authenticating the identity of communication parties.

Best Practices for Secure Radio Communication

- **Regularly Update Encryption Keys**: To prevent unauthorized access through key compromise.
- **Use Trusted Encryption Algorithms**: Ensure the use of well-established and secure encryption methods.
- **Stay Informed About Security Threats**: Keep abreast of potential vulnerabilities and emerging threats in radio communication security.

Conclusion

Securing radio communications is critical to protect sensitive information from eavesdropping and unauthorized access. This chapter provides a comprehensive overview of the methods and practices for securing radio communication systems, with a focus on amateur radio scenarios. As technology evolves and security threats become more sophisticated, the importance of implementing robust security measures in radio communication systems cannot be overstated. This knowledge is not only essential for individuals and organizations relying on secure radio communication but also forms a cornerstone for anyone involved in the design and deployment of secure radio communication systems.

Chapter 19: Troubleshooting and Maintenance

Troubleshooting and maintaining radio communication equipment are essential skills for ensuring reliable and effective operation. This chapter discusses the common issues that can arise with radio equipment, methods to diagnose and fix these issues, and regular maintenance practices to prevent future problems.

Understanding Troubleshooting and Maintenance

Troubleshooting involves identifying and resolving issues that impair the functioning of radio equipment. Maintenance, on the other hand, is the routine care and servicing of equipment to keep it operating efficiently and to prevent breakdowns.

Common Issues in Radio Communication Equipment

1. **Poor Reception or Transmission**: Can be due to antenna issues, interference, or equipment failure.
2. **Equipment Noise**: Caused by faulty components or external interference.
3. **Power Problems**: Issues with the power supply or battery.
4. **Frequency Drift**: The transmitter or receiver drifting off the correct frequency.

Diagnostic Tools and Techniques

- **SWR Meter**: Measures the standing wave ratio to assess antenna performance.
- **Multimeter**: Used to check for electrical faults and component integrity.
- **Spectrum Analyzer**: Analyzes the frequency spectrum for interference and signal quality.
- **Signal Generator**: Helps in testing and aligning receivers and transmitters.

Practical Example: Diagnosing and Repairing an Amateur Radio Transceiver

Consider an amateur radio operator encountering transmission issues with their transceiver:

1. **Initial Symptom Observation**: The operator notices that transmissions are weak and distorted.
2. **SWR Measurement**: Using an SWR meter, the operator checks the antenna system and finds that the SWR is higher than normal.
3. **Antenna Inspection**: Upon inspecting the antenna, a loose connection is discovered at the feed point.
4. **Repair and Retest**: The operator repairs the connection, rechecks the SWR (finding it now within the normal range), and then tests the transmission, which has significantly improved.

Regular Maintenance Practices

- **Visual Inspections**: Regularly inspect equipment for physical damage or wear.
- **Cleaning**: Keep equipment free of dust and moisture.
- **Connection Checks**: Ensure all connections are secure and corrosion-free.
- **Software Updates**: Keep any software or firmware updated to the latest version.

Tips for Effective Troubleshooting

- **Start Simple**: Check the most obvious and simple issues first.
- **Isolate the Problem**: Use a process of elimination to isolate where the problem lies.
- **Consult Documentation**: Refer to the equipment's manual for specific troubleshooting guidance.
- **Seek Help When Needed**: Don't hesitate to consult more experienced operators or professionals for complex issues.

Conclusion

Effective troubleshooting and regular maintenance are crucial for the longevity and reliability of radio communication equipment. This chapter provides a foundational understanding of the common issues faced in radio communication systems and outlines practical steps for diagnosing and addressing these problems. By incorporating these practices, radio operators can ensure their equipment remains in top working condition, ready for reliable communication whenever needed. As we advance in the field of radio communications, these skills become increasingly important, enabling users to manage and maintain complex and sophisticated radio systems effectively.

Chapter 20: The Future of Radio Communication

Exploring the future of radio communication involves looking at emerging trends, technological advancements, and the potential changes they might bring to the field. This chapter will delve into the foreseeable developments in radio technology, discussing innovations that are shaping the future of communication, and providing insights into their implications and applications.

Emerging Trends in Radio Communication

The future of radio communication is shaped by several key trends:

1. **Integration with Digital Technologies**: Increasing use of digital signal processing, software-defined radios, and integration with computer networks.
2. **Advancements in Antenna Technology**: Development of smart and adaptive antenna systems for more efficient signal transmission and reception.

3. **Enhanced Spectrum Efficiency**: Techniques like cognitive radio and dynamic frequency selection to optimize the use of the radio spectrum.
4. **IoT and M2M Communications**: Expansion of radio communication to support the Internet of Things (IoT) and machine-to-machine (M2M) communication.

Technological Advancements

- **Quantum Communication and Encryption**: Utilizing quantum properties to enhance security and develop new communication paradigms.
- **Artificial Intelligence in Radio Networks**: AI-driven optimization of network performance and predictive maintenance.
- **5G and Beyond**: Advancements in cellular networks offering higher speeds, lower latency, and massive connectivity.

Practical Example: Implementing a Cognitive Radio Network

Consider a scenario where a telecommunications company is deploying a cognitive radio network to optimize spectrum usage:

1. **Network Design**: The network is designed to dynamically identify unused spectrum bands and allocate them to users, improving overall spectrum efficiency.
2. **Implementation of AI Algorithms**: AI algorithms are implemented to analyze the radio environment, detect unused frequencies, and make real-time decisions on frequency allocation.
3. **Deployment of Cognitive Radios**: Users are equipped with cognitive radios capable of changing their operating frequencies based on AI recommendations.
4. **Testing and Optimization**: The network is tested in various environments to optimize its performance, ensuring reliable communication even in congested spectrum areas.

Challenges and Opportunities

- **Regulatory Evolution**: Regulations will need to evolve to accommodate new technologies and spectrum usage models.
- **Security Challenges**: Advanced security measures will be required to protect increasingly complex and interconnected radio networks.
- **Accessibility and Global Reach**: The potential to bridge communication gaps in remote and underserved areas.

Conclusion

The future of radio communication is poised at an exciting juncture, with technological advancements promising to revolutionize how we think about and use radio frequencies. This chapter provides a glimpse into the emerging trends and technologies shaping the future of radio communication, illustrated through the example of a cognitive radio network. As these advancements materialize, they hold the potential to address current limitations, open up new possibilities for communication, and create a more connected world. The journey ahead in radio communication is not only about technological innovation but also about adapting to and embracing these changes for a better future.

Conclusion:

The Evolving Landscape of Radio Communication

As we reach the conclusion of "The Radio Communication Handbook," it's evident that the field of radio communication is not just vast but dynamically evolving. The journey through various aspects of radio theory and practice has revealed the depth and breadth of this field, encompassing basic principles, advanced technologies, and a glimpse into future possibilities. This final chapter synthesizes the key takeaways and contemplates the future trajectory of radio communication.

Reflection on the Journey

The journey began with understanding the fundamentals of radio waves, which laid the groundwork for further exploration into more complex topics. Each chapter built upon the last, progressively delving into the technicalities of radio hardware, the intricacies of antenna design, the nuances of digital signal processing, and the critical aspects of security in radio communication.

Key Takeaways

1. **Foundational Principles**: The importance of understanding basic concepts such as wave propagation, antenna theory, and modulation techniques.
2. **Technological Advancements**: Appreciating the evolution from basic transmitters and receivers to sophisticated software-defined radios and advanced antenna systems.
3. **Practical Applications**: Realizing the significance of hands-on experience and practical application in mastering radio communication skills.

The Future of Radio Communication

Looking ahead, the future of radio communication is set to be shaped by several key factors:

- **Technological Innovation**: Continual advancements in technology will further enhance the capabilities of radio systems.
- **Regulatory Developments**: Changes in spectrum management and regulatory frameworks will impact how radio frequencies are utilized.
- **Integration with Emerging Fields**: The convergence of radio communication with areas like IoT, AI, and quantum computing.

Practical Example: A Future Community Radio Project

Imagine a future community radio project that integrates various aspects discussed in the book:

1. **Advanced Antenna System**: The project employs a smart antenna system capable of adaptive beamforming to optimize signal coverage and quality.
2. **SDR-Based Infrastructure**: Utilizing software-defined radios for flexible and efficient broadcasting, easily adaptable to different formats and standards.
3. **AI-Driven Content Delivery**: Implementing AI algorithms to analyze listener preferences and optimize content delivery.
4. **Spectrum Efficiency**: Using cognitive radio technology to dynamically access underutilized frequencies, ensuring optimal spectrum utilization.

Challenges and Opportunities Ahead

- **Adapting to Change**: The need to continuously learn and adapt to new technologies and methodologies.

- **Security and Privacy**: As radio communication becomes more sophisticated, ensuring the security and privacy of communications will be paramount.
- **Bridging the Digital Divide**: Leveraging advancements in radio communication to provide connectivity in underserved regions.

Final Thoughts

Radio communication, from its humble beginnings, has grown into a field rich with possibilities and opportunities. This book has aimed to provide a comprehensive guide through this evolving landscape, equipping readers with the knowledge and skills necessary to navigate and contribute to the world of radio communication. As we close this chapter, it's clear that the journey in radio communication is ongoing, filled with continuous learning, innovation, and exploration. The future beckons with the promise of new discoveries and advancements, inviting us all to be part of this exciting and ever-evolving field.

www.ingramcontent.com/pod-product-compliance
Lightning Source LLC
Chambersburg PA
CBHW062313220526
45479CB00004B/1150